Mental Health and Quality of Life of Adolescents with Physical, Intellectual and Developmental Disabilities

This timely volume addresses issues related to the mental health and health-related quality of life of adolescents through a study with three groups: those with physical, intellectual, and other developmental disabilities, specifically fetal alcohol spectrum disorder (FASD).

Investigating the physical, cognitive, and social-emotional dimension of adolescents' quality of life, the chapters explore the meaning of personal and social resources of adolescents with disability and their parents in the context of the Polish system of support for families with disabled children, further highlighting difficulties intensified by the COVID-19 pandemic.

Another field-defining work on the progression of mental health research for children and adolescents, this book will be a useful and timely contribution to researchers, post-graduate students, and scholars in the fields of developmental and social psychology, mental health research, adolescent psychotherapy, and disability. It will also be of interest to school counselors, parents, and caregivers.

Zenon Gajdzica, professor, special educator, Institute of Pedagogy, University of Silesia in Katowice, Poland.

Stanisława Byra, associate professor, special educator, Institute of Pedagogy, Maria Curie-Skłodowska University, Poland.

Anna Kołodziej-Zaleska, assistant professor, psychologist, Institute of Psychology, University of Silesia in Katowice, Poland.

Katarzyna Rutkowska, assistant professor, psychologist, Institute of Psychoogy, Maria Curie-Skłodowska University, Poland.

Daniela Dzienniak-Pulina, assistant professor, sociologist, Institute of Sociology, University of Silesia in Katowice, Poland.

The Mental Health and Well-being of Children and Adolescents

Series Editor: Garry Hornby
(University of Plymouth)

Mental health disorders in children and young people are increasing, with one in four under 16 experiencing mental health difficulties that will disrupt relationships, education, and work. In addition to this, one in ten under-16s suffers from a diagnosed disorder. Access to up-to-date research and appropriate interventions minimises the mental health challenges these children and adolescents face and reduces their potentially lifelong impact.

It has been internationally recognised that the scale of mental health research is low in relation to the burden of the disorder. This research-focused series will consist of titles that consider key issues affecting young people's mental health and wellbeing, exploring preventative measures, promoting positive behaviour, and sharing research to develop effective and efficient treatment.

Aimed primarily at researchers and postgraduate students, this series will also be of interest to practitioners in the mental health field, such as psychologists, and some in the field of education, such as counsellors, who would like to implement research-based findings in their clinical practice.

Books in the series include:

Navigating Students' Mental Health in the Wake of COVID-19
Using Public Health Crises to Inform Research and Practice
Edited by James M. Kauffman and Jeanmarie Badar

Mental Health and Quality of Life of Adolescents with Physical, Intellectual and Developmental Disabilities
Perspectives of Parents and Children
Zenon Gajdzica, Stanisława Byra, Anna Kołodziej-Zaleska,
Katarzyna Rutkowska and Daniela Dzienniak-Pulina

Please visit www.routledge.com/The-Mental-Health-and-Well-being-of-Children-and-Adolescents/book-series/MHWCA

Mental Health and Quality of Life of Adolescents with Physical, Intellectual and Developmental Disabilities

Perspectives of Parents and Children

Zenon Gajdzica, Stanisława Byra, Anna Kołodziej-Zaleska, Katarzyna Rutkowska and Daniela Dzienniak-Pulina

Routledge
Taylor & Francis Group
LONDON AND NEW YORK

First published 2024
by Routledge
4 Park Square, Milton Park, Abingdon, Oxon OX14 4RN

and by Routledge
605 Third Avenue, New York, NY 10158

Routledge is an imprint of the Taylor & Francis Group, an informa business

British Library Cataloguing-in-Publication Data
A catalogue record for this book is available from the British Library

Library of Congress Cataloguing-in-Publication Data
Names: Gajdzica, Zenon, author.
Title: Mental health and quality of life of adolescents with physical, intellectual and developmental disabilities: perspectives of parents and children / Zenon Gajdzica, Stanisława Byra, Anna Kołodziej-Zaleska, Katarzyna Rutkowska and Daniela Dzienniak-Pulina.
Description: Abingdon, Oxon; New York, NY : Routledge, 2024. | Series: The mental health and well-being of children and adolescents | Includes bibliographical references and index.
Identifiers: LCCN 2023010987 (print) | LCCN 2023010988 (ebook) | ISBN 9781032432953 (hardback) | ISBN 9781032435329 (paperback) | ISBN 9781003367772 (ebook)
Subjects: LCSH: Teenagers with disabilities--Mental health. | Teenagers with disabilities--Social conditions. | Fetal alcohol spectrum disorders--Patients--Mental health. | Fetal alcohol spectrum disorders--Patients--Social conditions. | Quality of life.
Classification: LCC HV1569.3.Y68 G34 2024 (print) | LCC HV1569.3.Y68 (ebook) | DDC 362.4083--dc23/eng/20230320
LC record available at https://lccn.loc.gov/2023010987
LC ebook record available at https://lccn.loc.gov/2023010988

ISBN: 978-1-032-43295-3 (hbk)
ISBN: 978-1-032-43532-9 (pbk)
ISBN: 978-1-003-36777-2 (ebk)

DOI: 10.4324/9781003367772

Typeset in Sabon
by MPS Limited, Dehradun

The research activities co-financed by the funds granted under the Research Excellence Initiative of the University of Silesia in Katowice

Contents

Figures and Tables

Figures

Tables

Series Editor's Foreword

This groundbreaking book was written towards the end of the global crisis caused by the coronavirus pandemic, the impact of which has increased stress and anxiety levels for everyone, but especially for children with special needs and their families. This has highlighted the importance of supporting and facilitating the mental health and wellbeing of children and adolescents, especially those with disabilities of various kinds. Although the pandemic has led to increased awareness of children's mental health needs, this has been an issue of great concern for some time.

The mental health and wellbeing of children and young people has become an increasing concern in recent years. For example, the UK government reported that 10% of young people aged between 5 and 16 years have a clinically significant mental health problem, whilst only 25% of those were receiving appropriate support and treatment (Cooper & Hornby, 2018). This situation has been referred to as one of "scandalous neglect" by Kauffman & Badar (2018). It is an important issue because, for 50% of those who go on to develop mental illness, the symptoms are clearly evident before the age of 14. This highlights the critical role of early identification of children's mental health problems and the provision of safe environments for the development of their wellbeing.

It is now 20 years since the need for an increased focus on children's mental health and wellbeing, particularly in schools, was acknowledged by the publication of the first of several books on the topic, which provides information on a wide range of mental health concerns (Atkinson & Hornby, 2002). One response to these publications has been the creation of this series of books, which is dedicated to addressing the mental health and wellbeing of children and young people. The key focus of books in this series is on evaluating the latest research available and disseminating evidence-based interventions and programs. This book is the sixth in this series.

The first book in the series addressed the issue of bullying in schools (Cowie & Myers, 2018), the second book examined various approaches for promoting the mental health of children in schools (Reupert, 2020), the third book focused specifically on the use of mindfulness meditation for facilitating the mental health and wellbeing of children and young people in schools and community settings (Singh & Singh Joy, 2021), the fourth book addressed bullying in schools from multiple perspectives (Rigby, 2022), and the fifth book focused on implications for children's mental health of the COVID-19 pandemic (Kauffman & Badar, 2023).

The current book presents findings from a research study of health-related quality of life of three groups of adolescents, those with physical disability, intellectual disability, and fetal alcohol spectrum disorder, as an example of a specific developmental disability. The research used a biopsychosocial model of disability and a dyadic approach, including the perspectives of parents and their children. It focused on personal, family, and social resources in maintaining health-related quality of life and was conducted with a Polish sample that takes into account the education and health care context in Poland. However, the theoretical background of the research is based on the international research literature so the research project is relevant to and will contribute extensively to the understanding of this topic worldwide.

Emeritus Professor Garry Hornby
University of Plymouth

References

Atkinson, M., & Hornby, G. (2002). *Mental health handbook for schools*. RoutledgeFalmer.

Cooper, P., & Hornby, G. (2018). Facing the challenges to mental health and wellbeing in schools. *Pastoral Care in Education*, *36*(3), 173–175.

Cowie, H., & Myers, C.-A. (Eds.) (2018). *School bullying and mental health: Risks, intervention and prevention*. Routledge.

Kauffman, J. M., & Badar, J. (2018). *The scandalous neglect of children's mental health: What schools can do*. Taylor & Francis.

Kauffman, J. M., & Badar, J. (Eds.) (2023). *Navigating students' mental health in the wake of Covid 19: Using public health crises to inform research and practice*. Routledge.

Reupert, A. (2020). *Mental health and academic learning in schools: Approaches for facilitating the wellbeing of children and young people*. Routledge.

Rigby, K. (2022). *Multiperspectivity on school bullying: One pair of eyes in not enough*. Routledge.

Singh, N. N., & Singh Joy, S. D. (2021). *Mindfulness-based interventions with children and adolescents: Research and practice*. Routledge.

List of Abbreviations

AAIDD	American Association on Intellectual and Development Disabilities
AAMR	American Association on Mental Retardation
ALQ	Adolescent Lifestyle Questionnaire
COVID-19	Coronavirus disease 2019
DSM	Diagnostic and Statistical Manual of Mental Disorders
FASD	Fetal Alcohol Spectrum Disorder
GUS	Central Statistical Office (in Polish: Główny Urząd Statystyczny)
HRQoL	Health-Related Quality of Life
ICD	International Classification of Diseases
ICF	International Classification of Functioning, Disability and Health
ICIDH	International Classification of Impairments, Disabilities and Handicaps
IQ	Intelligence Quotient
NGO	Non-Governmental Organization
NIK	Polish Supreme Audit Office (in Polish: Najwyższa Izba Kontroli)
OR	Optimal Regulation
PARPA	Polish National Agency for Solving Alcohol-Related Problems (in Polish: Polska Agencja Rozwiązywania Problemów Alkoholowych)
QoL	Quality of Life
RPD	Ombudsmen for Children (in Polish: Rzecznik Praw Dziecka)
SOR	Family Rating Scale (in. Polish Skala Oceny Rodziny)
WHO	World Health Organization
ŻWJR	Life Is Worth a Conversation (in Polish: Życie Warte Jest Rozmowy)

Chapter 1

Introduction

This book will address the issues of health and health-related quality of life of adolescents with an intellectual or physical disability and those with other developmental disabilities, in particular fetal alcohol spectrum disorder (FASD). The applied perspective focuses on the meaning of personal and social resources in maintaining health-related quality of life. The text is based on the findings of a research project that highlight positive and negative elements in adolescents' psychosocial development and behaviour that have substantial impact on their health-related and quality of life in the context of experiencing a disability.

The study to be reported in the book conducted with the guiding assumption that the understanding of health-related quality of life experienced by adolescents with intellectual disability, physical disability, and other developmental disabilities may be best understood by examining certain cognitive schemata and behaviour patterns in the family environment. Therefore, health-related quality of life and their determinants in the aforementioned groups are analysed using a dyadic approach in which the parental perspective is also taken into account. The juxtaposed perceptions of both adolescents and parents provides many interesting grounds for discussions aimed at an understanding of health-related quality of life. Such discussions are particularly justified in the context of the COVID-19 pandemic, which has posed a real threat to the health of young people with disabilities. The pandemic has significantly influenced mental health and quality of life, especially in vulnerable populations, like adolescents with disabilities.

The book contents encompass a wide range of related topics, presenting the complex context in which health-related quality of life is viewed by youth with disabilities. These are: evaluation of the health-related quality of life connected with adolescents' life in various fields: physical, emotional, family, peer, and educational; the meaning of personal resources: including ego-resiliency, lifestyle, self-rated health and disability acceptance; and social perspectives: financial situation, family cohesion and flexibility, meeting friends and using social media, in maintaining a good health-related quality

DOI: 10.4324/9781003367772-1

of life; the dyadic perspective: adolescents – parents, in understanding health-related quality of life in relation to the resources that one has; and, the overall impact of the pandemic on health-related quality of life of adolescents and their parents.

This book will present findings from a study of health-related quality of life of three groups of adolescents, those with a physical disability, intellectual disability, and other developmental disabilities, specifically FASD. A unique contribution of the book is presenting findings from research that used a dyadic approach, that is, including the perspectives of parents and their children, in the context of the COVID-19 pandemic. Applying the assumptions of the biopsychosocial concept of disability, the research involves youth with diverse disabilities: physical, cognitive, and social-emotional ones. The inclusion of youth with FASD is considered important due to their growing number in society and insufficient recognition of their psychosocial needs, as well as resources and possibilities of support.

Therefore, the groups invited to take part in the study were selected purposefully. The system of certification and diagnostics that functions in Poland and some other countries recognises disability mostly in the category of a limitation of particular resource. The aforementioned groups include:

- youth with physical disability with certified limitations in resources involving physical competencies;
- youth with intellectual disability with certified limitations in resources involving cognitive competencies;
- youth with FASD with diagnosed limitations in resources involving social-emotional competencies.

The authors' intention is to identify and compare the experiences of and resources of different groups of youth, as well as to consider them as regards the common and divergent resources – to emphasise common and divergent deficits, strengths, and needs.

The Polish system of support for families with disabled children has been evolving for some years. In practice, the consequences of its imperfection are still present and justify some attention. Underfunding, insufficient information about services available, lack of optimal solutions for the implementation of respite care, are just some of the issues that determine the quality of life of parents and guardians of children with disabilities. Additionally, the difficulties have been intensified by the COVID-19 pandemic in the access to medical care, psychological support, education, or community support.

The study is being conducted with a Polish sample and takes into account the Polish context (of e.g. education and health care). The book comprises of a presentation of the specificity of social functioning of Polish youth with physical disability, intellectual disability, and FASD, with a special focus on the institutional and non-institutional support systems, as well as their efficiency during the pandemic.

However, the theoretical background of the research is based on a review of the international research literature on the topic (biopsychosocial model of disability, health-related quality of life, resources). The research project is focused on personal, family, and social resources in maintaining health-related quality of life, which is relevant to and will contribute to research conducted worldwide on this topic. The book will be a voice in the debate on the universal (supranational) need of emphasising and implementing the biopsychosocial model in defining disabilities, especially in the face of the increasing number of young people who experience various disabilities.

Another issue pertains to the fact that existing systemic support does not respond to all the needs of such families, nor does it take into account all the hypothetical beneficiaries. One of such "systemically invisible" groups are families with FASD children. The number of diagnoses of FASD is growing. Yet, currently – the issues of children on the FASD do not comply with the classical definition of disability or illness. The status of children with FASD seems not to be recognised, which results in an insufficient number of available effective systemic solutions – especially in the educational space and in the field of support for families. In turn, this increases difficulties in access to systemic care and support solutions, that has been highlighted in the pandemic. Comparing the three indicated groups in regard to their experiences and resources, especially in relation to their health-related quality of life, will become the starting point for building support, based mostly on resources, not on limitations.

Therefore, the primary market will be researchers, post-graduate students, and educators of children and adolescents with disabilities. The book will be of interest to psychologists, nurses, social workers, rehabilitation therapists, and other specialists, such as school counselors, family therapists, and parent counselors, who provide clinical care to this population. The subject of the book will also be of interest to parents and caregivers.

Chapter 2

Youth with a disability from the biopsychosocial perspective – assumptions of the study

Introduction to the concept of disability

Adopting a particular worldview is the basis underlying the design of any research project. At its core are theories and sets of propositions used to derive and define fundamental research categories and problems, and even to design research tools (or select already existing ones). These theories are also usually employed as a tool to explain or interpret data collected during the investigations. In practice, this means using them repeatedly at different stages of the research. The design of the theoretical part of research projects, placed in the positivist paradigm, generally consists of a set of concepts/models/theories of varied extent, constituting a roadmap, as it were, for the aspects addressed by the studies. This chapter introduces the reader to the category of disability.

Disability as a social phenomenon has always been present in all cultures, at every stage of their development. Although it is generally associated with disorders and limitations, its definition has evolved in the process of social transformations. The understanding of disability is also embedded in culture and religion. This is why disability as a concept is invested with different content in different regions of the world. In addition, it draws the interest of many academic disciplines, from medical sciences to technical sciences, social sciences, and humanities. Consequently, it is perceived and defined in multifaceted ways.

Not so long ago, knowledge about disability was strongly determined by medicine and psychology. As a result of this approach, disability used to be equated with disease and described through the lens of bodily disorders (dysfunctionalities of individual organs) as well as of individual functionality, rooted in behavioural and cognitive concepts of the human being. This is illustrated not only by the changes in perception of persons with disabilities, but also by rehabilitation processes focusing primarily on correction and improvement (Garbat, 2015). Social transformations have guided the shift in the perception of disability, moving the focus from its causes to what makes it dynamic. This turn involved placing disability in the field of

DOI: 10.4324/9781003367772-2

social interaction and recognising its relative nature, depending on diverse points of reference. According to Reinhart Koselleck (2012), investing historical concepts with dynamics is linked to their wandering, whose symptoms include precisely the transition from a static to a dynamic nature. Another indicator of the changes in the definition and perception of disability is the latter's migration between the medical, psychological, and sociocultural dimensions. This transition is illustrated by clashes between paradigms in the fields of special needs education, clinical psychology, and sociology of disability, creating different (identical, parallel, and contradictory) worlds of persons with disabilities (Krause, 2010).

Generally, two concepts derived from two different ontological assumptions clash in defining disability.

The first concept defines it as an objectively measurable deviation from the physical norm (body impairment), leading to individual functional disorders. This approach determines the individual model of disability (or the closely related medical one). Its essence lies in referring indicators of disability to an objectively existing norm that determines the category of able-bodiedness. According to this point of view, the latter is a certain benchmark (norm), while disability can only be identified on the basis of objectively measurable deviations from the formally established standard. The adoption of such assumptions places disability studies within the traditional positivist line of research. The premise underlying this approach is that the world exists objectively, and that the essence of research is to discover cause-and-effect relationships. Persons with disabilities are subject to the same rules of functioning as all other people, while their uniqueness (exceptionality) is always considered in relation to objectively established abled-bodiedness, norms, and principles (Byra, 2019; Gajdzica, 2017; Haegele & Hodge, 2016; Krause, 2010; Olkin, 1999).

The other concept portrays disability as a social construct, as it were, perceived from an observer's point of view. In this approach, disability is not objectively measurable, as its indicators are determined by the social context (e.g. expectations, experiences, and emotions of specific individuals). The picture of disability is therefore formed on the basis of relationships between people and/or the environment. These assumptions provide the foundation underlying the social model of disability. It treats the latter essentially as a set of properties perceived subjectively, which makes it impossible to define unambiguous (undisputed) points of reference, such as an objectively indicated norm. Social concepts of disability are therefore designed on the basis of contextual variables: states, traits, and processes. Disability defined in this manner is difficult to generalise by adopting unambiguous standards for every culture. In this view, there are no general rules of functioning that could be discovered and that all people would be subject to. Adopting these assumptions places disability studies in the interpretative line of research (Barnes et al., 2010; Gajdzica, 2017; Krause, 2010; Oliver, 2013; Shakespeare, 2016).

Table 2.1 Social and individual models of disability

Criterion of comparison	*Individual model of disability*	*Social model of disability*
Approach to disability	personal tragedy	social issue
Essence of the problem	disease, physical impairment, occupational incapacitation, psychological maladjustment, lack of motivation and cooperation	dependence on professional assistance, lack of adequate support services, architectural barriers, economic barriers
Location of the phenomenon	personal dimension	in the organisation of society
Role of the disabled person	patient/client	consumer
Solution	professional intervention by doctors, physiatrists, therapists and vocational counsellors	exercising rights, counselling, self-help, removal of barriers
Control	by experts	self-control = possibilities of choosing
Expected results	adaptation of the individual	acceptance of the individual in society (social change)

(Source: Piasecki et al., 1998, p. 48).

The two distinct worlds generate different (or at least partly different) content categories relevant in their description. In other words, as already mentioned, concepts recognised as key are invested with different meaning. This is illustrated by the assumptions underlying the two disability models, presented in brief in Table 2.1.

In disability studies, the term "model" is usually used to describe the general approach to disability. It thus formulates merely a rough outline of disability, of its consequences and of the ways of working with people with disabilities and educating them (DeVidi & Klausen, 2017). This is how it is understood in the present study, although in order to show the nature of disability (including, among other things, its link to disease), we also perceive the "model" as the relationships of connected components (Forstner, 2022, p. 541).

Criticism of the extreme approaches and the search for universal concepts led to the development of the biopsychosocial model, which can be briefly summarised as:

> disease – impairment – disability – handicap
>
> (WHO, 1980, p. 11)

The basis for this model was the concept of disability published by Saad Z. Nagi (1965), revised in his subsequent publications (e.g. Nagi, 1991).

This concept fits within the framework of the health triad adapted from sociology: disease, illness, and sickness (Hofmann, 2016), and corresponds to the body, individual, and society triad mentioned by the World Health Organization (WHO, 2001). An important premise thereof is to capture all the main aspects of the disability phenomenon without narrowing its definition down to functional limitations (Forstner, 2022).

It is a dynamic concept of disability, with a linear progression of components. The first one is disease, a pathological change disrupting the body's natural physical and/or mental processes. Understood in this way, disease can lead to impairment, i.e. the loss of the normal anatomical, physiological, or mental structure (some or all of them). This results in a functional limitation in the performance (achievement) of basic bodily activities. In turn, this makes it difficult or impossible to perform culturally, legally, and socially expected roles and tasks (Nagi, 1991, pp. 320–323). This model was subjected to criticism, resulting in the creation of supplements and new varieties. As a result, three main areas were distinguished within it:

- Disease (Biomedical Body);
- Illness (Subjective Individual);
- Sickness (Society).

The biomedical and functionalist dimension refers to pathological anatomical changes and functional aspects. This area can be observed and measured fairly objectively.

The illness dimension, in turn, is linked to the individual perspective, affecting the general physical and mental state, and daily life. It is defined and interpreted subjectively. The subjective identity of disability is defined on its basis. In this dimension, it intersects with categories such as gender and sexuality.

Sickness, which is the third area, refers to the social dimension, i.e. to the social model of disability. It is closely linked to sociocultural barriers, prejudices in the assignment of social roles, exclusion, ableism, etc. (Forstner, 2022, p. 542).

The disability models created over the recent years are rooted in the ICIDH (International Classification of Impairments, Disabilities and Handicaps) reforms, and generally do not take into account the linear disablement process. The International Classification of Functioning, Disability and Health (ICF) is currently one of the most widely recognised model of disability within them. It consists of two main components.

The first one, disability and functioning, is situated in the area of broadly conceived health (meaning not only disease, illness, disorder, injury, but also natural states, such as pregnancy or age). Within it, the following components were distinguished: body functions and structure, as well as activities and participation. Body functions were defined as the individual processes of the human body systems, while structure refers to anatomical body parts such as organs, limbs, and their respective components. Areas of life were reflected in components identified as activity, i.e. the tasks performed or the actions undertaken by the individual, as well as participation, i.e. the individual's involvement in specific life situations.

The second component includes contextual factors, representing the environment in which the individual lives. These include two elements: environmental factors and personal factors that can influence the individual with a particular health condition, as well as their health status and health-related states (Bickenbach, 2014; Cieza & Stucki, 2008; Forstner, 2022; Kirenko, 2022; WHO, 2001).

This model was based on the assumption of interactivity between health status and contextual factors. It is worth emphasising that its introduction brought about two fundamental changes in the concept of functioning and disability. The first change concerns the terms used, bearing negative connotations in the past. The terms "impairment," "disability," and "handicap" were abandoned and replaced with "body functions" and "structures and participation." The second change manifested itself in perceiving disability as a concept representing the dynamic interaction between the individual and the environment (Byra et al., 2016; Dahl, 2002).

The approach to defining and measuring disability, presented above in brief, encompasses aspects of health, the related areas, as well as the environmental factors that make up the human experience of disability. The model also contributes to an understanding of the nature of health in relation to disability, from a view focused on the body and its functioning to social experiences. It can also serve as a tool for operationalising the broadly understood personal well-being, placed in the individual and social context (Cieza & Stucki, 2008).

In the following part of this chapter, we describe the three types of impediments to individual and social functioning that characterise the groups studied in the project described.

Mild intellectual disability

Understanding and defining intellectual disability is part of the transformations of the concept of disability described above. It already results clearly from the evaluation of the terms used to describe the condition (e.g. oligophrenia, feeble-mindedness, mental subnormality, idiocy, imbecility, moronism, mental retardation, mental handicap, and mental impairment). The literature offers many diverse approaches to intellectual disability. One of the simplest typologies presents this kind of disability in the following aspects:

- practical – considered with regard to the effective consequences of locating individuals with intellectual disabilities within the social structure. The

related concepts are useful in the legal and administrative area (as they make it possible to establish criteria for the assigning of the relevant legal status, allowing the individual to obtain specific support, among other things), and education (designing of specific strategies for separate or inclusive education);
- theoretical – oriented towards description and explanation of the disability status (with a focus on the aetiology of the disorder, the traits that are lacking, the functional characteristics, quality of life, resources and activities, as well as needs, including types of support) (Gajdzica, 2020).

In turn, Harris (2006) lists and characterises statistical, pathological, social, and developmental approaches. Speck (2015) presents the possible areas for considering intellectual disability in the medical genetic, psychological, sociological, and educational terms. The American Association on Intellectual and Development Disabilities Manual makes a distinction between social, clinical, intellectual, and dual criterion approaches (*Intellectual Disability ...* , 2010). In general, these approaches are reflected in the definitions of intellectual disability.

The American Association on Mental Retardation (AAMR) defined and described intellectual disability (mental retardation) using three components: intellectual functioning, adaptive behaviour, and systems of supports. Within each of these components, the severity of disability is measured on a continuum.

Intellectual functioning of people with intellectual disabilities, as interpreted by the AAMR, is "significantly below average," or below the level characterising 97% of the general population. On a standardised IQ test, the individual must score less than two standard deviations below the mean. As a result of this measurement, four degrees of intellectual disability are distinguished: mild (IQ 50–70), moderate (IQ 35–49), severe (IQ 21–34), and profound (IQ below 20).

Adaptive behaviour is a set of conceptual, social, and practical skills the individual has learnt to function in everyday life. They include practical skills such as eating, dressing, washing, moving around, preparing meals, using the telephone, managing money, taking medication, and doing household chores.

Systems of supports are treated as another defining feature of intellectual disability on the four levels of severity of its diverse types (personal development, learning and education, life at home, life in the community, employment, health and safety, conduct, social contacts, personal protection, and protection of rights). Support can be offered on any of the four levels of demand: intermittent, limited, extensive, and pervasive (AAMR, 2002; Smith, 2004).

In our work, we adopt the following assumption:

> A multidimensional framework for understanding intellectual disability depicts how human functioning and the manifestation of intellectual disability involve the dynamic, reciprocal, engagement, among intellectual ability, adaptive behavior, health, participation, context, and individualized supports.
>
> (*Intellectual Disability*, 2010, p. 13)

Thus, we assume that in this model, the functioning of a person with intellectual disabilities is determined by the dynamic relationships between intellectual abilities, participation, health, support, and adaptive behaviours.

Dimension 1. Intellectual Abilities – refers to intelligence perceived as general mental capacity. This includes reasoning, planning, problem solving, abstract thinking, understanding complex concepts, rapid learning, and experiential learning. Intelligence understood in this way is the ability to understand one's environment and the phenomena occurring therein.

Dimension 2. Adaptive Behaviour – is a set of cognitive, social, and practical skills. They are displayed and used in everyday life, i.e. in routine activities. The strengths and weaknesses of adaptive behaviour should be considered in relation to the individual's age and environment.

Dimension 3. Health – is understood here as full physical, mental, social, and spiritual wellbeing.

Dimension 4. Participation – is about how the individual functions within the community, how they take on certain social roles as well as establish and maintain relationships with other people. It therefore includes activities in the areas of home life, work, education, leisure, spiritual, and cultural life.

Dimension 5. Context – includes living conditions and is understood according to an ecological perspective. It therefore takes into account the microsystem (the closest environment), the mesosystem (neighbourhood, organisations providing education, services, and support), and the macrosystem (general cultural, political, and religious patterns). In this model, context is also considered in terms of the interacting environmental and personal factors. The description of context takes into account support, understood as the resources and strategies used to promote the individual's development, education, and interests to improve their wellbeing and functioning (after: AAIDD, 2010, pp. 14–18).

In view of the research presented further on in this work, we will focus on the least severe one of the four degrees of intellectual disability distinguished earlier.

The developmental descriptions of individuals with a mild intellectual disability usually emphasise that their development is close to normal and that the limitations do not manifest themselves distinctly. Therefore, in mainstream schools, children and young people with mild intellectual disabilities have often been perceived, for many years now, as neglected students from underprivileged backgrounds. Only a diagnosis made with appropriate diagnostic tools reveals their slight developmental disorders, especially in the cognitive area (Franiok, 2005; Speck, 2015; Wyczesany, 2002).

Children and young people with a mild intellectual disability do not generally differ from their peers in terms of appearance. Closer observation makes it possible to discern a slight lack of harmony in development, certain physical weakness, and a higher incidence of postural defects. Unless this disability is accompanied by signs of physical underdevelopment, upon first contact, such children/adolescents often give the impression of not deviating from the norm. It is difficult to find out about the degree of their intellectual disability during a routine conversation on everyday topics. This is particularly the case when the child/adolescent has a relatively rich vocabulary and ease of speech (Gajdzica, 2020; Chrzanowska, 2021; Wyczesany, 2002).

Children and young people with a mild intellectual disability are mostly described as capable of learning and of mastering a substantial part of the core curriculum in general education. However, albeit mainly in the medical and functional model, attention is drawn to the cognitive properties that characterise them, such as the following:

- Slowed cognitive and orientation processes.
- Thinking in a concrete terms and images.
- Limited abstract thinking, generalisation, comparison and cause-and-effect reasoning, inference and concept formation.
- More rigid and slower thinking, reduced criticism and reflection on the surrounding world, as well as reduced self-control capacity.
- Linking activity to the current situation and to learnt/habitual patterns of action.
- Adaptive concrete/image thinking to solve concrete problems.
- Delayed expression and comprehension of speech, limited vocabulary (after: Zasępa, 2016).

It is worth adding, however, that this is a very diverse group, and the difficulties indicated are not infrequently characterised by only a slight deviation from the cognitive abilities of able-bodied peers (Smith, 2004).

Despite the developmental limitations indicated above, one must not forget about the potential every person with mild intellectual disabilities has. In this regard, it is also worth remembering about their many talents that enable them to achieve success in various spheres, competing successfully against developmentally normal peers. In addition, it is worth emphasising that the vast majority of children and young people from this group attain a level of social development that enables them to function independently in society (Zasępa, 2016). In many cases, despite the limitations indicated, the level of resourcefulness achieved (especially with appropriate support and effective education) is comparable to that displayed by individuals within the intellectual norm. As a result, people with mild intellectual disabilities achieve relative independence in life. They perform work independently (albeit in jobs culturally reserved for them), fulfilling themselves as parents, and often actively participating in local social life. However, it is worth emphasising once again that this is a diverse group also in terms of their resourcefulness, and in practice many of its members continuously rely on support provided by family and aid institutions (Gajdzica, 2007; Chrzanowska, 2021; Speck, 2005). This support is particularly important during the coming-of-age period, when the individual enters roles typical of adolescents, but this is accompanied by the simultaneous intensified rebelliousness against the established social order, the formation of one's distinct identity, as well as by entering new social milieus. As a result, young people with mild intellectual disabilities are characterised by difficulties in socialisation typical of the developmental age, intensified by issues resulting from the properties of intellectual disability. The accumulation of these factors remains inextricably linked to quality of life and affects their mental health.

Physical disability

Physical disability is among the most representative categories of disability. This representative nature is determined by two aspects: the constantly increasing number of people worldwide with various locomotor system impairments, and its prototypical character. What this means is that, by virtue of the visible limitations that are clear upon contact with an individual who has them, this kind of disability is seen as typical and easily definable, representing disability in general (Byra, 2009).

Physical disability is most often described as any limitation of one's physical functioning, mobility and stamina, affecting significantly and on a long-term basis their ability to perform daily activities and fully participate in individual life experiences. It includes functional limitations in the elements that make up body structure (lower limbs, upper limbs, and spine) or body functions (physiological processes related to the locomotor system) (Majewicz, 2012). Physical disability can be temporary or permanent, and is a consequence of musculoskeletal system impairment resulting from an accident, injury, or chronic disease. It can be acquired or congenital. Regardless of whether the irregularities in the structure or function of the locomotor system are of the former or of the latter nature, they can lead to serious disruptions in almost all spheres of human functioning, most generally in the physical, mental, and social ones (Byra, 2012). At the same time, according to the ICF, musculoskeletal system impairment does not lead directly to disability, nor does it determine a specific level of the latter or the severity of the limitations resulting from it. In fact, the extent and dynamics of the impact of body impairment are determined by the interaction of personal and environmental factors that ultimately define the individual's life situation. This is because disability does not simply reflect the respective person's traits, but rather the difficulties they may experience in interacting with society due to the type of musculoskeletal impairment they have experienced (Bickenbach, 2019).

Due to the various types of possible locomotor system impairment, the population of people experiencing them is very diverse. The main criteria for physical disability categorisation include location of the impairment/dysfunction, its causes and scope, the dynamics, extent and depth of the limitations, as well as their duration. It is therefore accepted that physical disability can be a consequence of: spinal cord injury, stroke, cerebral palsy, spina bifida, arthritis, or muscular dystrophy. In addition, it may result from post-traumatic damage (e.g. to ligaments, tendons, muscles and skin, deformations accompanying dislocations, fractures, and amputations) or chronic diseases, directly or indirectly linked to the musculoskeletal system (i.e. rheumatic disease, cancer, infectious diseases, muscular dystrophies, multiple sclerosis, epilepsy, cystic fibrosis, poliomyelitis, or Parkinson's disease) (Kirenko, 2007). Physical consequences may include compromised large motor skills (mobility), or manifest themselves in small motor skills (difficulties related to writing and eating, fluctuating muscle tone, paralysis, loss or inability to use one or more limbs, etc.).

The previously mentioned criteria for categorising physical disability are supplemented by additional elements of individual and environmental factors that make up the life situation of the individual with a specific impairment. As a result, people with physical disabilities differ not only in terms of bodily impairment, but also in their level of functioning and daily coping with the activities they undertake (Kowalik, 2018). An intrinsic aspect characterising this group is therefore the degree of psychosocial adjustment, including both positive (developmental) elements and negative ones, preventing its members from making full use of their capacity. In the context of the existing theoretical approaches explaining the functioning of persons with physical disability, the category of adjustment provides relatively the broadest understanding of the process of coping with the consequences of experienced limitations, whether permanent or temporary. Having said that, it is also emphasised that such explanations do not lead to categorisation of people experiencing musculoskeletal impairments into adjusted and maladjusted ones, but rather to their placing on a broad continuum, ranging from maladjustment to full adjustment, defined, among other things, by a satisfactory quality of life. Attention is further drawn to the particular dynamics of the process following the injury, determined by numerous intrinsic and extrinsic factors (Livneh, 2021).

It is important to emphasise that the dynamics of the interactive links between factors facilitating or hindering the optimal functioning of a person with a motor impairment creates a slightly different basis for assessing the consequences of the limitations they have at different stages of their development. This means that an individual experiencing even permanent impairment of the structure or function of the musculoskeletal system may, over the course of their lifetime, have different attitudes towards the limitations experienced, making the significance of the latter depend on a broad context of interacting factors. The same configuration of factors may therefore affect the individual's level of functioning and perception of their own abilities during childhood, adolescence, adulthood, and old age (Livneh, 2021).

Adolescence, as a time of profound developmental changes: cognitive, emotional, social, and ones oriented towards the crystallisation of personality and identity, proceeds with similar difficulties in people with physical disabilities and in peers not experiencing such disabilities. Nevertheless, those growing up with physical disabilities may face some specific obstacles and have to overcome challenges in many areas of functioning. While some of these do not have a direct impact on the health and quality of daily functioning of adolescents, they are sufficiently critical/sensitive to have important implications for the progress of further developmental stages (Tuffrey, 2013). Significantly, reviews of the research conducted reveal that more severe physicla disability may no longer play as decisive a role among youth in the formation of self-esteem as less severe disability, expressed by minor physical impairments (Miyahara & Piek, 2006). A higher degree of impairment, generating a wider range of limitations, may establish relatively stable physical self-esteem, which may not prove decisive for global self-esteem. This is in contrast to the unstable, variable physical self-esteem determined by low-severity developmental impairments. The individual is then more likely to engage in activities enhancing the level of physical functioning, which may consequently have a dynamic effect on the adolescent's overall self-perception (Raustorp & Lindwall, 2015). Although physical disability does not directly translate into quality of life assessment in adolescents, young people differ in terms of objective and subjective measurements compared to their physically able-bodied peers. A thematic review of the literature shows that quality of life in children and adolescents with physical disability is mainly shaped by their beliefs and feelings, being accepted by society, being able to create an identity beyond their disability and permanent impairments, autonomy, and hope for the future (Ow et al., 2021).

Vulnerable areas of functioning for young people with disabilities, specific due to the limitations resulting from physical impairment, include in particular the following: difficulties in maintaining friendships and satisfying relationships with peers, often resulting in feelings of isolation and loneliness, lowered self-esteem (Diamond et al., 2007); fatigue and chronic pain (De la Vega et al., 2018); impaired sexual development due to functional limitations, intended and unintended social barriers, and unfavourable body image (Holland-Hall & Quint, 2017); and finally reduced participation in recreational activities having beneficial health and social outcomes (Powrie et al., 2015). The specific nature of the functioning of adolescents with disability can furthermore be defined in terms of the fulfilment of the developmental tasks assigned to adolescence. On the basis of their research, Behle & Pinquart (2015) found that young people growing up with physical disabilities differed in 3 out of 12 possible developmental tasks. Adolescents perceived lower achievement in terms of integration into the peer group, but higher achievement in the acquisition of school competences and of independence from their parents. Those with higher levels of disability were found to have lower achievements in terms of autonomy, in the development of a realistic self-perception, in establishing and maintaining romantic relationships, in gender role awareness, and in socio-civic awareness. In turn, adolescents growing up with a lower degree of physical disability achieved similar results in the performance of developmental tasks to their physically able-bodied peers. Importantly, no differences were found between these groups of adolescents in relation to tasks specifically identified with that developmental period, such as the acquisition of gender roles and identity formation (Pinquart & Pfeiffer, 2015). This confirms the significant convergence between the development of physical-disabled adolescents and that of their able-bodied peers, with the marked presence of specific areas, determined by the type and extent of the limitations resulting from the impairment and the adolescent's psychosocial situation.

Fetal alcohol spectrum disorder

FAS appears in the ICD-10 as Q86.0: Fetal alcohol syndrome. The disease entity was identified in 1973 by Kenneth Lyons Jones and David W. Smith, who proved that consumption of alcohol as a teratogen during pregnancy can damage the foetus (Jones & Smith, 1973). FAS is a syndrome of congenital somatic and neurological defects. The degree of impairments and disorders caused by alcohol consumption can vary. In the full-blown form, three categories can be listed that characterise people with FASD: craniofacial dysmorphia, delayed psychomotor development, and symptoms resulting from damage to the central nervous system. Full-blown FAS accounts for only 10% of all developmental disorders associated with foetal exposure to ethanol, described as fetal alcohol spectrum disorder (FASD) (Banach & Matejek 2019).

The foundation of the developmental difficulties of children with FASD are central nervous system (CNS) impairments, constituting primary disorders. Secondary disorders are related to the child's mental functioning and behaviour. The following are distinguished clinically in addition to full-blown FAS: fetal alcohol syndrome without confirmed intrauterine exposure to alcohol, incomplete fetal alcohol syndrome, alcohol-related birth defects, and alcohol-related neurodevelopmental disorders. Distinguishing these entities makes it possible to classify individuals according to separate clinical criteria and to adapt tailor-made forms of therapy to them (Banach & Matejek, 2019). Małgorzata Klecka, one of the forerunners of FASD research in Poland, writing about primary impairments in people on the FASD spectrum, emphasises that the prenatal effect of alcohol does not always cause primary disorders, just as encephalitis does not always lead to postnatal brain damage. However, once this damage occurs, it is lifelong (Klecka, 2020). Secondary disorders, in turn, are those with which the child is not born, but which develop during their life under the influence of the environment. This means that some of the consequences of FASD may manifest themselves at later stages in one's life. Citing research carried out for many years on children, adolescents and adults on the FASD spectrum by a team led by Streissguth (1997), it is possible to identify the typical disorders observed and studied, and the resulting consequences characterising the respective group of people. These include: mental health problems, interrupted schooling, trouble with the law, institutions taking over their care (psychiatric wards, educational and rehabilitation centres, prisons, addiction treatment units), inappropriate sexual behaviours, and alcohol and drug abuse. Persons with FASD are moreover characterised by significant attention deficits (80%) and hyperactivity (72%), which often places their diagnosis in the area of ADHD during their school years. In addition, members of this group are characterised by the expression of illogical thoughts, motor stereotypies, unawareness of what is going on around them, odd mannerisms and habits, facial tics and grimaces, compulsive behaviours, self-harm, loss of control, and temper tantrums (after: Klecka, 2020). To this list one can add impaired judgement of cause-and-effect relationships, and hypersensitivity to sound or touch. An important finding is that intellectual disability is not a characteristic feature of FASD. However, the problems mentioned above that characterise this group of children and young people lead to them being placed in special education.

Another problem that additionally burdens children and adolescents with FASD is that they are most often abandoned children, growing up in adoptive families, foster families, or orphanages. The trauma of abandonment and the difficulty of building relationships make their already difficult situation even more complicated. Research by Banach & Matejek (2017) shows that, despite the greater awareness of FASD among young people and the positive attitudes towards the spectrum, there is still too little knowledge about what its characteristics and consequences are. The lack of institutional support for families raising children with FASD, limited public awareness, as well as insufficient diagnostic competences of educators, social workers and often also psychologists, result in problems in recognising, diagnosing, and selecting therapy for children and adolescents with FASD. Another problem is the limited number of entities specialising in helping individuals and families affected by FASD, which in practice accumulates the difficulties. In many cases, families raising children with FASD are deprived of adequate support, as the disease is not taken into account in the institutional support system. Parents continue to struggle to find out where and how to get help and, as a result, often become aware of the disease too late.

It is important to emphasise that FASD affects not only the child, but also the whole family. The consequences of primary and secondary disorders cause the family to fall into dysfunctions (the family breaking apart; psychiatric treatment, also of the parents). In Poland, this is a group with huge needs, but it continues to be neglected. Unfortunately, due to the cause of the disorder, namely alcohol consumption during pregnancy, it is placed under social taboo, which results for instance in fear of the diagnosis itself or of the consequences of its disclosure). Social campaigns continue to be insufficiently promoted. In turn, children and adolescents with FASD may not display the disorder in a clearly visible manner, and when the symptoms are more pronounced, they are sometimes perceived as rebellious behaviour typical of their age. However, the intensity, scale, and lack of specific cognitive, social, and emotional competences make this group particularly vulnerable to addictions, conflicts with the law, and the development of mental disorders, which significantly affects quality of life for them and their families.

We treat this chapter as a complementary introduction to the contents of the book, which is why it has to include information about the research concept and process. The concept is presented below.

Assumptions of the research

Aim of the study

The research is aimed mostly at analysing health and health-related quality of life of adolescents with a physical disability, an intellectual disability, and FASD, in regard to the dyadic perspective of adolescents and their parents. Other aims include comparing the respondents' personal and social resources, as well as finding out which resources impact health-related quality of life. The specific research objectives focus on establishing: a) the rating of health and health-related quality of life in adolescents with disabilities and their parents; b) the levels of personal resources (ego-resiliency, lifestyles, self-rated health, and acceptance of disability) and of social resources (family cohesion and flexibility, assessment of the family's financial situation, direct and social media contacts with friends and acquaintances) in adolescents with disabilities and their parents; c) similarities and differences in the parent-adolescent dyads in terms of the rating of health-related quality of life and personal and social resources; and d) the significance of the personal and social resources in explaining health-related quality of life in adolescents with disabilities. The assumptions underlying the study are illustrated in Figure 2.1.

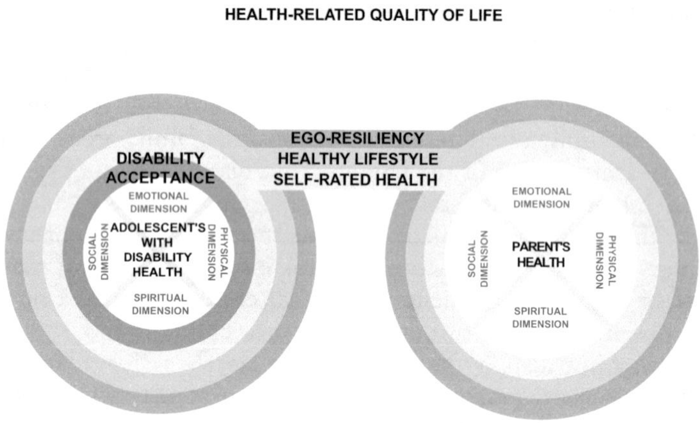

Figure 2.1 Tandem model – conceptualisation of health-related quality of life in dyadic perspective of adolescents with disability and their parents.

Method

Participants and procedure

The inclusion criteria for adolescents were: 1/ adolescents with physical disabilities, intellectual disabilities, or FASD; 2/ age between 16 and 19 years. For parents, the criteria were: 1/ having a child aged 16–19 with physical disabilities, intellectual disabilities, or FASD. All respondents (adolescents and their parents) read and confirmed the online consent form before completing the online survey. The study procedure was approved by the Ethical Committee of University of Silesia in Katowice (KEUS 142/ 06.2021). The research activities were co-financed with funds granted under the Research Excellence Initiative of the University of Silesia in Katowice.

The research participants were 120 parents and 114 adolescents. However, it was impossible to combine all the parent-child outcomes into a dyad, or the adolescent-parent pair studied pointed to a different physical or mental health difficulty of the child than the three categories we analysed (e.g. it was autism, a somatic illness, social anxiety). The following surveys had to be excluded: (n_{parents} = 22, and $\text{n}_{\text{adolescents}}$ = 16). Ultimately, 98 dyads were included in the study: parent-adolescent with a physical disability, an intellectual disability, or FASD.

The group of adolescents studied included 98 participants, of whom 59 were girls (60.2%) and 39 boys (39.8%). The mean age of the adolescents is 16.79 (M = 17.00; SD = 1.07). A vast majority of the respondents had siblings (93.9%) and lived with their parents and siblings (73.5%). Most respondents were students of secondary schools of general education (46.9%) and vocational schools (43.9%), while the rest were primary school pupils (6.1%) and technical secondary school students (3%). More than half of the respondents (51.0%) attended a mainstream school, 27.6% a special school, 19.4% an integrated school, and two respondents followed compulsory education in an individual form. Most research participants had physical disabilities (62.2%), while the others had mild intellectual disabilities (26.5%) and FASD (11.2%). A majority of the respondents (77.6%) indicated not suffering from a chronic disease.

The group of parents studied included 98 participants: 76 mothers (77.6%) and 22 fathers (22.4%). The mean age of the parents was 46.43 (M = 46,00; SD = 5.51). A majority of the parents surveyed lived in an urban area (66.3%), and 33.7% in rural areas. A vast majority were married (86.7%), while the remaining parents were either divorced (9.2%) or widows/widowers (4.1%). The educational structure in the case of the parents surveyed was as follows: higher (45.9%), secondary (38.85), vocational (11.2%), and primary (4.1%). A vast majority of the parents were employed (86.7%). Biological parents (91.8%) prevailed by far in the study, with the others being foster parents (4.1%), adoptive parents (2.0%), and legal guardians (2.0%). A majority of the respondents raised their child together with the other parent (83.7%), and 16.3% were single parents. Most respondents reported bringing up two children (45.9%; 31,6% reported three; 8.2% reported four; 8,2% reported one; 4,1% reported five; and 1% reported 7–8). Almost none of respondents (98%), except two parents, had a disability, and 89.8% of respondents did not have any chronic disease.

The online questionnaire was completed through LimeSurvey, an online survey system intended for scientific research. The study was carried out through contact with educational and rehabilitation institutions, as well as some associations and foundations supporting youth with physical or intellectual disability and with FASD, and their families.

Measures

Health-related quality of life was measured using KIDSCREEN-27 (Health-Related Quality of Life Questionnaire, HRQLQ) in a version intended for adolescents and for parents. The questionnaire contains 27 items to assess five areas of quality of life (subscales: physical wellbeing, psychological wellbeing, autonomy and parents, peers and social support, and school environment) (KIDSCREEN Group Europe, 2006; Ravens-Sieberer et al., 2005; 2007; Robitail et al., 2007). The respondent answers taking into account the past week ("Overall, how would you rate your health during the past week?"; "Did you feel well and were you physically fit during the past week?"), rating the frequency as: never, rarely, quite often, often, or always, or rating the intensity as: not at all, a little bit, moderately, very much, or to a very large extent. In turn, respondents would rate their general health as: excellent, very good, good, fair, or bad (Mazur et al., 2011). The questionnaire has satisfactory psychometric properties. The scales and subscales were internally consistent. Cronbach's α in the adolescent group is .921 and in the individual subscales; it was as follows: physical wellbeing .814; psychological wellbeing .838; autonomy and parents .855; peers and social support .818; and school environment .856. In the parent group, Cronbach's α was .973 for the parents surveyed, and in the individual subscales: physical wellbeing .765; psychological wellbeing .834; autonomy and parents .781; peers and social support .882; and school environment .856.

Ego-resiliency was measured with the Polish adaptation of the Ego-Resiliency Scale (ER89; Block & Kremen, 1996; adapted by Kołodziej-Zaleska & Przybyła-Basista, 2018). The Polish version of the questionnaire (ER89-R12) was abridged to finally include 12 items rated on a 4-point response scale, with scores ranging from 1 ("Does not apply at all") to 4 ("Applies very strongly"). Its psychometric parameters (reliability, stability, validity) are satisfactory. Moreover, the ER89-R12 is useful in studies on people experiencing various crises in their lives (Kołodziej-Zaleska et al., 2023). The results of exploratory and confirmatory factor analyses indicate that the revised version of ER89-R12 has a two-factor structure: "Optimal Regulation," OR (example item: "I quickly get over and recover from being startled") and "Openness to Life Experiences," OL (example item: "I like to take different paths to familiar places"), in accordance with what was proposed by Alessandri et al. (2007). It is possible to obtain an overall score in the questionnaire, as well as scores for individual subscales. The higher the score, the greater the ego-resiliency. Cronbach's α in the group of adolescents surveyed is .799, and .786 in the parent group.

Lifestyle was measured using the Adolescent Lifestyle Questionnaire (ALQ) by A. J. Gillis, elaborated by M. Duda (2016); the tool was adapted to measure adult lifestyle, i.e. that of the adults participating in the research presented in the book. The questionnaire consists of 43 items (e.g. I exercise vigorously 20–30 minutes a day, at least three times a week; I set goals for myself in life; I avoid alcohol consumption), which the respondent rates on a scale from 1 – never to 5 – almost always. It includes seven subscales: physical participation, nutrition, social support, stress management, identity awareness, general health practice, and safety. The scale demonstrates satisfactory reliability coefficients in both the adolescent and parent study groups, with Cronbach's α for the total score being .889 for the adolescents and .901 for the parents. In turn, the reliability coefficients of all the subscales range from .763 to .917 in the adolescent group, but two of the subscales have lower reliability: stress management and general health practice. In the parent group, Cronbach's α for all the subscales ranges from

.726 to .914, but, just like in the adolescent group, two scales have lower reliability: once again stress management and security.

Family cohesion and flexibility was measured using David Olson's FACES-IV in a Polish adaptation by A. Margasiński (2015) called Skala Oceny Rodziny – SOR (Family Rating Scale). The questionnaire consists of 62 items forming eight scales: balanced cohesion, balanced flexibility, disengagement, enmeshment, rigidity, chaos, family communication, and family life satisfaction. Two scales were used in the research: balanced cohesion, referred to in the study as family cohesion (e.g. "Family members participate in joint family activities even though they have their own interests") and balanced flexibility, referred to as family flexibility (e.g. "My family can change if need be"). Responses to all items are rated on a scale from 1 to 5, with 1 – completely disagree and 5 – completely agree (the remaining scales are formed from statements whose truthfulness in relation to the family is rated by the participant on a 5-point scale from 1 – completely agree to 5 – completely disagree) (Margasiński, 2015). The scales used have satisfactory reliability coefficients for the adolescent group studied (Cronbach's α for the balanced cohesion scale is .849, and for the balanced flexibility scale it is .812), as well as in the parent group (Cronbach's α for the balanced cohesion scale is .860, and for the balanced flexibility scale it is .793).

A questionnaire prepared by the authors (used to collect additional sociodemographic data and other data including self-rated health, acceptance of disability, as well as frequency of contacts with friends: direct and using social media).

The analyses also used sociogeographical data obtained from the questionnaire, as well as data on health, illness, disability, and use of medical and psychological assistance by the respondents.

Study design

The collected data were analysed using SPSS statistical software version 26 and JASP 0.16.0.0. Descriptive statistics were used to describe the basic characteristics of the participants. Data were reported as mean (*M*) and standard deviation (*SD*) for continuous variables. Nominal data are presented as numbers and percentages. In order to compare independent samples (subgroups of adolescents with intellectual disability, with physical disability, and with FASD) or dependent samples (adolescent-parent dyads in all surveyed dyads and in three subgroups of dyads), parametric or nonparametric tests were used. The differences were evaluated using χ^2, independent sample *t*-tests, the Kruskal-Wallis *H*, paired *t*-test, and nonparametric paired difference: the Wilcoxon signed-rank test as appropriate.

We also checked *r*-Pearson's correlation coefficient between all variables adopted in our model and between all dimensions of health-related quality of life. Regression analysis and mediation were conducted to verify the predictors and mediators of adolescents' health-related quality of life among their personal and their social resources. The indirect effect was tested using the bootstrapping technique, a non-parametric procedure based on random substitution sampling and producing point estimates and bias-corrected confidence intervals for the indirect effect. Mediation analysis was conducted with a PROCESS macro for SPSS with 5,000 bootstraps and bias correction (Hayes, 2013). The acceptable confidence interval was 95%. Mediation was statistically significant, where the result did not include zero. The criterion for statistical significance was $p < 0.05$ for all analyses.

References

Alessandri, G., Vecchione, G.M., Steca, P., Caprara, M.G., & Capara, G.V. (2007). A revised version of Kremen and Block's Ego Resiliency Scale in an Italian sample. *TPM*, *14*, 165–183.

American Association on Mental Retardation. (2002). *Mental Retardation: Definition, Classification, and System of Supports*. (10th edn). Washington DC: AAMR.

Banach, M., & Matejek, J. (2017). Uczniowie szkół ponadgimnazjalnych o Spektrum Poalkoholowym Uszkodzeń Płodu (FASD) [Upper-Secondary School Students on Fetal Alcohol Spectrum Disorder (FASD)]. *Wychowanie w rodzinie* [*Education in the Family*], *XVI*(2), 174–189. 10.23734/wwr20172.173.189.

Banach, M., & Matejek, J. (2019). Edukacja dziecka z FASD w szkole – propozycje metodycznego działania – ograniczenia i możliwości [School Education of Children with FASD – Proposed Methodological Action – Limitations and Possibilities] *Szkoła - Zawód - Praca* [*School - Profession - Labour*], *18*, 122–135.

Barnes, C., Mercer, G., & Shakespeare, T. (2010). The social model of disability. In A. Giddens & P. Sutton (eds.), *Sociology: Introductory readings*, 3rd edn. (161–166). Cambridge: Polity Press.

Behle, A.E., & Pinquart, M. (2015). Perceived attainment of developmental tasks in adolescents with and without physical disabilities. *Journal of Developmental and Physical Disabilities*, *27*, 773–787.

Bickenbach, J.E. (2014). The international classifcation of functioning, disability and health and its relationship to disability studies. In N. Watson, A. Roulstone & C. Thomas (eds.), *Routledge Handbook of Disability Studies* (51–66). Routledge Taylor & Francis Group.

Bickenbach, J.E. (2019). The ICF and its relationship to disability studies. In N. Watson & S. Vehmas (eds.), *Routledge Handbook of Disability Studies*. Routledge Taylor & Francis Group.

Block, J.L. & Kremen, A.M. (1996). IQ and ego-resiliency: Conceptual and empirical connections and separateness. *Journal of Personality and Social Psychology*, *40*, 349–361.

Byra, S. (2012). *Przystosowanie do życia z niepełnosprawnością ruchową i chorobą przewlekłą. Struktura i uwarunkowanie* [*Adaptation to Life with Physical Disability and Chronic Disease. Structure and Determinants*]. Wydawnictwo Uniwersytetu Marie Curie-Skłodowskiej.

Byra, S. (2009). Prototypowa kategoryzacja osób z niepełnosprawnością [Prototypical Categorisation of Persons with Disabilities]. *Człowiek – Niepełnosprawność – Społeczeństwo* [*Humans – Disability – Society*], *1*, 61–76.

Byra, S. (2019). *Niepełnosprawność ruchowa w paradygmacie pozytywnie ukierunkowanym* [*Physical Disability in a Positively Oriented Paradigm*]. Wydawnictwo Uniwersytetu Marii Curie-Skłodowskiej.

Byra, S., Boczkowska, M., & Duda, M. (2016), Współczesne konteksty znaczeniowe terminu „niepełnosprawność" – implikacje Międzynarodowej Klasyfikacji Funkcjonowania, Niepełnosprawności i Zdrowia (ICF) [Contemporary Contexts of Meaning of the Term "Disability" – Implications of the International Classification of Functioning, Disability and Health (ICF)]. *Człowiek – Niepełnosprawność – Społeczeństwo* [*Humans – Disability – Society*], *4*, 15–31.

Chrzanowska, I. (2021), *Pedagogika specjalna* [*Special Education*]. Impuls.

Cieza, A., & Stucki, G. (2008). The international classification of functioning disability and health: Its development process and content validity. *European Journal of Physical and Rehabilitation Medicine*, *44*, 303–313.

Dahl, T.H. (2002). International classification of functioning, disability, and health: An introduction and discussion of its potential impact on rehabilitation services and research. *Journal of Rehabilitation Medicine*, *34*, 201–204.

De la Vega, R., Racine, M., Castarlenas, E., Solé, E., Roy, R., Jensen, M.P., Miró, J., & Cane, D. (2018). The role of sleep quality and fatique on the benefits of an interdyscyplinary treatment for adults with chronic pain. *PAIN Practice*, *19*, 354–362. 10.1111/papr.12746.

DeVidi, D., & Klausen, C. (2017). No mere difference. *Dialogue*, *56*, 357–379.

Diamond, K.E., Huang, H., & Steed, E.A. (2007). The development of social competence in children with disabilities. In P.K. Smith & C.H. Hart (eds.), *The Wiley-Blackwell Handbook of Childhood Social Development* (2nd ed., 627–645). Wiley.

Duda, M. (2016). *Poczucie jakości życia młodzieży z problemami zdrowotnymi* [*Perceived Quality of Life in Adolescents with Health Problems*]. Wydawnictwo Uniwersytetu Marii Curie-Skłodowskiej.

Forstner, M. (2022). Conceptual models of disability: The development of the consideration of non-biomedical aspects. *Disabilities*, *2*, 540–563. 10.3390/disabilities 2030039.

Franiok, P. (2005). *Vzdělávání osob s mentálním postižením.* Ostavská univerzita v Ostravie.

Gajdzica, Z. (2007). *Edukacyjne konteksty bezradności społecznej osób z lekkim upośledzeniem umysłowym* [*Educational Contexts of Social Helplessness in People with Mild Mental Disability*]. Wydawnictwo Uniwersytetu Śląskiego.

Gajdzica, Z. (2017). Wybrane pułapki niewspółmierności w badaniach świata osób z niepełnosprawnością [Selected pitfalls of incommensurability in research on the world of persons with disabilities]. In M. Dudzikowa & S. Juszczyk (eds.), *Pułapki epistemologiczne i metodologiczne w badaniach nad edukacją. Jak sobie z nimi radzić?* [*Epistemological and Methodological Pitfalls in Studies on Education. How to Cope with Them?*] (212–223). Wydawnictwo Uniwersytetu Śląskiego.

Gajdzica, Z. (2020). *Uczeń z lekką niepełnosprawnością intelektualną w szkole ogólnodostępnej. Nauczyciele o (nie)zmienianej sytuacji w kontekście kultury szkoły inkluzyjnej* [*Students with Mild Intellectual Disability in Mainstream Schools. Teachers on the (Non-)Changeable Situation in the Context of Inclusive School Culture*]. Wydawnictwo Naukowe PWN.

Garbat, M. (2015). *Historia niepełnosprawności. Geneza i rozwój rehabilitacji, pomocy technicznych oraz wsparcia społecznego osób z niepełnosprawnościami* [*History of Disability. Origin and Development of Rehabilitation, Technical Aids and Social Support for Persons with Disabilities*]. Nove Res.

Haegele, J.A., & Hodge, S. (2016) Disability discourse: Overview and critiques of the medical and social models, *Quest*, *68*, 193–206. 10.1080/00336297.2016.1143849.

Harris, J.C. (2006). *Intellectual Disability: Understanding Its Development, Causes, Classification, Evaluation, and Treatment*. Oxford University Press.

Hayes, A.F. (2013). *Introduction to Mediation, Moderation, and Conditional Process Analysis: A Regression-Based Approach*. The Guilford Press.

Hofmann, B. (2016). *Disease, Illness, and Sickness. The Routledge Companion to Philosophy of Medicine*. Routledge.

Holland-Hall, C., & Quint, E.H. (2017). Sexuality and disability in adolescents. *Pediatric Clinics in North America*, *64*, 435–449. 10.1016/j.pcl.2016.11.011.

Intellectual Disability (2010). *Definition, Classification, and System of Supports*. (11th edn). Washington DC: American Association on Intellectual and Development Disabilities.

Jones, K., & Smith, D. (1973). Recognition of the fetal alcohol syndrome in early infancy. *The Lancet*, *302*, 999–1001.

KIDSCREEN Group Europe (2006). *The KIDSCREEN Questionnaires Quality of Life Questionnaires for Children and Adolescents*. Handbook. Lengerich: Pabst Science Publishers.

Kirenko, J. (2007) *Indywidualna i społeczna percepcja niepełnosprawności* [*Individual and Social Perception of Disability*]. Wydawnictwo Uniwersytetu Marii Curie-Skłodowskiej.

Kirenko, J. (2022). *Aspiracje rodzicielskie wobec dzieci z niepełnosprawnościami. Struktura i uwarunkowania* [*Parental Aspirations for Children with Disabilities. Structure and Determinants*]. Wydawnictwo Uniwersytetu Marii Curie-Skłodowskiej.

Klecka, M. (2020). *Fascynujące dzieci* [*Fascinating Children*]. Ośrodek Fastryga.

Kołodziej-Zaleska A., Ilska M., Brandt-Salmeri A., Jazłowska A., & Przybyła-Basista H. (2023). How to measure ego-resiliency in the face of various life-changing crises: Measurement invariance, convergent and discriminant validity and reliability of the Polish version of the Revised Ego-Resiliency Scale (ER89-R12), *PeerJ*, *11*, e14499. 10.7717/peerj.14499.

Kołodziej-Zaleska, A., & Przybyła-Basista, H. (2018). Ego-resiliency jako zasób osobisty – narzędzie pomiaru i jego wykorzystanie w badaniach interdyscyplinarnych [Ego-Resiliency as a Personal Resource – Measurement Tool and Its Use in Interdisciplinary Research]. *Czasopismo Psychologiczne* [*Psychology Periodical*], *24*, 159–170.

Koselleck. R. (2012). *Semantyka historyczna* [*Historical Semantics*]. Wydawnictwo Poznańskie.

Kowalik, S. (2018). *Stosowana psychologia rehabilitacji* [*Applied Psychology of Rehabilitation*]. Wydawnictwo Naukowe Scholar.

Krause. A. (2010). *Współczesne paradygmaty pedagogiki specjalnej* [*Contemporary Paradigms of Special Education*]. Impuls
Livneh, H. (2021). Psychosocial adaptation to chronic illness and disability: An updated and expanded conceptual framework. *Rehabilitation Counseling Bulletin*, *65*. 10.1177/003435522110348.
Majewicz P. (2012). *Psychospołeczna adaptacja osób z niepełnosprawnością ruchową w okresie dorosłości* [*Psychosocial Adaptation of Persons with Physical Disability in Adulthood*]. Wydawnictwo Naukowe Uniwersytetu Pedagogicznego.
Margasiński, A. (2015). The polish adaptation of FACES IV-SOR. *Polish Journal of Applied Psychology*, *13*, 43–66.
Mazur J., Małkowska-Szkutnik A., Dzielska A., & Tabak I. (2011). *Polska wersja kwestionariuszy do badania jakości życia związanej ze zdrowiem dzieci i młodzieży (KIDSCREEN)* [*Polish Version of Questionnaires for the Study of Health-Related Quality of Life in Children and Adolescents (KIDSCREEN)*]. Instytut Matki i Dziecka.
Miyahara, M., & Piek, J. (2006). Self-esteem of children and adolescents with physical disabilitie: Quantitative evidence from meta-analysis. *Journal of Developmental and Physical Disabiltiies*, *18*, 219–234. 10.1007/s10882-006-9014-8.
Nagi, S. (1965). *Some Conceptual Issues in Disability and Rehabilitation*. American Sociological Association.
Nagi, S.Z. (1991). A disability concepts revisited: Implication for prevention. In A. Pope, A. Tarlow (eds.), *Disability in America; Toward a National Agenda for Prevention* (309–327). Washington: National Academies Press.
Oliver, M. (2013). The social model of disability: Thirty years on. *Disability & Society*, *28*, 1024–1026. 10.1080/09687599.2013.818773.
Olkin, R. (1999). *What psychotherapists should know about disability*. Guilford Press.
Ow, N., Appau, A., Matout, M., & Mayo N.E. (2021). What is QOL in children and adolescents with physical disabilities? A thematic synthesis of pediatric QOL literaturę. *Quality of Life Research*, *30*, 1233–1248. 10.1007/s11136-021-02769-6.
Piasecki, M., Besowski, S., & Czech, R. (1998). Społeczny model niepełnosprawności [Social model of disability]. *Problemy Rehabilitacji Społecznej i Zawodowej* [*Problems of Social and Professional Rehabilitation*], *1*, 47–52.
Pinquart, M., & Pfeiffer, J.P. (2015). Solving developmental tasks in adolescents with a chronic physical illness or physical/sensory disability: A meta-analysis. *International Journal of Disability, Development and Education*, *62*, 249–264. 10.1080/1034912X.2015.1020922.
Powrie, B., Kolehmainen, N., Turpin, M., Ziviani, J., & Copley, J. (2015). The meaning of leisure for children and young people with physical disabilities: A systematic evidence synthesis. *Developmental Medicine & Child Neurology*, *57*, 993–1010. 10.1111/dmcn.12788.
Raustorp, A., & Lindwall, M. (2015). Physical self-esteem - A ten-year follow-up study from early adolescence to early adulthood. *International Journal of Adolescent Medicine and Health*, *27*, 31–39.
Ravens-Sieberer, U., Auquier, P., Erhart, M., Gosch, A., Rajmil, L., Bruil, J., Power, M., Duer, W., Cloetta, B., Czemy, L., Mazur, J., Czimbalmos, A., Tountas, Y.,

Hagquist, C., Kilroe, J., & European KIDSCREEN Group (2007). The KIDSCREEN-27 quality of life measure for children and adolescents: Psychometric results from a cross-cultural survey in 13 European countries. *Quality of Life Research: An International Journal of Quality of Life Aspects of Treatment, Care and Rehabilitation*, *16*, 1347–1356. 10.1007/s11136-007-9240-2.

Ravens-Sieberer, U., Gosch, A., Rajmil, L., Erhart, M., Bruil, J., Duer, W., Auquier, P., Power, M., Abel, T., Czemy, L., Mazur, J., Czimbalmos, A., Tountas, Y., Hagquist, C., Kilroe, J., & Kidscreen Group, E. (2005). KIDSCREEN-52 quality-of-life measure for children and adolescents. *Expert Review of Pharmacoeconomics & Outcomes Research*, *5*(3), 353–364. 10.1586/14737167.5.3.353.

Robitail, S., Ravens-Sieberer, U., Simeoni, M.C., Rajmil, L., Bruil, J., Power, M., Duer, W., Cloetta, B., Czemy, L., Mazur, J., Czimbalmos, A., Tountas, Y., Hagquist, C., Kilroe, J., & Auquier, P. (2007). Testing the structural and cross-cultural validity of the KIDSCREEN-27 quality of life questionnaire. *Quality of Life Research*, *16*, 1335–1345. 10.1007/s11136-007-9241-1.

Shakespeare, T. (2016). The social model of disability. In L.J. Davis (ed.), *The Disability Studies Reader*, 4th edn. (214–221). Routledge Taylor & Francis Group.

Smith, D.D. (2004). *Introduction to Special Education: Teaching in an Age of Opportunity Study Guide*, (5th edition). IDEA.

Speck, O. (2005), *Niepełnosprawni w społeczeństwie. Podstawy ortopedagogiki* [*Disabled Persons in Society. Fundamentals of Orthopedagogy*]. GWP.

Speck, O. (2015). *Osoby z niepełnosprawnością intelektualną. Podręcznik dla celów wychowawczych i edukacyjnych* [*Persons with Intellectual Disability. Textbook for Education and Teaching Purposes*]. Harmonia Universalis.

Streissguth, A.P. (1997). *Fetal Alcohol Syndrom. A Guide for Families and Communities*. Brooks.

Streissguth, A.P., & Dehaene, P. (1993). Fetal alcohol syndrome in twins of alcoholic mothers; concordance of diagnosis and IQ. *American Journal of Medical Genetic*, *47*, 857–862.

Tuffrey, C. (2013). Adolescents with physical disability: Seeing the individual in context. *Archives of Disease in Childhood*, *98*, 373–377. 10.1136/archdischild-2 012-302839.

WHO (1980). *International Classification of Impairments, Disabilities, and Handicaps: A Manual of Classification Relating to the Consequences of Disease*. Geneva, Switzerland: WHO.

WHO (2001). *ICF - International Classification of Functioning, Disability and Health Functioning, Disability and Health*. Geneva, Switzerland: WHO.

Wyczesany, J. (2002). *Pedagogika upośledzonych umysłowo. Od tradycji do współczesności* [*Pedagogy of the Mentally Disabled. From Tradition to the Present Day*]. Impuls.

Zasępa, E. (2016). *Osoba z niepełnosprawnością intelektualną. Procesy poznawcze* [*A Person with Intellectual Disability. Cognitive Processes*]. Impuls.

Chapter 3

Mental health evaluation by adolescents with a disability and by their parents

Jan Kochanowski's short poem *On Health*, written in the 16th century, is a classic work of Polish literature emphasising the timeless value of health.

> My good and noble health, thou matter'st more than wealth.
> None know'th thy worth until thou fad'st, and we fall ill.
> And every man can see, in stark reality,
> And every man will say:
> 'Tis health I need today.'"

As per the above quote, in the past, as today, health has usually been unanimously mentioned as one of the most important values in human life, and as a desirable state (Wollmann, 2001). Its definitions, however, tend to vary. They are determined by various factors. The starting point is provided by the different models of health formulated on the basis of the currently available knowledge and the beliefs developed. In the individual context, the circumstances in which the definition of health is formed are important. From the point of view of the aspects addressed in this work, a particular situation in which people seek to define it involves health- and/or life-threatening circumstances, such as pandemic, war or the experience of illness and disability, whether one's own or of a loved one. "Everyone sets their own price on life and health (...) the price of health increases when its resources diminish, it fluctuates when health and life compete against other values, and especially when they come into drastic conflict with them" (Demel, 1989, p. 240).

The starting point is usually the definition of health provided by the World Health Organization (WHO), which was enshrined in the latter's Constitution in 1946 and finally entered into force in 1948: "a state of complete physical, mental and social well-being and not merely the absence of disease or infirmity" (WHO, 2014, p. 1). The WHO definition of health emphasised the importance of the multidimensionality of health, as a conglomerate of physical, psychological, and social aspects (Card, 2017).

DOI: 10.4324/9781003367772-3

Referring to the assumptions underlying antireductionism (put forward by Frankl, among others), a fourth aspect, namely the noetic/spiritual element, should be added to the three areas mentioned above (Kropińska, 2000). Consequently, the following four dimensions describe health:

- physical – somatic health, considered as the correct functioning of body systems;
- psychological – the emotional sphere (including coping with stress, self-awareness, insight) the mind (optimal cognitive functioning), translating into a particular mental structure of the human individual;
- social – having (building and maintaining) correct and satisfactory relationships with others, performing social roles, feeling of belonging to specific groups, and contributing to one's identification in relation to this very social context;
- spiritual – related to the individual's spirituality realised on the basis of/with the contribution of religious doctrines and/or an individual value system, a credo (Kluczyńska, 2015; Wilczek-Rużyczka & Kwak, 2022). This provision simultaneously confirmed the right of every human being to enjoy the highest possible and attainable level of health (Ostrzyżek & Marcinkowski, 2012).

The WHO definition formally initiated a process of moving away from the reductionist, biomedical model of health that had been in place until then (for nearly 200 years). It opened up a new chapter in the perception of health, and it definitely deserves credit for that. It laid the foundations for a biopsychosocial model of health. However, the nearly 80-year-old WHO definition is no longer in line with the changing reality and with new scientific perspectives (Card, 2017).

The biomedical model seems to be useful to a certain extent, and tends to be applied relatively frequently for the purposes of medical certificates, procedures or diagnosis in health care. It defines the patient's condition following clear norms, i.e. diagnostic criteria. They are clear, but very dichotomous and reductionist, recalling health behaviourism (Carvalho et al., 2008; Cianciara & Piotrowicz, 2018; Misselbrook, 2014). Its consequence is often the medicalisation of life. States of well-being, previously not considered in terms of negative well-being, have started to be interpreted as health problems driving the pharmaceutical industry (Illich, 1975; Lancet, 2009). From the patient's point of view, in turn, the biopsychosocial perspective emerges as a much friendlier approach (Misselbrook, 2014). The biopsychosocial/holistic-functional/holistic model was developed at the end of the 20th century and became the basic trend in thinking about the human being (Dolińska-Zygmunt, 2001).

A certain novelty appeared in the holistic philosophy (in relation to biomedical assumptions): an additional important dimension, no longer situated within the individual, but external with regard to the latter. The environmental context of the model emphasises the significance of the surroundings, of coping with problems whose source lies in the external environment and, ultimately, of adapting to the requirements of the individual's environment; this is referred to as the adaptive model, assuming the possibility of positive physical/physiological, mental, and social adaptation to changes in the environment (Cianciara & Piotrowicz, 2018; Menatti et al., 2022).

This approach to the relationship between health and the environment is evident for instance in strategies developed across various sectors, emphasising the importance of the synergic combination of interdisciplinary solutions for the sake of health. An example is the "One Health" idea, integrating the aspects of ecology, culture, community, as well as local and global needs and concerns into sustainable health-oriented activity (One Health High-Level Expert Panel, 2022). Taking into account the socioeconomic, cultural, and environmental determinants of health is important for collective prevention, health promotion, healthy lifestyle, and optimal health care, dedicated in particular to people who, due to their personal limitations, experience specific inequalities in this area (Cianciara & Piotrowicz, 2018).

There is no consensus around the existing WHO definition of health. Among other things, it has been criticised for an overly idealistic vision. Other objections have concerned the political determinants of the definition of health. According to researchers, the definitional study drafted by League of Nations veteran Raymond Gautier was based on a controversial publication by medical historian Sigerist, presenting socialist trends in Soviet medicine (after: Larsen, 2022). The classic WHO definition has also been challenged with regard to the definition of health formulated in situations of chronic illness and disability. They exclude the individual from the "healthy" status. Full well-being for persons with experiences of disability and disorders seems straight out impossible if one follows the WHO definition. Thus, the latter, due to its reductionist nature, becomes useless (Sturmberg, 2013; Leonardi, 2018; van Druten et al., 2022). Finally, the WHO definition refers to a certain state. Meanwhile, health (in its various dimensions) is subject to transformations. It is a dynamic process, both in relation to the individual's health over the life course, and in relation to community health transformations, challenges and health issues appearing across generations, such as ageing of the population and various changes in the course of diseases affecting people (Huber et al., 2011).

Another important aspect (especially from a developmental perspective, "towards health") is that of health needs (De Freitas et al., 2022). Their determination, both from an individual and collective viewpoint, is important for designing and optimising interventions and planning aid policy for health-promoting impacts. Meanwhile, there is a lack of clear scientific definitions, and consequently also of clear guidelines for organising and targeting contemporary health-promoting practice, based on values; postulating equality and freedom from stigma, among other things (Card, 2017).

The observations cited above discredit in a way the classic WHO definition by pointing to its theoretical and practical shortcomings. A fuller definition is needed, approaching health as individually experienced well-being in a holistic dimension (mental and physical well-being). Understood in this manner, health does not refer to a dichotomy, but to a certain continuum on which disease or disability are not key for the individual's determination of their state of health (Card, 2017).

In addition to the biomedical model referred to above, the WHO definition of health, and the biopsychosocial model, there is also the proposition that health be approached as a dynamic, goal-oriented, value-based process, as development, as the potential to exist/to be in spite of the obstacles, and/or with the resources and capabilities to cope with these obstacles (Misselbrook, 2014). Health is also sometimes defined as capabilities. Thus, the theory identifies, in a sense, the human being with a source of health-promoting potentials (Nussbaum, 2011). This concept also refers in a certain ways to the trend (close to us during the preparation of this work) emphasising the health-determining potentials that exist in the human being.

When addressing the aspect of health determinants, it seems necessary to refer to a classic concept from the Lalonde Report. In 1974, Marc Lalonde, the Canadian Minister of National Health and Welfare, presented a document (which went down in the history of health thought as the Lalonde Report) in which he identified "health fields," i.e. factors determining health (Lalonde, 1974). It is estimated that the individual's lifestyle has the greatest impact on their health, determining even over 50% of the latter. Lifestyle is the totality of behaviours undertaken by the individual and controllable by the latter. The physical environment is not insignificant either (about 21% of the impacts on health; this is an area on which the individual generally has no influence), genetic factors (including personal characteristics, such as age and gender; approx. 16%), and health care (nearly 10%) (Lalonde, 1974; Woźniak et al., 2015).

Another alternative way of thinking about health is Aaron Antonovsky's salutogenetic concept. For this author, the central construct is a sense of coherence, representing a health-promoting attitude towards stress, towards one's own resources, and towards the process of coping with specific challenges. Sense of coherence makes it possible to interpret various events the individual encounters in terms of their comprehensibility, meaningfulness, and manageability. It is the result of the analysis that the individual performs through the lens of these three dimensions that makes them interpret a specific event/experience as positive or negative. Understood in this way, sense of coherence determines health and quality of life. Salutogenesis explains the cause of health, not the reason for disease (Antonovsky, 1987). According to the author, sense of coherence is established at a relative level around the age of 30. "It is with entry into adulthood, with long-range commitment to persons, social roles and work that the experiences of childhood and adolescence are re-enforced or reversed in both directions" (Antonovsky, 1995, p. 106). Significantly, especially from the point of view of the research presented in this publication, the family factor is the most important for the development of "salutogenetic" resources. Of key importance, although not entirely determinant, for the development of a child's sense of coherence is the quality of the parent-child relationship, family cohesion (Braun-Lewensohn et al., 2016; Garcia-Moya et al., 2013). The salutogenetic concept has been successfully applied regardless of the cultural context: its nature is international. Its value is recognised in analyses of the quality of life in people with chronic diseases is recognised (Apers et al., 2016; Delgado, 2007).

In the salutogenetic concept, sense of coherence is identified with attitude (Antonovsky, 1987). The literature contains an interesting reference to the three key dimensions of A. Antonovsky's sense of coherence. They are linked to the three components of attitude (Mądrzycki, 1977; Wojciszke, 2004):

- the cognitive component (beliefs, assumptions, expectations, knowledge) – sense of comprehensibility (perception of external and internal signals as ones that make sense and are clear and explainable);
- the behavioural component (a tendency towards certain behaviours and actions) – sense of manageability (perception of resources as sufficient to cope with incoming stimuli);
- the emotional-motivational component (affective, sensory-judgmental; emotional attitude, feelings) – a sense of meaningfulness (feeling that life has meaning on an emotional level, sense of being involved in an effective coping process), constituting a key factor of coherence (Łuszczyńska-Cieślak, 2001a, 2001b). This may represent an extension of the understanding of attitudes towards stress/health (Rutkowska, 2008).

Similar dimensions can be found among the determinants of health awareness, which in turn determines the presentation of specific health behaviours. This is known as the Information-Motivation-Behavioural Skills Model. It takes into account knowledge about health, the skills making it possible to build autonomy and self-efficacy (communicative skills – in the area of interpersonal relations, but also in the use of the media and other sources of knowledge) and motivation (intrinsic and extrinsic, which also includes the ability to use social support; this aspect moreover relates to the importance of socialisation, the influence of parents/guardians and the individual's value/spiritual system) (Fisher et al., 2003; Joseph & Fleary, 2021).

Health awareness, mentioned above, is one of the key aspects in the context of care for health. A period of intensive learning of responsibility, also for one's health, is adolescence, important in the context of the research topic presented in work. The literature points to inadequate knowledge of health awareness issues, emphasising at the same time the high demand for such knowledge (Fleary & Joseph, 2020; Joseph & Fleary, 2021). While emphasising the importance of developing and enforcing responsibility for one's own health, it should be noted (and this might be, in fact, particularly relevant from the point of view of the research presented here) that there are groups of people (for instance seniors and/or persons with disabilities) with relatively less possibilities or competences to manage their own health potential (Jambores et al., 2016).

This review is not an exhaustive presentation of all approaches to health. Over 120 definitions of health alone have been counted (Domaradzki, 2013). Attempts to formulate them have been made by experts for instance in the field of medical sciences, humanities and social sciences, often involving inter-disciplinary, intersectoral cooperation. However, the efforts so far, despite some interesting proposals, have failed to produce a single valid definition (Larson, 1999). There is a need to establish a single, new coherent definition of health as a goal, embedded in the holistic philosophy and matching our contemporary times and the related challenges. This is extremely important from the point of view of health care recipients and providers. It will improve the effectiveness and adequacy of targeted systemic interventions for the sake of health (Leonardi, 2018; van Druten et al., 2022).

An interesting and inspiring overview, taking into account the specific transformations and chronology of the terminological redefinition of health is presented below:

- "WHO – 1948 – Health is a state of complete physical, mental and social well-being and not merely the absence of disease or infirmity;
- WHO – 1986 – Health is a resource for everyday life, not the objective of living. Health is a positive concept emphasizing social and personal resources, as well as physical capacities;
- WHO – 2001 – Health is considered distinct from function and disability. Health conditions, environmental factors, and personal factors influence disability. Disability is an umbrella term that refers to impairments, activity limitations, and participation restrictions;
- Sartorius, 2006 – Health is a state of balance whereby individuals with disease or impairment are considered healthy by their ability to establish an internal equilibrium that allows them to get the most they can from their life despite the presence of disease or infirmity;
- The Lancet, 2009 – Health is dynamic adaptation to stressors akin to resilience (Schulkin, 2004) and sense of coherence (Antonovsky, 1979);
- Huber et al., 2011, 2016 – Health is dynamic based on one's ability to adapt and to self-manage" to maintain and restore one's sense of integrity, equilibrium and sense of well-being. Six proposed dimensions of positive

health are: bodily functions, mental functions and perception, existential, quality of life, social and societal participation, and daily functioning;
- Halfon et al., 2014 – Health as creating capacities to achieve goals, satisfy needs, fortify reserves;
- Authors. – 2020 – Health is the dynamic balance of physical, mental, social, and existential well-being in adapting to conditions of life and the environment." (Krahn 2021, p. 3)

The attempts to summarise the deliberations and investigations so far lead to the emergence of a general direction in defining health. It can be considered in two broad categories:

- the predisposition, resource, or capability to comprehensively develop and cope with different situations;
- the process of adaptation, seeking, and maintaining a relative balance in a dynamically changing reality. (Heszen-Niejodek et al., 2000)

The literature continues to present the multi-directional discussions on definitions of health. Many of them emphasise the need to take into account not only the facts (objective health) and the various factors, but above all, with the patient-centred, goal-focused care in mind, the subjective opinions of those constructing the definitions of health as they describe their own condition (subjective health). This seems particularly important in the context of a group of people who experience on a daily basis the confrontation between health and disability, limitations, disorders, and chronic diseases, especially in the distinctive period of adolescence (Card, 2017; Lynn et al., 2015; Reuben & Tinetti, 2012).

However, the lack of unambiguous definitions reached in the area of broadly understood health, combined with the importance of the issue and the need to develop health awareness and to formulate a systemic response to health needs (especially in the group of people with special needs) led us to undertake research on key concepts around health aspects. An additional factor making this topic particularly important is the context of the research, namely the pandemic and the outbreak of war in Ukraine, Poland's neighbouring country. At the same time, the turnabout we are witnessing in thinking about health, the reconceptualisation of health on a continuum, showing it as determined by various factors (personal, social, environmental), being a dynamic system of balance and adaptation, has been one of the inspirations for a research-based and theoretical investigation of the aspects of health-related quality of life in a group of persons with disabilities. With the ICF concept, the experience of disability as a trait (rather than as a deficit) does not have to change the definition of health, and above all, the sense of being healthy.

Consequently, we invited young people with disabilities and FASD and their parents to participate in the study. In the course of our research work, we verified the extent to which respondents agreed with the WHO definition. They were also invited to write down their own proposed understanding of the concept (see Table 3.1).

The following stage of the survey involved self-assessment of their health: in general, but also in the four key areas/aspects: physical, mental, social, and spiritual. In Table 3.2, we present data on the health of adolescents with intellectual disabilities, physical disabilities, and FASD, and their parents. Table 3.2 also shows the results of comparisons of adolescent-parent dyads in the area of selected variables concerning health, illness and treatment. Non-parametric test for the matched sample was used.

The results presented indicate that adolescents and parents agree to an equal extent with the WHO definition of health. They also rate their own family's healthy lifestyle similarly (see Table 3.1). However, the self-rated health in general and in the distinguished areas of physical, mental, social, and spiritual health is different between adolescents with intellectual disabilities/physical disabilities/FASD and their parents. According to the results, adolescents rate their health lower in all areas compared to their parents.

In addition, the adolescent group includes has a higher share of individuals using the help of specialist physicians and a significantly higher proportion of people with chronic illnesses than the parent group. At the same time, the difference between adolescents and their parents in terms of the use of psychological or psychiatric help turned out to be statistically insignificant, as opposed to the difference in the use of pharmacological/psychiatric treatment, with a higher percentage of adolescents using it compared to their parents. A vast majority of the adolescents surveyed described themselves as disabled persons, while almost none of the parents felt disabled (see Table 3.2).

A starting point of sorts for the investigations into the theme of the research is the aspect of defining health and the related context of defining disability, both in the group of adolescents and their parents. Formulating a definition of health is, in line with Pender's health promotion model we refer to more extensively in the final section of the work, crucial for the health-promoting behaviours chosen and implemented (Buck & Ryan-Wenger, 2003; Heydari & Khorashadizadeh, 2014). This, in turn, can provide an important backdrop for health-related quality of life.

Particularly important is how people with disabilities define health. Disability (in spite of the ICF assumptions we present) does build (and continues to do so, despite a number of changes that have taken place) a specific reference to the states recognised within the framework of the biomedical model. Being able to step out of this pattern, thus creating a definition of health that relates to the biopsychosocial concept, and reflecting oneself in it, presents persons with disabilities with an opportunity to see (and experience) themselves as healthy people. This, in turn, is of key

Table 3.1 Health defined by teenagers with intellectual disability, physical disability, and FASD, and their parents

	Adolescents with intellectual disabilty, physical disability, and FASD (n = *98)*	*Parents of adolescents with intellectual disabilty, physical disability and FASD* (n = *98)*
One of the most popular definitions of health is that health is a state of complete physical, mental, and social well-being and not merely the absence of disease or infirmity.	84 teenagers (85.7%) agree with this definition. Eight teenagers (8.2%) have no opinion, and six (6.1%) disagree with the definition, giving their own definitions of health.	82 parents (83.7%) agree with this definition. Six parents (6.1%) have no opinion, and ten parents (10.2%) disagree, giving their own definitions of health.
	W = .06, *p* = .949	
Respondents' own definitions of health	• The highest value • Health is joy • Able-bodiedness • Something important • The most important thing • Health • Physical and mental wellbeing • I don't get sick, I have the strength and desire to do things, go to the swimming pool and hang out with my friends • Everything	• A valued asset more important than wealth • Someone who's independent and able to take care of their own life is healthy. An exception is an incurable disease that destroys the body. One we have no control of. • A state in which I have no worries or ailments • Physical and mental wellbeing • It's a state of moderate happiness • Health is the most important thing because without it we are unable to function and think normally • The best thing • A sense of security • Health is everything to me: when you're healthy, you can move, you can exercise, work, study, take on different challenges, etc. • For me, health is about feeling good, not being ill, having a good lifestyle, e.g. do sports. • Something very important

Note: W - *The Wilcoxon signed-rank test based on negative ranks.*

Table 3.2 Health of teenagers with intellectual disability, physical disability, and FASD, and their parents: Results of non-parametric paired difference test in all surveyed dyads

	Adolescents with intellectual disabilty, physical disability, and FASD (n = *98)*	*Parents of adolescents with intellectual disabilty, physical disability and FASD* (n = *98)*
General self-rated health	Bad *n* = 0(0%) Not very good *n* = 21(21.4%) Good *n* = 60(61.2%) Very good *n* = 13(13.3%) Excellent *n* = 4(4.1%) $W = -3.36$, p = **<.001**	Bad *n* = 3(3.1%) Not very good *n* = 4(4.1%) Good *n* = 49(50.0%) Very good *n* = 41(41.8%) Excellent *n* = 1(1.0%)
Physical health	Very bad *n* = 2(2.0%) Bad *n* = 14(14.3%) Average *n* = 46(46.9%) Good *n* = 26(26.5%) Very good *n* = 10(10.2%) $W = -5.88$, p = **<.001**	Very bad *n* = 0(0%) Bad *n* = 3(3.1%) Average *n* = 12(12.2%) Good *n* = 54(55.1%) Very good *n* = 29(29.6%)
Mental health	Very bad *n* = 1(1%) Bad *n* = 4(4.1%) Average *n* = 20(20.4%) Good *n* = 60(61.2%) Very good *n* = 12(12.2%) $W = -4.36$, p = **<.001**	Very bad *n* = 0(0%) Bad *n* = 3(3.1%) Average *n* = 7(7.1%) Good *n* = 50(51%) Very good *n* = 38(38.8%)
Social health	Very bad *n* = 1(1%) Bad *n* = 5(5.1%) Average *n* = 16(16.3%) Good *n* = 55(56.1%) Very good *n* = 21(21.4%) $W = -2.89$, p = **.004**	Very bad *n* = 1(1%) Bad *n* = 1(1%) Average *n* = 7(7.1%) Good *n* = 56(57.1%) Very good *n* = 33(33.7%)
Spiritual health	Very bad *n* = 1(1%) Bad *n* = 5(5.1%) Average *n* = 29(29.6%) Good *n* = 52(53.1%) Very good *n* = 11(11.2%) $W = -4.97$, p = **<.001**	Very bad *n* = 0(0%) Bad *n* = 1(1%) Average *n* = 9(9.2%) Good *n* = 52(53.1%) Very good *n* = 36(36.7%)
Healthy lifestyle of one's family	Definitely not *n* = 1(1%) Rather not n = 4(4.1%) No opinion *n* = 10(10.2%) Rather yes *n* = 65(66.3%) Definitely yes *n* = 18(18.4%) $W = -.006$, $p = .995$	Definitely not *n* = 0(0%) Rather not n = 6(6.1%) No opinion *n* = 5(5.1%) Rather yes *n* = 72(73.5%) Definitely yes *n* = 15(15.3%)
Chronic disease	Yes *n* = 22(22.4%) No *n* = 76(77.6%) $\chi^2 = 4.65$, $df = 1$, $\mathbf{p = .031}$	Yes *n* = 10(10.2%) No *n* = 88(89.8%)
Specialist physician care	Yes *n* = 71(72.4%) No *n* = 27(27.6%) $\chi^2 = 54.72$, $df = 1$, $\mathbf{p = <.001}$	Yes *n* = 9(9.2%) No *n* = 89(90.8%)

(Continued)

Table 3.2 (Continued)

	Adolescents with intellectual disabilty, physical disability, and FASD (n = 98)	*Parents of adolescents with intellectual disabilty, physical disability and FASD (n = 98)*
Psychological/ psychiatric help*	Yes *n* = 13(13.3%) No *n* = 85(86.7%) χ^2 = 2.12, *df* = 1, *p* = .143	Yes *n* = 3(3.1%) No *n* = 95(96.9%)
Pharmacological psychiatric treatment	Yes *n* = 12(12.2%) No *n* = 86(87.8%) χ^2 = 4.27, *df* = 1, ***p* = .035**	Yes *n* = 3(3.1%) No *n* = 95(96.9%)
Disability (according to own assessment)	Yes *n* = 79(80.6%) No *n* = 19(19.4%) χ^2 = 75.01, *df* = 1, ***p* = <.001**	Yes *n* = 2(2.0%) No *n* = 96(98%)

Note: W - *The Wilcoxon signed-rank test based on negative ranks.*

* In the case of surveyed adolescents, additional help on top of the standard psychological and educational assistance at school.

importance for seeing oneself in society as a full, autonomous person (Nazli, 2012; Krahn et al., 2021). The results of our research confirm this viewpoint in the youth group. Despite having and experiencing disabilities, the majority of the respondents rate their health at least as good.

The issue of defining health presented in the first part of this chapter is essentially centred around the WHO definition. According to the arguments appearing in the literature, which we have cited above, this definition is not perfect. It leads to a number of objections and triggers numerous discussions. It opens up a holistic perspective in the reflection on health. The results of our research show that a vast majority of both adolescents and parents (over 80% of respondents in both groups) agree with this definition, seeing health as multidimensional well-being. Both groups included individuals who attempted to formulate a definition themselves. Most often (in 9 out of 20 children and parents) these recorded statements involved looking at health in terms of value, with an emphasis on its priceless nature, for example: health as "the greatest value," "the most important thing," "everything," "a valued asset more important than wealth." It can be noticed that personal definitions of health formulated by parents are relatively more numerous (compared to the adolescent group), and more complete.

We do not know whether the way in which respondents define health could have been related in some way to their self-assessment. That was not studied in our research. Detailed investigations may be worth undertaking in this area. In turn, the results of our research showed a difference in self-assessment of health by young people (74 respondents rated their health in positive terms, as good, very good, or excellent) and by parents (91 considered their health to be at least good). Following consistently the WHO definition of health cited above, the trend was maintained in the context of assessing one's health in different areas; parents rated their health better in the physical, mental, social, and spiritual aspects. The following chapters will provide more insight into the reflection on the matter in the context of resources important for a potential sense of wellbeing.

One of the aspects we are curious about is the number of respondents using psychological and/or psychiatric care. This was respectively 12–13 among the adolescents, and 3 among the adults. In relation to the problematic issue of accessibility of mental health care, it is difficult to clearly determine whether our diagnosis corresponds to the actual needs of individuals, or rather to the capabilities offered by the systemic solutions currently available in Poland.

According to the Report by the Ombudsman for Children (2021), an issue of particular importance in assessing the quality of life of young people is currently the area of psychological well-being. "In the opinion of the Board of Experts advising the Ombudsman for Children, it is among the most important ones, especially in the context of the pandemic threat and the experience of social isolation" (Raport RPD, 2021, p. 3). The results of research conducted in Poland for the above report show that 14% of children in the second year of secondary school require significant intervention with regard to mental functioning. One-fifth of respondents in this age group function below the norm in this area. In our research, bad and very bad self-rated health was declared by five persons, which is almost three times less compared to the general population of young people of a similar age.

A report by the Supreme Audit Office (NIK) of 2020 shows that in Poland, around 630,000 children and young people under the age of 18 require help from the psychological, psychotherapeutic, and psychiatric treatment system. This number, as one would expect, has increased after the pandemic period and due to a number of other challenges that have emerged. An alarming example of these upward trends is provided by reports on suicide rates. According to data from the National Police Headquarters in Poland, nearly 1,500 young people attempted suicide in 2021. Over the previous year, the increase in suicidal behaviours was as high as 77%. In comparison, 152 suicidal behaviours were reported in 2012, i.e. ten times fewer than in 2021 (NIK, 2020; ŻWJR, 2021). "According to the WHO, in the 15–29 age group, suicide is the second cause of death (after accidents) in most highly developed countries (and in some even the first)" (Solecka, 2022, p. 6). These data are highly worrying and underline the alarming reports on the mental condition of young people in general. At the same time, they reflect the high need for specialised psychological, psychotherapeutic, and psychiatric care. Above all, however, they reveal a deeper need, namely to build autonomy and self-esteem, two key components of mental health and well-being (Falissard et al., 2017).

According to the Central Register of Physicians, in 2020 in Poland there were 419, and currently, in 2022, there are 466 physicians[1] with a specialisation in child and adolescent psychiatry (NIK, 2020; ŻWJR, 2021). Although there are more specialists in the field of psychological and psychotherapeutic interventions, the market for these services in Poland has many shortcomings, especially in terms of regulation. While a part of the professional community organises psychological and psychotherapeutic help in line with the good practices and recommendations of the Polish Psychological Association and the Polish Psychiatric Association, the absence of a law on the psychological profession and the lack of adequate regulations in the field psychotherapy makes the services offered differ significantly in terms of scope and quality. At the same time, an increasing number of children and young people require help.

In the context of this information, the question arises, therefore, as to whether the young people who participated in our research did not have to face experiences requiring psychological, psychotherapeutic, or psychiatric support, whether they had already used such help (and with what result?), whether they had been unable to benefit from such help for example due to the current difficulty to access it, or whether there are other factors that hinder access (including misconceptions of young people and/or their parents about broadly perceived mental help, lack of awareness of such types of help, lack of funds to pay for private visits/therapy in this area, fatigue/overload with other forms of therapy). The results of our research are therefore accompanied by a number of questions, serving as a pretext for signalling and highlighting the rather unrewarding topic of the systemic inadequacies related to psychological, psychotherapeutic, and psychiatric care. However, we are convinced that looking after the mental health of the respondents, especially in challenging times such as ours, is one of the priorities of interventions aimed at improving health-related quality of life. Our suggestions are specified in detail in the final chapter of this publication.

Following the current WHO definition, in the model used for our research we assumed health to be tantamount to complete well-being including aspects of physical, social, and psychological functioning. According to the information presented in Chapter 2, among others, the health context also comprises spirituality. Existing research would only signal this context. Nevertheless, we do recognise the importance of spirituality for health-related quality of life.

According to our research results, three times as many parents compared to adolescents rate their spiritual health as very good, and five times fewer adults compared to their children rate this aspect as bad and very bad. The data collected justify the extension of the research field.

Spirituality is an important aspect of human culture-forming attitudes. It determines people's drive to develop, adapt, and change. It is certainly a broader concept than that of religiosity, combined with it (Skowronek & Pasek, 2013). The contemporary transformations of religiosity and spirituality in the life of people in Poland have been extremely dynamic. They also generate many forms of expression of experiencing spirituality, which generally falls within three areas: church religiosity, non-religiosity, and "new spirituality" (Beck, 2004; Mariański, 2021).

Theories exist linking the trend, noticeable a few years ago, towards improving quality of life and prosperity to the secularisation trend. The current socioeconomic situation in Poland (pandemic, war in neighbouring Ukraine, economic crisis, and the spectre of even greater inflation), as well as difficult individual and family experiences may cause people to see it in spirituality (or perhaps in religiosity/in the sacred) a source of support against their fears. This is an interesting aspect, especially in view of the special historical role religion used to play in Polish society and, at the same time, the transformation of Polish people's religiosity. While spirituality is a certain inner experience, the ability to draw on one's own resources, religion is an externally established formula adopted by the individual to understand meanings, sense, and values. People usually learn in their closest environment, which is the family (Mariański, 2021; Zwierżdżyński, 2010). Religiosity actually develops through positive relationships with one's parents/guardians. Any change in the family system influences the perception of key religious concepts. People resort to religiosity also in situations of transgression or, precisely, faced with difficult experiences such as crises (Mariański, 2021; Zwierżdżyński, 2010). Religiosity changes as one develops, and correlates strongly with the characteristics of the stages of human development. The adolescents surveyed were in the following periods:

- period of autonomous religiosity (12–17 years) – a time of intensive change, revision of previous attitudes and emergence of one's own religiosity (often devoid of practices during this period);
- period of religious authenticity (18–24 years) – creating one's own worldview and building one's own practices.

The aspects cited in this passage show how important spirituality and religiosity can be for the individual and how much it is related to the family context. A parent influencing the child's spirituality, the child-parent relationship determining the development and form of spirituality and, finally, the perception and experience of the image of the parent versus God show the undisputed connection and the exchange of sorts between the parent's and the child's concept of religiosity/values. Similarly, we can assume that a similar intra-family transfer occurs in terms of health as a value. This is an interesting aspect in light of the results of our research. While the adolescents and their parents surveyed differ in terms of self-rated health, of the experiences of (current) use of psychological/psychiatric care and, above all, of having a disability or chronic disease, the definition of health, as well as the perceived lifestyle of the family (i.e. variables included in the set of key determinants of health) is relatively similar in the dyads, with no significant differences recorded in the children's and the parents' opinions.

The selected aspects of mental or spiritual health presented above refer to contexts related to the family, to relationships, and therefore to the social context. In the following chapters, selected aspects related to the social functioning of our respondents will be analysed in detail.

Note

1 Information published by the Polish Supreme Chamber of Physicians at https://nil.org.pl/aktualnosci/6368-psychiatria-dzieci-i-mlodziezy-nie-moze-byc-samotna-wyspa (accessed: 28 Nov 2022).

References

Antonovsky, A. (1979). *Health, Stress and Coping: New Perspectives on Mental and Physical Well-Being*. Ch. 6. Jossey-Bass.

Antonovsky, A. (1987). *Unraveling the Mystery of Health: How People Manage Stress and Stay Well*. Jossey-Bass Social and behavioral Science Series.

Antonovsky, A. (1995). Poczucie koherencji jako determinanta zdrowia [Sense of Coherence as a Health Determinant]. In I. Heszen-Niejodek & H. Sęk (eds.), *Psychologia zdrowia* [*Health Psychology*]. (206–231). Wydawnictwo Naukowe PWN.

Apers, S., Rassart, J., Luyckx, K., Oris, L., Goossens, E., Budts, W., Moons, P., & I-DETACH Investigators (2016). Bringing Antonovsky's salutogenic theory to life: A qualitative inquiry into the experiences of young people with congenital heart disease. *International Journal of Qualitative Studies on Health and Well-being*, *11*, 29346. 10.3402/qhw.v11.29346.

Beck, U. (2004). *Społeczeństwo ryzyka. W drodze do innej nowoczesności* [*Risk Society: Towards a New Modernity*]. Wydawnictwo Scholar.

Braun-Lewensohn, O., Idan, O., Lindström, B., & Margalit, M. (2016). Salutogenesis: Sense of coherence in adolescence. In M.B. Mittelmark et al. (eds.), *The Handbook of Salutogenesis*. (123–136). Springer.

Buck, J.S., & Ryan-Wenger, N.A. (2003). Early adolescents' definition of health: The development of a new taxonomy. *Journal of Theory Construction & Testing*, *7*, 50–55.

Card, A.J. (2017). Moving beyond the WHO definition of health: A new perspective for an aging world and the emerging era of value-based care. *World Medical & Health Policy*, *9*, 127–137.

Carvalho, G.S., Dantas, C., Rauma, A.L., Luzi, D., Ruggieri, R., Bogner, F., Geier, C., Caussidier, C., Berger, D., & Clément, P. (2008). Comparing health education approaches in textbooks of sixteen countries. *Science Education International*, *19*, 133–146.

Cianciara, D., & Piotrowicz, M. (2018). The theoretical order as a means of professionalizing health promotion. *Zdrowie Publiczne i Zarządzanie* [*Public Health and Management*], *16*, 202–214.

De Freitas, G.C., das Flores, J.A., & de Camargo, Jr. K.R. (2022). "Health needs": Reflections on the (in)definition of a concept. *Saúde e Sociedade São Paulo*, *31*, 2–9. 10.1590/S0104-12902022200983.

Delgado, C. (2007). Sense of coherence, spirituality, stress and quality of life in chronic illness. *Journal of Nursing Scholarship*, *39*(3), 229–234.

Demel, M. (1989). Pedagogika zdrowia [Health pedagogy]. In L. Turos (ed.), *Pedagogika ogólna i subdyscypliny* [*General Pedagogy and Subdisciplines*] (236–254). Wydawnictwo Akademickie Żak.

Dolińska-Zygmunt, G. (2001). Teoretyczne podstawy refleksji o zdrowiu [Theoretical foundations of reflection on health]. In G. Dolińska-Zygmunt (ed.), *Podstawy psychologii zdrowia* [*Health Psychology Fundamentals*] (11–18). Wydawnictwo Uniwersytetu Wrocławskiego.

Domaradzki, J. (2013). O definicjach zdrowia i choroby [On definitions of health and disease]. *Folia Medica Lodziensia*, *40*, 5–29.

Falissard, B., Monégat, M., & Harper, G. (2017). Psychiatry, mental health, mental disability: Time for some necessary clarifications. *European Child & Adolescent Psychiatry*, *26*(10), 1151–1154. 10.1007/s00787-017-1037-4.

Fisher, W.A., Fisher, J.D., & Harman, J. (2003). The information-motivation-behavioral skills model: A general social psychological approach to understanding and promoting health behavior. In J. Suls & K.A. Wallston (eds.), *Social Psychological Foundations of Health and Illness* (82–106). Blackwell Publishing.

Fleary, S.A., & Joseph, P. (2020). Adolescents' health literacy and decision-making: A qualitative study. *American Journal of Health Behaviour*, *44*, 392–408. 10.5993/AJHB.44.4.3.

Garcia-Moya, I., Moreno, C., & Jimenez-Iglesias, A. (2013). Understanding the joint effects of family and other developmental contexts on the sense of coherence (SOC): A personfocused analysis using the classification tree. *Journal of Adolescence*, *36*. 10.1016/j.adolescence.2013.07.007.

Halfon, N., Long, P., Chang, D.I., Hester, J., Inkelas, M., & Rodgers, A. (2014). Applying a 3.0 transformation framework to guide large-scale health system reform. *Health Affairs*, *33*. 10.1377/hlthaff.2014.0485.

Heszen-Niejodek, I., Kądzielawa, D., & Toeplitz-Wiśniewska, M. (2000). Zdrowie i choroba [Health and Illness]. In J. Strelau (ed.), *Psychologia. Podręcznik akademicki. Jednostka w społeczeństwie i elementy psychologii stosowanej* [*Psychology. An Academic Textbook. The Individual in Society and Elements of Applied Psychology*] (441–819). Wydawnictwo GWP.

Heydari, A., & Khorashadizadeh, F. (2014). Pender's health promotion model in medical research. *JPMA*. The *Journal of the Pakistan Medical Association*, *64*, 1067–1074.

Huber, M., van Vliet, M., Giezenberg, M., Winkens B., Heerkens Y., Dagnelie P.C., & Knottnerus J.A. (2016). Towards a 'patient-centred' operationalisation of the new dynamic concept of health: A mixed methods study. *BMJ Open*. 6. 10.1136/bmjopen-2015-010091.

Huber, M., Knottnerus, J.A., Green, L., van der Horst, H., Jadad, A.R., Kromhout, D., Leonard, B., Lorig, K., Loureiro, M.I., van der Meer, J.W., Schnabel, P., Smith, R., van Weel, C., & Smid, H. (2011). How should we define health? *BMJ Open, 343*. 10.1136/bmj.d4163. PMID: 21791490.

Illich, I. (1975). The medicalization of life. *Journal of Medical Ethics, 1*, 73–77.

Jambroes, M., Nederland, T., Kaljouw, M., Van Vliet, K., Essink-Bot, M.L., & Ruwaard, D. (2016). Implications of health as "the ability to adapt and self-manage" for public health policy: A qualitative study. *European Journal of Public Health, 26*, 412–416.

Joseph, P., & Fleary, S.A. (2021). The way you interpret health: Adolescent definitions and perceptions of health literacy. *Journal of School Health, 91*, 599–607. 10.1111/josh.13050.

Kluczyńska, Z. (2015). Zdrowie psychiczne – wybrane definicje i koncepcje wyjaśniające [Mental Health – Selected Definitions and Explanatory Concepts]. In E. Sokołowska, E. Zabłocka-Żytka, E. Kluczyńska & J. Wojda-Kornacka (eds.), *Zdrowie psychiczne młodych dorosłych. Wybrane zagadnienia* [*Mental Health of Young Adults. Selected Aspects*] (25–38). Wydawnictwo Difin.

Krahn, G.L., Robinson, A., Murray, A.J., Havercamp, S.M., Havercamp, S., Andridge, R., Arnold, L.R., Barnhill, J., Bodle, S., Boerner, E., Bonardi, A., Bourne, M.L., Brown, Ch., Buck, A., Burkett, S., Chapman, R., Cobranchi, Ch, Cole, Ch., Davies, D., Dresbach, T., Farr, J., Lee Fay, M., Fletcher, R., Gertz, R., Hollway, J., Izzo, M., Krahn, Lawrence-Slater, R., Lecavalier, L., Murray, A., Page, K., Perry, S., Poling, A., Rabidoux, P., Rice, R., Robinson, A., Rosencrans, M., Ryan, M., Sanford, Ch., Schaeffer, C., Seeley, J., Shogren, K., Stepp, K., Straughter, M., Sucheston-Campbell, L., Tassé, M.J., Taylor, Ch., Walton, K., Wehmeyer, M., Williams, C., & Witwer, A. (2021). It's time to reconsider how we define health: Perspective from disability and chronic condition. *Disability and Health Journal, 14*, 101129. 10.1016/j.dhjo.2021.101129.

Kropińska, I. (2000). Przekonania zdrowotne. *W poszukiwaniu perspektywy pedagogicznej [Health Beliefs. In Search of a Pedagogical Perspective]*. Wydawnictwo Uczelniane WSP.

Lalonde, M. (1974). A new perspective on the health of Canadians. *Minister of Supply and Services Canada*. Retrieved from Public Health Agency of Canada. http://www.phac-aspc.gc.ca/ph-sp/pdf/perspect-eng.pdf [access: 29.10.2022].

Lancet (2009). What is health? The ability to adapt. Editorial. *The Lancet, 373*, 781. 10.1016/S0140-6736(09)60456-6.

Larsen, L.T. (2022). Not merely the absence of disease: A genealogy of the WHO's positive health definition. *History of the Human Sciences, 35*, 111–131. 10.1177/0952695121995355.

Larson, J.S. (1999). The conceptualization of health. *Medical Care Research and Review, 56*(2), 123–136. 10.1177/107755879905600201.

Leonardi, F. (2018). The definition of health: Towards new perspectives. *International Journal of Social Determinants of Health Services, 48*, 735–748.

Lynn, J., McKethan, A., & Jha, A.K. (2015). Value-based payments require valuing what matters to patients. *Journal of the American Medical Association, 314*, 1445–1446. 10.1001/jama.2015.8909.

Łuszczyńska-Cieślak, A. (2001a). Czym jest dla psychologa poczucie koherencji? [What is the sense of coherence for a psychologist?]. *Promocja Zdrowia. Nauki*

Społeczne i Medycyna [*Health Promotion. Social Sciences and Medicine*], VIII, *20*, 56–68.

Łuszczyńska-Cieślak, A. (2001b). Trudności dotyczące badań nad poczuciem koherencji [Difficulties concerning research on sense of coherence]. In H. Sęk & T. Pasikowski (eds.), *Zdrowie – stres – zasoby. O znaczeniu poczucia koherencji dla zdrowia* [*Health – Stress – Resources. On the Importance of Sense of Coherence for Health*] (57–68). Wydawnictwo Fundacji Humaniora.

Mariański, J. (2021). O nowej duchowości – próba opisu zjawiska [On new spirituality – An attempt to describe the phenomenon]. *Nauki O Wychowaniu. Studia Interdyscyplinarne* [*Education Sciences. Interdisciplinary Studies*], *12*, 40–68. 10.18778/2450-4491.12.04.

Mądrzycki, T. (1977). *Psychologiczne prawidłowości kształtowania się postaw* [*Psychological Regularities of Attitude Development*]. WSiP.

Menatti, L., Bich, L., & Saborido, C. (2022). Health and environment from adaptation to adaptivity: A situated relational account. *History and Philosophy of the Life Sciences*, *44*. 10.1007/s40656-022-00515-w.

Misselbrook, D. (2014). W is for wellbeing and the WHO definition of health. *British Journal of General Practice*, *64*, 582. 10.3399/bjgp14X682381.

Nazli, A. (2012). "I'm healthy": Construction of health in disability. *Disability and Health Journal*, *5*, 233–240. 10.1016/j.dhjo.2012.06.001.

NIK – Najwyższa Izba Kontroli [Supreme Audit Office] (2020). *Informacja o wynikach kontroli. Dostępność lecznictwa psychiatrycznego dla dzieci i młodzieży – w latach 2017–2019* [*Information on Audit Results. Availability of Psychiatric Treatment for Children and Adolescents in the Years 2017–2019*]. Departament Zdrowia NIK.

Nussbaum, M.C. (2011) *Creating Capabilities: The Human Development Approach*. Harvard University Press.

One Health High-Level Expert Panel (OHHLEP), Adisasmito, W.B., Almuhairi, S., Behravesh, C.B., Bilivogui, P., Bukachi, S.A., Casas, N., Cediel Becerra, N., Charron, D.F., Chaudhary, A., Ciacci Zanella, J.R., Cunningham, A.A., Dar, O., Debnath, N., Dungu, B., Farag, E., Gao, G.F., Hayman, D., Khaitsa, M., Koopmans, M., & Zhou, L. (2022). One health: A new definition for a sustainable and healthy future. *PLoS Pathogens*, *18*, e1010537. 10.1371/journal.ppat.1010537.

Ostrzyżek, A., & Marcinkowski, J.T. (2012). Jakość życia jako pozytywny wskaźnik zdrowia [Quality of life as a positive health indicator]. *Hygeia Public Health*, *47*, 408–411.

Raport RPD - Raport Rzecznika Praw Dziecka (2021). Ogólnopolskie badanie jakości życia dzieci i młodzieży w Polsce. Obszar nr 3 – Samopoczucie psychiczne [Children's ombudsman report (2021). *Nationwide Research on the Quality of Life of Children and Adolescents in Poland*. Area no. 3 – Mental Well-Being]. https://www.nik.gov.pl/plik/id,22730,vp,25429.pdf [access: 30 Nov 2022].

Reuben, D.B., & Tinetti, M.E. (2012). Goal-oriented patient care—An alternative health outcomes paradigm. *The New England Journal of Medicine*, *366*, 777–779.

Rutkowska, K. (2008). Postawy zdrowotne studentów pedagogiki [Health attitudes of pedagogy students]. In A. Grabowiec, J. Bogucki & A. Bochniarz (eds.), *Zdrowa szkoła – zdrowy uczeń. Edukacja wobec współczesnych zagrożeń zdrowia* [*Healthy School – Healthy Student. Education Faced with Contemporary Threats to Health*] (199–208). NeuroCentrum.

Sartorius, N. (2006). The meanings of health and its promotion. *Croatian Medical Journal*, *47*, 662–664.

Schulkin, J. (Ed.). (2004). *Allostasis, Homeostasis, and the Costs of Physiological Adaptation*. Cambridge University Press. 10.1017/cbo9781316257081.

Skowronek, K., & Pasek, Z. (2013) Wstęp. Czy istnieje duchowość bez sacrum? Kilka słów o duchowości niereligijnej [Introduction. Does spirituality without the sacred exist? Some remarks on non-religious spirituality] In Z. Pasek, K. Skowronek & R. Tyrała (eds.), *Pozareligijne wymiary duchowości* [*Dimensions of Spirituality Outside Religion*] (7–16). Wydawnictwo Libron.

Solecka, M. (2022). Psychiatria dzieci i młodzieży – światy (nie)równoległe [Psychiatry for Children and Adolescents – (Non)Parallel Worlds]. *Puls – Miesięcznik Okręgowej Izby Lekarskiej w Warszawie* [*Pulse – Warsaw Regional Chamber of Physicians Monthly*], *326*, 5–6.

Sturmberg, J.P. (2013). Think health—speak health—achieve Health. *OA Family Medicine*, *1*, 1–8.

The Lancet (2009). What is health? The ability to adapt. Editorial. *The Lancet*, *373*, 781. 10.1016/S0140-6736(09)60456-6.

van Druten, V.P., Bartels, E.A., van de Mheen, D., de Vries E., Kerckhoffs A.P.M., & Nahar-van Venrooj, L.M.W. (2022). Concepts of health in different contexts: A scoping review. *BMC Health Services Research*, *22*. 10.1186/s12913-022-07702-2.

WHO (2014). Basic documents. https://apps.who.int/gb/bd/PDF/bd48/basic-documents-48th-edition-en.pdf [access: 12.10.2022].

Wilczek-Rużyczka, E., & Kwak, M. (2022). *Zdrowie psychiczne – współczesne zagrożenia i możliwości wzmacniania* [*Mental Health – Contemporary Threats and Opportunities for Reinforcement*]. Wydawnictwo PZWL.

Wojciszke, B. (2004). *Człowiek wśród ludzi. Zarys psychologii społecznej* [*The Human Individual Among People. An Outline of Social Psychology*]. Wydawnictwo Naukowe Scholar.

Wollmann, M. (2001). Zdrowie jako wartość pedagogiczna i przedmiot wychowania. Cz. 1 [Health as a pedagogical value and as a subject matter of education. Part 1]. *Edukacja Dorosłych* [*Education of Adults*], *1*, 49–56.

Woźniak, M., Brukwicka, I., Kopański, Z., Kollar, R., Kollarova, M., & Bajger, B. (2015). Zdrowie jednostki i zbiorowości [Individual and collective health]. *Journal of Clinical Healthcare*, *4*, 1–3.

Zwierżdżyński, M.K. (2010). Religia – duchowość – postmodernizm. Problem znaczeń [Religion – Spirituality – Postmodernism. The problem of meanings] In M. Libiszowska-Żółtkowska & S. Grotowska (eds.), *Religijność i duchowość – dawne i nowe formy* [*Religiosity and Spirituality – Past and New Forms*] (79–93). Zakład Wydawniczy Nomos.

ŻWJR - Życie Warte Jest Rozmowy (2021). Raport za lata 2012–2021 Zachowania samobójcze wśród dzieci i młodzieży [Life Is Worth a Conversation (2021). Report for the Years 2012–2021 Suicidal Behaviours Among Children and Adolescents]. https://zwjr.pl/artykuly/raport-dotyczacy-zachowan-samobojczych-mlodziezy [access: 29 Nov 2022].

Chapter 4

Health-related quality of life of youth with a disability in the physical, emotional, family, peer, and educational context

Health-related quality of life – Introduction

Health-related quality of life (HRQoL) is a complex construct, difficult to define in an unambiguous manner. Its emergence was a result of relating the concept of quality of life to health and illness (Felce & Perry, 1995; Guyatt et al., 1993; Schipper, 1990). The term "health-related quality of life" (HRQoL) narrows QoL to aspects relevant to health; however, HRQoL is a comprehensive and complex concept for which no universally accepted definition is available (Fayers & Machin, 2000).

The World Health Organization defines quality of life (QoL) "as an individual's perception of their position in life in the context of the culture and value systems in which they live and in relation to their goals, expectations, standards and concerns" (WHO, 1995, 1997). Due to the very broad context of this definition, greater emphasis is placed in medical science on understanding quality of life related to health. In this respect, the definition of health proposed by the WHO (2014) is deemed as valid, namely that health "is a state of complete physical, mental and social well-being and not merely the absence of disease or infirmity." The mindset associated with health-related quality of life can be seen as a sign of shifting away from a problem-centred or psychopathology-oriented attitude, and towards the positive aspects of health, and its protection and prevention. The HRQoL concept as such was initially developed and operationalised in the context of the adult population and referred to the impact of disease or injury, the treatment undertaken, or the health care policy in place on individual quality of life (see Drotar, 2014). The HRQoL assessment is also a valuable criterion for assessing the effectiveness of treatment. It makes it easy to plan and organise short- and long-term care and estimate the risk of death or additional hospitalisations, which is of particular importance in the treatment of chronic diseases (Radecka, 2015). Researchers investigating HRQoL in the sick adult population focused on the consequences of cutting-edge technology in medicine, the efforts made to minimise costs, and to assess incidence in a population living longer than in the past (Drotar, 2014).

DOI: 10.4324/9781003367772-4

Theoretical models of HRQoL show great complexity and indicate that a sense of health is one of the primary determinants of quality of life. In defining HRQoL, the multidimensional nature of the concept is emphasised, as it can be understood as a latent construct encompassing physical and mental functioning, the social roles performed, as well as various aspects of physical, psychological, and social wellbeing (Bullinger, 1991; Calman, 1987; Spilker, 1990). It is moreover pointed out that "health-related quality of life," as opposed to "quality of life," can include both the objective and the subjective perspective in each area (Testa & Simonson, 1996; see also: de Wit & Hajos, 2013). Objective assessment focuses on what the individual person can do, and is important in determining health status (de Wit & Hajos, 2013). At the same time, medical sciences point to the need to take into account, in addition to objective health parameters, the subjective assessment made by the patient as key for the treatment and recovery process (Davis et al., 2018). Health-related quality of life has become a key indicator for planning and undertaking prevention and intervention measures, as incidence and mortality rates alone have been considered insufficient (Mazur et al., 2011). Thus, HRQoL has become an important variable in itself, independently of the medical results.

Health-related quality of life in a developmental age population: Advantages, difficulties, and measurement

HRQoL was not considered in the past in clinical trials involving children. However, there has been a shift in approach (Clarke & Eiser, 2004), and attention to health-related quality-of-life aspects in children has evolved since the 1980s (de Wit & Hajos, 2013). Before 2000, researchers (e.g. Bullinger & Ravens-Sieberer, 1995) would point out that, as opposed to adults, children's health-related quality of life was a newly discovered, important aspect in paediatric research. Simultaneously, they emphasised at the time the need to intensify research into HRQoL in children.

Currently, the assessment of health-related quality of life is becoming an increasingly important aspect of paediatric research in different contexts, both in healthy child populations and in clinical trials (e.g. Ravens-Sieberer et al., 2014). Consequently, the number of measurement tools available to assess children's HRQoL is also growing (Drotar, 2014; Solans et al., 2008). However, most specific tools collect information from legal representatives/guardians, mainly parents (Rajmil et al., 2013).

Early attempts to assess children's quality of life relied on data provided by mothers, as children were considered unreliable as respondents. It turned out, though, that children and parents did not always have similar views, for example on the impact of disease (de Wit & Hajos, 2013). As children grow, they begin to interpret their own health and their own quality of life independently, often differently from their parents. Research shows that parents and children agree more on objective aspects of HRQoL (i.e. physical functioning) than on subjective aspects such as emotional and social functioning (Eiser & Morse, 2001a; Janse et al., 2008). According to studies, concordance in HRQoL assessment in parent-child pairs is moderate to low and tends to decrease as the children get older (Rajmil et al., 2013).

In paediatric care, it is assumed that parents can provide information about the impact of disease and treatment on the child, but it is recognised increasingly often that the child's perspective is different and equally important. Regardless of whether the focus is placed on clinical assessment or on research findings, HRQoL assessments in children and parents will differ (Eiser & Morse, 2001a). Consequently, a child's HRQoL should be taken into account in decisions concerning their care and treatment (de Wit & Hajos, 2013). It may still seem arguable, for example, to what extent children's language abilities (especially of younger children or children with developmental difficulties, disorders, or disabilities), as well as their ability to understand questions and to generalise are sufficient to allow them to answer the questionnaire questions. The same can be said for the extent to which children's responses will be related to the need for approval from parents or other adults. Nevertheless, it is pointed out that refraining from using children's self-assessment represents a major departure from the accepted definition of HRQoL as a subjective measure (Mazur et al., 2011).

In clinical practice, focusing on children's HRQoL means that health care professionals should take into account the child's perspective, understanding of the situation, views on health, disease, and treatment. In the case of children and adolescents, HRQoL assessment makes it possible to acquire useful information about the health status of children with chronic illness, disability, and mental problems, as well as to potentially improve clinical decision making, improving understanding of the consequences and experiences of different diseases, disabilities, and disorders from the point of view of children and adolescents (Drotar, 2014). Any comprehensive assessment of a child's health-related quality of life will include information from both the child and the legal guardian/parent (Eiser & Morse, 2001a). It may also take into account information from third parties, such as teachers and doctors (Mazur et al., 2011; Morrow et al., 2012).

Currently, there is an abundance of research available on HRQoL assessed by children. Studies have been conducted both in normative populations (e.g. Ravens-Sieberer et al., 2007a, 2007b; 2010; Schlarmann et al., 2008) and among children with disabilities, chronic illnesses, or mental disorders (e.g. Kalyva et al., 2011; Law et al., 2014; Morrow et al., 2012; Riley et al., 2006). The following health aspects are taken into account in relation to populations in the developmental age: (1) in the area of physical health: general vital energy, somatic symptoms and complaints, ability to perform daily activities to a degree comparable to peers; (2) in the area of mental health: positive and negative emotions, self-perception, self-esteem, behaviour, concentration, cognitive abilities; (3) in the area of social relations: relationships with parents, ability to make friends, contacts with other children, functioning in the school environment. Children's daily functioning and the associated feelings of limitation they experience are investigated (Mazur et al., 2011). When assessing children's HRQoL according to their own rating, either well-being or functioning is considered, and dimensions such as family life, social life, children's activities, school, leisure, health, or functioning as well as the child's emotional reaction to the level of functioning are assessed (Davis et al., 2018). The assessment of functioning takes into account the following aspects: mobility (capacity for moving around), self-care (capacity for looking after oneself in terms of washing or dressing), performing usual activities (exemplified by attending school, sport and leisure activities, playing, doing things with family or friends), pain or discomfort (to what extent they are felt), being worried, sad, or unhappy (to what extent the respondent feels anxious and depressed) (Domellöf et al., 2013). Rosenbaum and colleagues (2007) suggest that in the case of functional limitations, adolescents' perceptions of their holistic wellbeing do not correspond directly to their functional health status.

Also relevant is the theoretical model of HRQoL as discrepancy by Calman (1984), according to which quality of life measures the difference between the hopes and expectations of the individual and the latter's experience in a particular time. It concerns the difference between perceived and actual goals, and it is an assessment of the potential for growth. This model has been adopted, for example, in studies of children with asthma (Eiser et al., 1999). In this approach, poorer quality of life results from a discrepancy between the individual's actual and ideal self (Eiser et al., 2000). The discrepancy between the actual and the desired state is used to determine quality of life (Collier et al., 2000). However, the discrepancy-based measure may affect self-esteem in children with disabilities and is therefore considered inappropriate for use in research concerning such children (Davis et al., 2018). At the same time, it can be too complicated, too complex, and contain too much information, thus preventing engagement and adequate responses from children with disabilities.

The problem with the tools for measuring children's HRQoL in a group of children with chronic illness and the difficulties related to the measurement are highlighted by Eiser and Morse (2001a). The problem, as mentioned above, is that children often do not share adults' views on the aetiology, course, and treatment of the disease. They may interpret the questions differently and apply a different time perspective. Additionally, their ability to use rating scales, understand language, and complete long questionnaires may be hindered by age, as well as cognitive or emotional development (Eiser & Morse, 2001b).

Understanding and measuring health-related quality of life in our study

In the definition we adopted, health-related quality of life is a multidimensional construct covering physical, emotional, mental, social, and behavioural components of well-being and functioning as perceived by patients and/or other individuals (KIDSCREEN, 2022). These are general health-related indicators of quality of life, relating to both healthy and chronically ill populations. A developmental approach based on research reports on HRQoL and on the development of tools to measure this construct (Bullinger & Ravens-Sieberer, 1995; Eiser & Morse, 2001b) was adopted to conceptualise quality of life.

The dimensions of HRQoL taken into account include: physical and psychological wellbeing, autonomy and parents, peers and social support, and school environment. Physical health refers to a child's (in our case: a teenager's) level of physical activity, energy, and fitness. Psychological wellbeing refers to positive emotions and satisfaction with life as well as the absence of experiencing loneliness and sadness. Autonomy and parents refers to the relationships with parents and the atmosphere at home. It is linked to interactions and feelings, it reveals whether the child, in our case a teenager, feels loved, supported, and treated fairly by the parents. This aspect also concerns the child's/teenager's perception of their level of autonomy, their capacity to make decisions about themselves, as well as financial aspects. Peers and social support is a dimension referring to the child's/teenager's relationships with other people of the same age, as well as to the perceived social support received from them. School environment is an HRQoL dimension that determines the child's/teenager's cognitive abilities, the ability to learn and concentrate, and their feelings towards school. Relationships with teachers are also studied (Mazur et al., 2011; Ravens-Sieberer et al., 2007a, 2007b; Robitail et al., 2007).

The dimensions described above are measured using the KIDSCREEN questionnaire, which is a tool for measuring HRQoL in children and adolescents developed simultaneously in more than a dozen countries (including Poland) and tested on a large representative, multinational sample of children and adolescents. This way of measuring HRQoL makes sure that different points of view are taken into account, prevents the impact of potential cultural aspects regarding the content of the measurement tool, makes it possible to make valid cross-cultural comparisons, and furthermore guarantees that the content is appropriate for different cultures (Ravens-Sieberer et al., 2007a; 2010; 2014). KIDSCREEN-27 in the middle version was used in our research. It consists of 27 items measuring, as described above, the dimensions of physical wellbeing, psychological wellbeing, autonomy and parents, peers and social support, and school environment (Mazur et al., 2011; Ravens-Sieberer et al., 2007a; Robitail et al., 2007).

Measuring HRQoL using scales addressed to children is quite challenging. Among the number of problems related to measuring children's quality of life, Eiser & Morse (2001a) list discrepancies between children's and parents' assessments; limited availability of self-completion measures for children; lack of precision in the content of the QoL dimensions; and the cultural adequacy of measures developed for children in countries other than their place of origin (Eiser & Morse, 2001b). KIDSCREEN is indicated as one of the few questionnaires that smooths out the flaws listed above, has clearly and precisely defined HRQoL dimensions, enables comparisons in parent-child dyads or parent-child-teacher triads within the same dimensions, is a questionnaire developed in cross-cultural research, has good psychometric properties, and also enables cross-cultural comparison (Davis et al. 2018; Ravens-Sieberer et al., 2007a, 2007b). Content for the questionnaire was developed using a literature review; expert opinions; and focus groups with children, adolescents, and parents (KIDSCREEN, 2022; Mazur et al., 2011). At the same time, it is pointed out that KIDSCREEN is suitable for studying children with illnesses and disabilities due to the sheer content of the items. Authors (Davis et al., 2018) performing a review of the available HRQoL measurement tools wrote: "Nine of the instruments were deemed to be suitable to be completed by a child with a disability. These were short in length and had simple questions and rating scales. For example, KIDSCREEN employs simple, five-point Likert-type rating scales, and has been used in a large study with children with cerebral palsy in which 61% of the children were able to self-report." This is all the more important since HRQoL measurement, especially for chronically ill children, children with disabilities, or with mental health problems, is significant not only for describing their current situation and health needs, but also for evaluating the clinical interventions undertaken (Ravens-Sieberer et al., 2007b).

Health-related quality of life and its dimensions in the presented sample of adolescents

The means and standard deviations in our study of adolescents with an intellectual disability, a physical disability, and FASD using KIDSCREEN are presented in Table 3.1. The HRQoL dimensions were intercorrelated, with the correlation results shown in Table 4.1. Correlations between the individual HRQoL dimensions and the overall score on the questionnaire range from 0.59 to 0.82, while the correlations between the scales range from 0.28 to 0.56 (see also Table 4.1).

Health-related quality of life and age of surveyed adolescents

Correlations between health-related quality of life and its individual dimensions and age were found to be statistically insignificant. The *r*-Pearson's correlation results are indicated below:

Table 4.1 Correlation between each dimensions of health-related quality of life and the general HRQoL score and descriptive statistics in the group of surveyed adolescents

	Physical wellbeing	*Psychological wellbeing*	*Autonomy and parent*	*Peers and social support*	*School environment*	*Health-related quality of life*
Physical wellbeing	–	–	–	–	–	–
Psychological wellbeing	.439***	–	–	–	–	–
Autonomy and parent	.476***	.407***	–	–	–	–
Peers and social support	.412***	.391***	.564***	–	–	–
School environment	.099	.283**	.425***	.476***	–	–
Health-related quality of life	.708***	.648***	.852***	.768***	.595***	–
Descriptive statistics *M(SD)*	12.18(3.92)	18.95(2.37)	23.72(4.83)	12.60(2.80)	13.86(2.87)	81.31(12.29)

Notes: n = 98; *r-Pearson's correlation.*
** $p < .01$;
*** $p < .001$;
M – Mean; SD – Standard Deviation

- For the general HRQoL score $r = -1.34$, $p = 189$.
- For physical wellbeing $r = -.04$, $p = 680$.
- For psychological wellbeing $r = -.08$, $p = 447$.
- For autonomy and parents $r = -.14$, $p = 153$.
- For peers and social support $r = -.11$, $p = .289$.
- For school environment $r = -.10$, $p = 322$.

Health-related quality of life and sex of surveyed adolescents

The results of the comparisons of means between boys and girls in the adolescent group studied, carried out using the *t*-student test, did not indicate any differences in either the total score or the individual HRQoL dimensions, with the exception of the autonomy and parents dimension. In this dimension, gender differences are present and the results indicate that girls rate their health-related quality of life worse than boys, taking into account their own autonomy and relationship with their parents. The results for the individual dimensions are presented below:

- For the general HRQoL score: $t = -1.43$ $p = .156$
  - $M_{boys} = 83.49$, $SD_{boys} = 14.49$; $M_{girls} = 79.88$, $SD_{girls} = 10.47$
- For physical wellbeing: $t = -1.74$ $p = .087$
  - $M_{boys} = 13.08$, $SD_{boys} = 4.61$; $M_{girls} = 11.59$, $SD_{girls} = 3.31$
- For psychological wellbeing $t = -1.49$, $p = .140$
  - $M_{boys} = 19.38$, $SD_{boys} = 2.51$; $M_{girls} = 18.66$, $SD_{girls} = 2.24$
- For autonomy and parents $t = -2.12$, $\mathbf{p = .037}$
  - $M_{boys} = 24.97$, $SD_{boys} = 4.38$; $M_{girls} = 22.89$, $SD_{girls} = 5.25$
- For peers and social support $t = .33$, $p = .743$
  - $M_{boys} = 12.49$ $SD_{boys} = 3.15$; $M_{girls} = 12.68$, $SD_{girls} = 2.57$
- For school environment $t = .82$, $p = .414$
  - $M_{boys} = 13.56$, $SD_{boys} = 3.36$; $M_{girls} = 14.05$, $SD_{girls} = 2.50$

Health-related quality of life and financial situation of surveyed adolescents

Correlations between health-related quality of life and financial situation were found to be statistically significant in almost all HRQoL dimensions. The *r*-Pearson's correlation results are indicated below:

- For the general HRQoL score $r = .44$, $p = <.001$
- For physical wellbeing $r = 2.8$, $p = .005$.
- For psychological wellbeing $r = 16$, $p = 102$.
- For autonomy and parents $r = .44$, $p = <.001$.
- For peers and social support $r = .36$, $p = <.001$
- For school environment $r = .294$, $p = .003$

Health-related quality of life and the type of disability of surveyed adolescents

The results of the comparisons between the three groups of adolescents studied showed that adolescents with physical disabilities had a lower health-related quality of life in the general score and in the autonomy and parents dimension as compared to the group of adolescents with intellectual disability (see Table 4.1). They also had a lower quality of life in the physical wellbeing dimension compared to both other groups of respondents: adolescents with intellectual disability and with FASD. Adolescents with FASD, in turn, displayed lower health-related quality of life in the school environment dimension compared to adolescents with intellectual and physical disability (see Table 4.2).

The results presented above regarding adolescents' HRQoL remain consistent with other studies conducted using KIDSCREEN (Ravens-Sieberer et al., 2010). For example, in cross-cultural studies, the interscale correlation of KIDSCREEN was similar to the interscale correlation in our study. For the 27-item version of the questionnaire, the correlations ranged from 0.36 to 0.59 for the self-report, and from 0.33 to 0.57 for proxy report (Ravens-Sieberer et al., 2010).

Our research results indicate that there is no relationship between the age of the adolescents studied and HRQoL. However, referring to developmental psychology knowledge (Bee, 2004; Schaffer & Kipp, 2015), one can assume that adolescence, as a developmental period associated with many relatively difficult developmental tasks, may contribute to the deterioration of health-related quality of life assessments. Longitudinal studies indicate a reduction in HRQoL in the period from childhood until adolescence (Meade & Dowswell, 2016; Rajmil et al., 2013). Children have higher HRQOL than adolescents in many aspects (Bisegger et al., 2005). However, our research is cross-sectional and no such conclusions can be drawn on its basis. At the same time, it only covers late adolescents. It is perhaps the small age variation within the study group that makes it impossible to see the relationship between age and HRQoL.

Comparing the HRQoL of boys and girls, in turn, one can notice gender differences, but only in one HRQoL dimension. The boys surveyed have higher quality of life than the girls in the areas of independence, leisure, and relations with parents. A similar relationship is indicated by other studies,

Table 4.2 Differences between adolescent with an intellectual disability, a physical disability, and FASD in each dimensions of HRQoL: Results of the Kruskal-Wallis H test

HRQoL	H(df)	p	Average rank		p	
Physical Wellbeing	45.32(2)	**.001**	intellectual	74.63	physical-FASD	**<.001**
			physical	34.57	physical-intellectual	**<.001**
			FASD	72.86	FASD-intellectual	.861
Psychological wellbeing	3.76 (2)	.152	intellectual	58.10	physical-FASD	.498
			physical	45.44	physical-intellectual	.055
			FASD	51.68	FASD-intellectual	.526
Autonomy and parents	8.10(2)	**.011**	intellectual	63.52	physical-FASD	.558
			physical	43.61	physical-intellectual	**.003**
			FASD	49.05	FASD-intellectual	.156
Peers and social support	1.90(2)	.387	intellectual	54.94	physical-FASD	.447
			physical	48.61	physical-intellectual	.337
			FASD	41.9	FASD-intellectual	.188
School environment	21.64(2)	**<.001**	intellectual	54.62	Physical-FASD	**<.001**
			physical	54.03	physical-intellectual	.930
			FASD	12.27	FASD-intellectual	**<.001**
HRQoL	14.14(2)	**<.001**	intellectual	67.25	physical-FASD	.576
			physical	42.30	physical-intellectual	**<.001**
			FASD	47.50	FASD-intellectual	.053

Notes: Intellectual – adolescents with intellectual disability; physical – adolescent with physical disability; FASD – adolescents with FASD

but the gender differences there are more wide-ranging, encompassing not only autonomy, but also physical and mental health (Meade & Dowswell, 2016). Boys scored higher than girls in those areas too, studied using KIDSCREEN. Other research indicates that with age, girls score lower on HRQoL than boys (Bisegger et al., 2005). In general, it can be concluded that the female gender was associated with significantly lower global health, mental health, and general health perceptions scores (Arrington-Sanders et al., 2006). Our research indicates that girls with disabilities experience lower quality of life related to autonomy and independence, and rate their relationships with their parents lower compared to boys.

Looking at other variables from the sociodemographic area that are relevant to young people's HRQoL, it can be concluded that HRQoL is related to the respondents' self-assessment of their financial situation. The correlations between the variables are positive and indicate that the higher the respondents rate their financial standing, the higher their quality of life. Other studies indicate that children from families in the lower socioeconomic categories having poorer HRQoL and family SES is an important factor associated with HRQOL in young patients with heart disease (Xiang et al., 2019). According to research by Von Rueden and colleagues (2006), exposure to low parental educational status may result in a decreased HRQoL in childhood, whereas reduced access to material resources may lead to a lower HRQoL especially in adolescence (von Rueden et al., 2006).

The presented analyses of the comparisons between adolescents in a breakdown by disability type indicated that adolescents with physical disabilities assessed health-related quality of life lower compared to the other groups surveyed; the largest number of differences can be seen in the comparison to adolescents with intellectual disabilities. In other studies, adolescents with physical disabilities are mainly compared to a normative group, and in such a comparison the results also indicate lower health-related quality of life, and lower self-rated health (Law et al., 2014; Liptak et al., 2001; McCullough et al., 2013). Children with physical disabilities differ from the normative group on parent ratings of their physical and psychosocial health, but they received lower scores in the physical dimension of health-related quality-of-life than in the psychosocial dimension (Law et al., 2014). However, our research indicated that children with physical disabilities had a lower quality of life in the psychosocial area related to their autonomy, independence, and relationships with their parents.

Few studies compare adolescents' health-related quality of life taking into account the type of disability. The study by Biggs & Carter (2016) compared health-related quality of life in adolescents with autism and intellectual disability, but using the parent proxy version of KIDSCREEN-27. The young people with autism and with intellectual disability surveyed in that study had a lower score than a normative sample in the dimensions of physical wellbeing, psychological wellbeing, and peers and social support. For both groups of young people, the lowest ratings were reported in the social support and peers dimension (Biggs & Carter, 2016). Other researchers find large differences in HRQoL between children with mental health problems and children without such problems, but only average or small differences in HRQoL between children with chronic diseases and children without such diseases, and between children with self-rated good and poor physical health (Hirschfeld et al., 2020). Our research points to the differences occurring in relation to the type of disability. In such a comparison, adolescents with physical disabilities appear to be a group experiencing lower health-related quality of life in at least two of its dimensions, especially if we compare this group to adolescents with intellectual disabilities. Adolescents with physical disability feel less able, active, and energetic, but also experience a lower level of autonomy and lower ability to decide for themselves, and rate the financial aspects of their functioning lower.

At the same time, our analyses indicate differences between young people with disabilities and young people with FASD. The results are difficult to relate to other research findings, as the HRQoL of adolescents with FASD is not addressed often. Studies indicate that children and youth with FASD have significantly lower HRQoL than children and youth from the general population (Stade et al., 2006). We also know that lower HRQoL also applies to young adults with FASD (Gyllencreutz et al., 2022). Our research indicates that young people with FASD score lower on only one HRQoL dimension: school environment. It can be assumed that adolescents with FASD rate their cognitive abilities, as well as their ability to learn and concentrate lower. At the same time, their feelings towards school and their relationships with teachers are presumably worse than those of young people with intellectual and physical disabilities. Although the group we studied was not very large, the result of the comparisons points to a certain interesting problem. Adolescents with FASD, due to the brain damage that accompanies the syndrome, may face many functional difficulties, and their functioning in the educational process depends on their health condition, the environment they live in, and the demands placed on them (Jadczak-Szumiło et al., 2018). The lower health-related quality of life experienced in the area related to school environment may be linked, on the one hand, to the cognitive problems resulting from the spectrum of disorders experienced due to foetal exposure to alcohol. On the other hand, it can be linked to the school environment itself. Perhaps the problem consists in the functioning of adolescents with FASD in schools, their difficulties with learning and social relationships, and perhaps in the lack of systemic solutions, of understanding on the part of teachers, of knowledge about FASD, as well as in the downplaying of the problems and in failing to attribute the right importance to them. The issue of FASD in Poland has been appearing recently in publications, few of which, however, are more widely known in the school environment (Banach & Matejek, 2017; Jadczak-Szumiło et al., 2018; Liszcz, 2011).

References

Arrington-Sanders, R., Yi, M.S., Tsevat, J., Wilmott, R.W., Mrus, J.M., & Britto, M.T. (2006). Gender differences in health-related quality of life of adolescents with cystic fibrosis. *Health Quality of Life Outcomes*, *4*, 1–8. 10.1186/1477-7525-4-5.

Banach, M., & Matejek, J. (2017). Uczniowie szkół ponadgimnazjalnych o Spektrum Poalkoholowym Uszkodzeń Płodu (FASD) [Upper-Secondary School Students on Fetal Alcohol Spectrum Disorder (FASD)]. *Wychowanie w rodzinie* [*Education in the Family*], *XVI*(2), 174–189. 10.23734/wwr20172.173.189.

Bee, H. (2004). *Psychologia rozwoju człowieka [Lifespan Development]*. Wydawnictwo Zyska i S-ka.

Biggs, E.E. & Carter, E.W. (2016). Quality of life for transition-age youth with autism or intellectual disability. *Journal of Autism Developmental Disorder*, *46*, 190–204. 10.1007/s10803-015-2563-x

Bisegger, C., Cloetta, B., von Rueden, U., Abel, T., Ravens-Sieberer, U., & European Kidscreen Group. (2005). Health-related quality of life: Gender differences in childhood and adolescence. *Sozial- und Praventivmedizin*, *50*, 281–291. 10.1007/s00038-005-4094-2

Bullinger, M. (1991). Quality of life – Definition, conceptualization and implications – A methodologists view. *Theoretic Surgery*, *6*, 143–149.

Bullinger, M. & Ravens-Sieberer, U. (1995). General principles, methods and areas of application of quality of life research in children. *Praxis der Kinderpsychologie und Kinderpsychiatrie*, *44*, 391–399.

Calman, K. (1987). Definitions and dimensions of quality of life. In N. Aaronson, J. Beckman, J. Bernheim & R. Zittoun (Eds.), *The quality of life of cancer patients* (81–97). Raven.

Calman, K.C. (1984). Quality of life in cancer patients – An hypothesis. *Journal of Medical Ethics*, *10*, 124–127.

Clarke, S.A., & Eiser, C. (2004). The measurement of health-related quality of life (QOL) in paediatric clinical trials: A systematic review. *Health and Quality of Life Outcomes*, *2*(1), 66.

Collier, J., MacKinlay, D., & Phillips, D. (2000). Norm values for the generic children's quality of life measure (GCQ) from a large school-based sample. *Quality of Life Research*, *9*, 617–623. 10.1023/A:1008915700210

Davis, E., Young, D., Gilson, K.-M., Swift, E., Chan, J., Gibbs, L., Tonmukayakul, U., Reddihough, D., & Williams, K. (2018). A rights-based approach for service providers to measure the quality of life of children with a disability. *Value in Health*, *21*, 1419–1427. 10.1016/j.jval.2018.05.009

de Wit, M., & Hajos, T. (2013). Health-related quality of life. In M.D. Gellman & J.R. Turner (eds.), *Encyclopedia of behavioral medicine*. Springer. 10.1007/978-1-4419-1005-9_753

Domellöf, E., Hedlund, L., & Odman, P. (2013). Health-related quality of life of children and adolescents with functional disabilities in a northern Swedish county. *Quality of Life Research: An International Journal of Quality of Life Aspects of Treatment, Care and Rehabilitation*, *23*, 1877–1882. 10.1007/s11136-013-0613-4.

Drotar, D. (2014). *Measuring health-related quality of life in children and adolescents implications for research and practice*. Psychology Press.

Eiser, C., & Morse, R. (2001a). Can parents rate their child's health-related quality of life? Results of a systematic review. *Quality of Life Research*, *10*, 347–357.

Eiser, C. & Morse, R. (2001b). A review of measures of quality of life for children with chronic illness. *Archives of Disease in Childhood*, *84*, 205-211. 10.1136/adc.84.6.487.

Eiser, C., Cotter, I., Oades, P., Seamark, D., & Smith, R. (1999). Health-related quality-of-life measures for children. *International Journal of Cancer*, *83*, 87–90. 10.1002/(SICI)1097-0215(1999)83:12+<87::AID-IJC16>3.0.CO;2-O.

Eiser, C., Vance, Y.H., & Seamark, D. (2000). The development of a theoretically driven generic measure of quality of life for children aged 6–12 years: A preliminary report. *Child: Care, Health and Development*, *26*, 445–456. 10.1046/j.1365-2214.2000.00177.x

Fayers, P., & Machin, D. (2000). Quality of life. *Assessment, analysis and interpretation*. Wiley.

Felce, D., & Perry, J. (1995). Quality of life: Its definition and measurement. *Research in Developmental Disability*, *16*, 51–74.

Guyatt, G.H., Feeny, D.H., & Patrick, D.L. (1993). Measuring health-related quality of life. *Annals of Internal Medicine*, *118*, 622–629.

Gyllencreutz, E., Aring, E., Landgren, V., Landgren, M., & Grönlund, M. (2022). Visual perception problems and quality of life in young adults with foetal alcohol spectrum disorders. *Acta Ophthalmolgica*, *100*, 115–121. 10.1111/aos.14868

Hirschfeld, G., von Brachel, R., & Thiele, C. (2020). Screening for health-related quality of life in children and adolescents: Optimal cut points for the KIDSCREEN-10 for epidemiological studies. *Quality of Life Research*, *29*, 529–536. 10.1007/s11136-019-02324-4.

Jadczak-Szumiło, T., Kałmajska-Lisz, K. & Liszcz, K. (2018). *Jak wspomagać dziecko z FASD w edukacji* [*How to Support a Child with FASD in Education*]. http://www.ciazabezalkoholu.pl [access: 5 December 2022].

Janse, A.J., Sinnema, G., Uiterwaal, C.S., Kimpen, J.L., & Gemke, R.J. (2008). Quality of life in chronic illness: Children, parents and paediatricians have different, but stable perceptions. *Acta Paediatrica*, 97, 1118–1124. DOI: 10.1093/eurpub/ckv206

Kalyva, E., Malakonaki, E., Eiser, C., & Mamoulakis, D. (2011), Health-related quality of life (HRQoL) of children with type 1 diabetes mellitus (T1DM): Self and parental perceptions. *Pediatric Diabetes*, *12*, 34–40. 10.1111/j.1399-5448.2010.00653.x

KIDSCREEN (2022). https://www.kidscreen.org/english/measurement-model/ [access: 5 December 2022].

Law, M., Hanna, S., Anaby, D. Kertoy, M., King, G., & Xuet, L. (2014). Health-related quality of life of children with physical disabilities: A longitudinal study. *BMC Pediatric*, *14*, 1–10. 10.1186/1471-2431-14-26

Liptak, G.S., O'Donnell, M., Conaway, M., Chumlea, W.C., Wolrey, G., Henderson, R.C., Fung, E., Stallings, V.A., Samson-Fang, L., Calvert, R., Rosenbaum, P., & Stevenson, R.D. (2001). Health status of children with moderate to severe cerebral palsy. *Developmental Medicine & Child Neurology*, *43*, 364–370. 10.1017/S001216220100069X.

Liszcz, K. (2011). *Dziecko z FAS w szkole i w domu [The child with FAS in school and in home]*. Wydawnictwo Rubikon.

Mazur J., Małkowska-Szkutnik A., Dzielska A., & Tabak I. (2011). *Polska wersja kwestionariuszy do badania jakości życia związanej ze zdrowiem dzieci i młodzieży (KIDSCREEN) [Polish Version of Questionnaires for the Study of Health-Related Quality of Life in Children and Adolescents (KIDSCREEN)]*. Instytut Matki i Dziecka.

McCullough, N., Parkes, J., Kerr, C., & McDowell, B.C. (2013). The health of children and young people with cerebral palsy: A longitudinal, population-based study. *International Journal of Nursing Studies*, *50*, 747–756. 10.1016/j.ijnurstu.2011.01.011.

Meade, T., & Dowswell, E. (2016). Adolescents'health-related quality of life (HRQoL) changes over time: A three year longitudinal study. *Health Quality of Life Outcomes*, *14* 10.1186/s12955-016-0415-9.

Morrow, A.M., Hayen, A., Quine, S., Scheinberg, A., & Craig, J.C. (2012). A comparison of doctors', parents' and children's reports of health states and health-related quality of life in children with chronic conditions. *Child: Care, health and development*, *38*, 186–195. 10.1111.

Radecka, B. (2015). Jakość życia uwarunkowana zdrowiem – znaczenie i sposoby oceny u chorych na nowotwory [Health-Determined Quality of Life – Significance and Methods of Assessment in Cancer Patients]. *Current Gynecologic Oncology*, *13*, 172–179. 10.15557/CGO.2015.0019.

Rajmil, L., López, A.R., López-Aguilà, S., & Alonso, J. (2013). Parent–child agreement on health-related quality of life (HRQOL): A longitudinal study. *Health Qual Life Outcomes*, *11*, 101. 10.1186/1477-7525-11-101

Ravens-Sieberer, U., Auquier, P., Erhart, M., Gosch, A., Rajmil, L., Bruil, J., Power, M., Duer, W., Cloetta, B., Czemy, L., Mazur, J., Czimbalmos, A., Tountas, Y., Hagquist, C., Kilroe, J., & European KIDSCREEN Group (2007a). The KIDSCREEN-27 quality of life measure for children and adolescents: Psychometric results from a cross-cultural survey in 13 European countries. *Quality of Life Research: An International Journal of Quality of Life Aspects of Treatment, Care and Rehabilitation*, *16*, 1347–1356. 10.1007/s11136-007-9240-2

Ravens-Sieberer, U., Erhart, M., Rajmil, L. Herdman M., Auqier P., Bruil J., Power M., Duer W., Abel T., Czemy L., Mazur J., Czimbalmos A., Tountas Y., Hagqiust C., Kilroe J., & European KIDSCREEN Group (2010). Reliability, construct and criterion validity of the KIDSCREEN-10 score: A short measure for children and adolescents' well-being and health-related quality of life. *Quality of Life Research*, *19*, 1487–1500. 10.1007/s11136-010-9706-5

Ravens-Sieberer, U., Herdman, M., Devine, J., Otto, C., Bullinger, M., Rose, M., & Klasen, F. (2014). The European KIDSCREEN approach to measure quality of life and well-being in children: Development, current application, and future advances. *Quality of Life Research*, *23*, 791–803. 10.1007/s11136-013-0428-3

Ravens-Sieberer, U., Schmidt, S., Gosch, A., Erhart, M., Petersen, C., & Bullinger, M. (2007b). Measuring subjective health in children and adolescents: Results of the European KIDSCREEN/DISABKIDS Project. *GMS Psycho-Social Medicine*, *4*. https://www.ncbi.nlm.nih.gov/pmc/articles/PMC2736532/

Riley, A.W., Spiel, G., Coghill, D., Döpfner, M., Falissard, B., Lorenzo, M.J., Preuss, U., Ralstoon, S.J., & ADORE Study GROPUP. (2006). Factors related to Health-Related Quality of Life (HRQoL) among children with ADHD in Europe at entry into treatment. *European Child & Adolescents Psychiatry*, *15*, i38–i45. 10.1007/s00787-006-1006-9

Robitail, S., Ravens-Sieberer, U., Simeoni, M.C., Rajmil, L., Bruil, J., Power, M., Duer, W., Cloetta, B., Czemy, L., Mazur, J., Czimbalmos, A., Tountas, Y., Hagquist, C., Kilroe, J., & Auquier, P. (2007). Testing the structural and cross-cultural validity of the KIDSCREEN-27 quality of life questionnaire. *Quality of Life Research*, *16*, 1335–1345. 10.1007/s11136-007-9241-1

Rosenbaum, P.L., Livingston, M.H., Palisano, R.J., Galuppi, B.E. & Russell, D.J. (2007). Quality of life and health-related quality of life of adolescents with cerebral palsy. *Developmental Medicine & Child Neurology*, *49*, 516–521. 10.1111/j.1469-8749.2007.00516.x

Schaffer, H.R. & Kipp, K. (2015). *Psychologia rozwoju. Od dziecka do dorosłości* [*Psychology of Development. From Childhood to Adulthood*]. Harmonia Universalis.

Schipper, H.(1990). Quality of life: Principles of the clinical paradigm. *Journal of Psychosocial Oncology*, *8*, 171–185.

Schlarmann, J.G., Metzing-Blau, S., & Schnepp, W. (2008). The use of health-related quality of life (HRQOL) in children and adolescents as an outcome criterion to evaluate family oriented support for young carers in Germany: An integrative review of the literature. *BMC Public Health*, *8*, 414. 10.1186/1471-2458-8-414

Solans, M., Pane, S., Estrada, M.D., Serra-Sutton, V., Berra, S., Herdman, M., Alonso J., & Rajmil S. (2008). Health-related quality of life measurement in children and adolescents: A systematic review of generic and disease-specific instruments. *Value in Health*, *11*, 742–764. 10.1111/j.1524-4733.2007.00293.x.

Spilker, B. (1990). *Quality of life assessment in clinical trials*. Raven.

Stade, B.C., Stevens, B., Ungar, W.J., Beyene, J., & Koren, G. (2006). Health-related quality of life of Canadian children and youth prenatally exposed to alcohol. *Health and Quality of Life Outcomes*, *4*, 81. 10.1186/1477-7525-4-81

Testa, M.A., & Simonson, D.C. (1996). Assessment of quality-of-life outcomes. *The New England Journal of Medicine*, *334*, 835–840.

von Rueden, U., Gosch, A., Rajmil, L., Bisegger, C., & Ravens-Sieberer, U. (2006). Socioeconomic determinants of health related quality of life in childhood and adolescence: Results from a European study. *Journal of Epidemiology and Community Health*, *60*, 130–135. 10.1136/jech.2005.039792.

WHO (1995). The WHOQOL Group: The World Health Organization quality of life assessment (WHOQOL): Position paper from the World Health Organization. *Social Science Medicine*, *41*, 1403–1409.

WHO (1997). WHOQOL. Measuring quality of life. Division of mental health and prevention of substance abuse. https://apps.who.int/iris/handle/10665/63482 [access: 12 October 2022].

WHO (2014). Basic documents. https://apps.who.int/gb/bd/PDF/bd48/basic-documents-48th-edition-en.pdf [access: 12 October 2022].

Xiang, L., Su, Z., Liu, Y., Huang, Y., Zhang, X., Li, S., & Zhang, H. (2019). Impact of family socioeconomic status on health-related quality of life in children with critical congenital heart disease. *Journal of the American Heart Association*, *8*(1), e010616. 10.1161/JAHA.118.010616.

Chapter 5

Evaluation of health-related quality of life

Perspectives of adolescents with a disability and of parents

The period of adolescence represents the interface between childhood and adulthood. The teenager, although still dependent in many respects like a child, especially on parents and school, looks and seeks to behave more and more like an adult. At the same time, adolescents experience intense changes whose nature is biological (especially in the physical and sexual maturation area), social (experiencing new roles, building social maturity), and psychological (new cognitive functions, personality changes, transformations in the area of morality, identity constitution) (Gurba, 2006, 2009). A process of intense restructuring and reintegration of earlier cognitive methods and ways of thinking takes place. New mechanisms of perceiving oneself and the world emerge in the young person's mind. The marked youthful egocentrism is associated with greater interest in oneself. At the same time, the area of self-knowledge expands. The notion of the self stabilises, which is reflected in the shaping of identity. While earlier, the key source of self-knowledge for the young person were adults, during adolescence peers become the point of reference and, above all, the "social mirror" for intense comparisons (Obuchowska, 2006; Oleszkowicz & Misztela, 2010). The relationship with the parent (especially the mother) is particularly important for the adolescent's self-esteem. A good and secure early childhood attachment relationship can develop into a resource that helps in the developmental process of separation and individuation. This is facilitated by newly acquired skills, including insight and awareness of one's autonomy needs (Liberska et al., 2016; Nomaguchi, 2008). It is the process of separation that offers

> the possibility to become emotionally independent from adults and to gain the autonomy which is so necessary for the formation of personal identity and for constructing a mature vision of oneself, at the same time maintaining a warm relationship with one's parents, based on treating each other as partners.
>
> (Oleszkowicz & Misztela, 2010, p. 66)

Conversely, insecure bonds hinder constructive detachment, and bring about the risk of remaining overly dependent or of rupturing the relationship

DOI: 10.4324/9781003367772-5

(Li et al., 2015; Liberska et al., 2016). On the one hand, adolescents are on the threshold of adulthood, while on the other hand, they experience a confrontation with the demands of that same adulthood. The process is dynamic. Some fluctuations, related to internal or external factors, seem to be natural (Brzezińska, 2000; Brzezińska & Krzywicki, 2001). This can be accompanied by various crises and conflicts, of intrapersonal and interpersonal nature, occurring especially in relationships with adults, including the parents. Sometimes, conflicts between an adolescent child and their parent, due to the emotional proximity, are particularly strong (Olearczyk, 2009). However, there are reasons to believe that, due to certain sociocultural transformations, adolescence progresses relatively more peacefully in the postmodern families of today (Biernat, 2014). It is also worth adding in this context that the phenomenon of deferred adulthood can currently be observed. The age of entry into adulthood has been increasing over the recent decades (Brzezińska et al., 2011). In the macroscale, the process itself has been perceived as a complex and multidimensional phenomenon for centuries now. However, in liquid modernity/postmodernity, it becomes a particularly difficult challenge to relatively stabilise the transformations involving fragmentation and individualisation (Bauman, 2006; Kudlińska-Chróścicka, 2019).

In turn, on the individual level, the relationship with the parent involves a number of changes and is a dynamic process, but on the other hand, paradoxically, it simultaneously provides relatively stable factors that determine the continuity of individual development. These elements include the specific framework of the family environment, the cultural environment, and the system of values transmitted by the parents (Gurba, 2009). In our opinion, an important category emerging in the space of the parent-child relationships, with a potential for constancy and stability, and at the same time with a dynamic that allows development to take place, is health-related quality of life.

It is definitely a valuable experience for the adaptation process. In a changing reality, it is necessary to maintain and recognise relative constancy, a sense of separateness and of self, while at the same time flexibly adapting to such intense changes, both in the outside world and the intrapsychic ones associated with developmental transformations in the life cycle. This underscores the role of timing, i.e. capturing moments of experience and developmental opportunities for health now and for the future (Palisano et al., 2020). Hence, the study of health-related quality of life aspects in unique developmental period such as adolescence and in a group such as that of persons with disabilities and FASD is particularly justified.

According to the ICF classification, but also in relation to the developmental approach to analysing the functioning of people with intellectual disabilities, we assume that there are no contraindications to the transfer knowledge from developmental psychology of non-disabled people to describing and explaining the functioning of persons with disabilities (and by way of analogy, also of those with physical disabilities and FASD). This also entitles us to use diagnostic methods dedicated to the general population in our research (Hodapp et al., 1998). The KIDSCREEN-27 – Health-Related Quality of Life Questionnaire used in this study is precisely such a tool. Adolescents completed self-ratings of individual dimensions of health-related quality of life. We asked their parents, in turn, to rate their perceived quality of life related to their children's health. Below, we present our research findings reflecting the confrontation between the point of view of the adolescents and of their parents.

We used the paired *t*-test in order to compare adolescent-parent dyads in the assessment of health-related quality of life. We compared the self-rated health-related quality of life of the adolescents with the self-rated health-related quality of life of their parents. We took into account each dimension of HRQoL and verified the differences between adolescents and parents 1) in dyads within the entire study group, 2) in dyads divided into subgroups due to the type of disability of the adolescents. The results of the analyses are presented in Tables 5.1–5.4.

Comparisons of the adolescent-parent dyads surveyed carried out in the whole group showed that adolescents and parents did not differ in the assessment of most health-related quality-of-life dimensions, which means that the assessment of the health-related quality of life of adolescents with intellectual disabilities, physical disabilities, and FASD made by parents is similar to the assessment made by adolescents. Assessment is similar in the

Table 5.1 Differences in the assessment of health-related quality of life in adolescent-parent dyads: Results of paired *t*-test in all surveyed dyads

All adolescent-parent dyads surveyed (n = 98 adolescents with intellectual disability, physical disability, and FASD, and n = 98 parents)

HRQoL	*Groups*	$M(SD)_{DS}$	M(SD)	t(df)	p
Physical wellbeing	adolescents	12.18(3.82)	.06(2.87)	.21(97)	.833
	parents	12.12(3.50)			
Psychological wellbeing	adolescents	18.95(2.37)	.15(2.50)	.61(97)	.545
	parents	18.79(2.18)			
Autonomy and parent relations	adolescents	23.72(4.83)	**−1.48(4.79)**	**−3.06(97)**	**.003**
	parents	25.20(3.84)			
Peers and social support	adolescents	12.60(2.80)	**.62(2.83)**	**2.17(97)**	**.032**
	parents	11.98(2.62)			
School environment	adolescents	13.86(2.87)	−.10(2.77)	−.36(97)	.717
	parents	13.96(2.98)			
HRQoL	adolescents	81.31(12.29)	−.74(10.61)	−.69(97)	.489
	parents	82.06(9.37)			

Note: $M(SD)_{DS}$ *– Means and standard deviations (descriptive statistics).*

Table 5.2 Differences in the assessment of health-related quality of life in adolescent with intellectual disability-parent dyads: Results of paired *t*-test

Adolescent with intellectual disability-parent dyads (n = 26 adolescents with intellectual disability and n = 26 parents)

HRQoL	*Groups*	$M(SD)_{DS}$	M(SD)	t(df)	p
Physical wellbeing	adolescents	15.65(4.15)	.65(4.35)	.77(25)	.451
	parents	15.00(3.03)			
Psychological wellbeing	adolescents	19.85(2.43)	.31(3.00)	.52(25)	.606
	parents	19.54(2.39)			
Autonomy and parent relations	adolescents	26.31(5.66)	−.173(5.57)	-1.58(25)	.126
	parents	28.04(4.62)			
Peers and social support	adolescents	13.32(3.89)	**2.00(3.79)**	**2.69(25)**	**.013**
	parents	11.31(3.38)			
School environment	adolescents	14.69(3.02)	.00(3.21)	.00(25)	1.00
	parents	14.69(2.60)			
HRQoL	adolescents	89.81(14.61)	1.23(15.09)	.42(25)	0.681
	parents	88.58(10.57)			

Note: $M(SD)_{DS}$ *– Means and standard deviations (descriptive statistics).*

Table 5.3 Differences in the assessment of health-related quality of life in adolescent with physical disability-parent dyads: Results of paired *t*-test

Adolescent with physical disability-parent dyads (n = 61 adolescents with intellectual disability and n = 61 parents)

HRQoL	*Groups*	$M(SD)_{DS}$	M(SD)	t(df)	p
Physical wellbeing	adolescents	10.13(1.80)	−.10(1.85)	−.41(60)	.679
	parents	10.23(1.81)			
Psychological wellbeing	adolescents	18.54(2.15)	.013(2.28)	.45(60)	.654
	parents	18.41(2.07)			
Autonomy and parent relations	adolescents	22.70(3.67)	**−1.29(3.89)**	**−2.60(60)**	**.012**
	parents	24.00(2.95)			
Peers and social support	adolescents	12.44(1.99)	.20(1.93)	.80(60)	.439
	parents	12.25(2.04)			
School environment	adolescents	14.28(2.10)	−.13(2.43)	−.42(60)	.675
	parents	14.41(2.29)			
HRQoL	adolescents	78.10(8.14)	−-1.20(7.61)	−1.23(60)	.224
	parents	79.29(6.51)			

Note: $M(SD)_{DS}$ *– Means and standard deviations (descriptive statistics).*

overall HRQoL score, physical wellbeing, psychological wellbeing, and school environment (see Table 5.1). Statistically significant differences can be seen in the results of two dimensions of health-related quality of life: autonomy and parent relations, and peers and social support. Parents of

Table 5.4 Differences in the assessment of health-related quality of life in adolescent with FASD-parent dyads: Results of paired *t*-test

Adolescent with FASD-parent dyads (n = 11 adolescents with intellectual disability and n = 11 parents)					
HRQoL	*Groups*	$M(SD)_{DS}$	M(SD)	t(df)	p
Physical wellbeing	adolescents	15.36(4.31)	−.45	−.46(10)	.654
	parents	15.82(4.21)			
Psychological wellbeing	adolescents	19.09(2.98)	−.09	−12(10)	.910
	parents	19.18(1.89)			
Autonomy and parent relations	adolescents	23.27(6.47)	−1.91	−.87(10)	.407
	parents	25.18(2.82)			
Peers and social support	adolescents	11.82(3.51)	−.27	−.25(10)	.804
	parents	12.09(3.33)			
School environment	adolescents	9.54(2.70)	−.18	−.16(10)	.872
	parents	9.73(3.90)			
HRQoL	adolescents	79.09(16.66)	−2.91	−.77(10)	.460
	parents	82.00(12.69)			

Note: $M(SD)_{DS}$ *– Means and standard deviations (descriptive statistics).*

teenagers with intellectual disabilities, physical disabilities, and FASD rate the health-related quality of life of their children higher than the teenagers themselves in the area of autonomy and parents relations (see Table 5.1). On the other hand, adolescents with intellectual disabilities, physical disabilities, and FASD assess their health-related quality of life higher than their parents in the area of peers and social support.

Analyses conducted by subgroups of dyads due to the type of disability of adolescents indicated that among the teenagers with intellectual disabilities-parent dyads, there was one statistically significant difference. Parents of teenagers with intellectual disabilities rated the health-related quality of life of their children lower in the area of peers and social support than the adolescents with intellectual disabilities themselves (see Table 5.2).

Similarly, among the adolescents with physical disability-parent dyads, one of the HRQoL dimensions turned out to differentiate parents and children, but it was a different dimension than in the previous group. The results indicated that parents of teenagers with a physical disability rate the health-related quality of life of the teenagers higher in the area of autonomy and parent relations than the adolescents themselves (see Table 5.3). In the case of adolescents with FASD-parent dyads, no difference in HRQoL dimensions turned out to be statistically significant (see Table 5.4).

It is worth looking at the adolescents and their parents participating in the research from a macro- and microscale perspective. This broader context shows us that nowadays, social structures, including the family, are changing more dynamically than ever before. Lifestyle is also undergoing transformations. It is becoming a central category. The postmodern trend is evident. Individualism becomes increasingly marked. Figures of authority are losing their importance. Social support is also weakening. On the one hand, this gives the individual more freedom of choice. On the other hand, the changing reality does not allow one to prepare for such transformations in an optimum way; one is often surprised (Biernat, 2014; Brzezińska & Piotrowski, 2009). This broader context also includes the extremely difficult and intense social experiences the adolescent, the family, and the society at large participate in. The pandemic, the war in Ukraine, the economic crisis, the vexing deficiencies of systemic solutions in the field of care, therapy, rehabilitation, prevention, education, etc., have all emerged in a relatively brief period, and at relatively short intervals.

In the microscale dimension, there is a number of individual experiences the adolescent with a disability and their family face. These include all the dynamic transformations and development challenges discussed above. It is also the context of disability, of experiencing it, accepting it, and adjusting to it.

> In the case of a family in which there is a child with a disability, family functions are most often disrupted, and the realisation of roles, which are more difficult in this case, requires a particular amount of effort and involves a great psychological burden.
>
> (Bakiera & Stelter, 2010)

It is worth noting that in a systemic, interaction-based approach, influence is exerted not only by the parents on the children, but also in the opposite direction. The parents, who are usually the main (though not the only) creators of the upbringing process, also experience changes related to their new role and their involvement in the child's socialisation process (Bakiera, 2008).

Even these merely signalled factors in the macro- and microscale make it possible to see a number of vertical and horizontal stressors in the lives of the families studied (Sikorski, 2021). In the course of their development, the child or adolescent receiving care in the field of broadly understood health changes, and so do, with these natural transformations, the needs for interventions from the medical, psychological, and social fields. The offer dedicated to the child in the individual dimension should be updated to be adjusted to the child's evolving needs. However, it should be remembered that the legal guardian, i.e. the parent, making key decisions in the case of underage children, also plays the role of recipient/consumer of these interventions. This highlights the importance of analysing the point of view not only of children, but also of their parents (Macdonald et al., 2007).

Hence, our intention in the dyadic research is to draw attention to this broader context. We are also aware, in line with positive concepts, that the resources needed for coping as well as for maintaining and enhancing quality of life (also health-related quality of life) are found within the family, in important relationships.

> The family is the primary and at the same time the strongest system people belong to. (...) Every family experiences a flow of stress, the latter being understood here not as a destructive phenomenon, but above all as an opportunity for further development and adaptation to the changing conditions inside as well as outside the family.
>
> (Gąsior, 2014, p. 79)

Successful adaptation to challenges and coping with problems depend to a large extent on activating potential resources from the physical, psychological, environmental, and spiritual areas (Szymańska, 2015), from what we interpret in this publication as holistically understood health.

Analyses of our research findings reveal a number of similarities in the self-rating of health-related quality of life between adolescents and their parents. This may signal a certain compatibility and good child-parent relationships. This hypothesis becomes more likely from the point of view of the nature of our research and the specificities of our sampling method. The very fact that the parent and the child enrolled in the study and participated together, their motivation, and the joint coding of the responses sent may suggest a relatively favourable, developmental child-parent relationship.

Another aspect that may explain the relatively high compatibility of respondents between the parents and the children is the fact that more mothers than fathers took part in the study. In the Polish reality, the care provider for a child with disabilities is relatively more often the mother (Bakiera & Stelter, 2010). This can arguably build a special bond between the mother and the child with a disability. Another aspect, already mentioned above, is the fact that the relationship with the mother may have a greater effect on the level of self-esteem (Kiang & Bhattacharjee, 2019; Nomaguchi, 2008). In the case of our research, this concerned self-esteem in the sense of self-assessment of health-related quality of life. Finally, this compatible vision of the adolescent's health-related quality of life may also be an expression of the process of adaptation to, reconciliation with, and acceptance of the particular disability-related condition (Byra, 2017), and thus a certain way of working through, and consequently a more insightful view of quality of life.

Considering these numerous points of compatibility in the estimates related to the assessment of functioning in the individual areas of quality of life, the theme of autonomy and social support/peers and friends draws our attention. In the entire sample of adolescents with disabilities, the aspect of autonomy is rated significantly higher by the young people (compared to their parents). Adolescents are going through a developmental period, when thinking about one's own autonomy is particularly important. It is a crossroads: on the one hand, depending on one's parents, on the other hand, looking towards autonomous adulthood. At this point in their development, both directions are important to them. Importantly, the perception of autonomy by others (especially parents and friends) is an important determinant of a certain readiness to undertake different activities. Interestingly, the perception of autonomy by others, and support for autonomy coming from them (from figures important for the child, i.e. parents, teachers, peers) is more effective than exerting direct pressure (Sicilia et al., 2020). Support for autonomy, or more broadly a parenting model that supports the child's needs, is one of the factors (alongside, among others, a warm, kind relationship) that also has a positive influence on adolescents' wellbeing (Bülowet al., 2022; Perlberg et al., 2021). Thus, once again, the importance of a good relationship with the parent emerges as a driver of successful development (Kiang & Bhattacharjee, 2019). Supporting autonomy is by no means tantamount to withdrawing from the relationship with the child, with distancing. Focusing on autonomy and supporting it will be another positive developmental signal, as it makes it possible to focus also on the future. Moreover, it has high value added in the rehabilitation process. It is in process, too, that such activities should be consistently implemented/continued with the participation of doctors and therapists (Hilberink et al., 2020). We can thus assume that the development and promotion of autonomy will also have a positive impact on health-related quality of life.

Considering the adolescents' self-assessment, parents seem to underestimate their children's level of functioning in the area of support received from others (including friends). This regularity applies to the results of the whole group (all the dyads), but also emerges in the group of adolescents with intellectual disabilities. It might be due to the child's social functioning becoming increasingly private/intimate. The adolescent spends more time outside the home, outside the direct care of the parent, and their relationships with peers take place essentially without parental involvement. Thus, such an outcome may simply result from the parent's certain lack of knowledge about the quality of the child's relations with peers, or from a one-sided attitude towards the child's limitations. A child receiving a diagnosis (a "negative" one that highlights the deficits and impairments) becomes, as it were, branded with a negative label. The stereotype of the dysfunctional child can be so strong that it makes it difficult to see the resources and potentials in the child and their environment (Szymańska, 2015).

In recent years, there has been a noticeable shift in the perception of children and adolescents with disabilities in the literature. Much more attention is paid to the aspect of their experience and development of self-determination. It is noted that the role of families, of parents in the process, has been insufficiently explored (Shogren & Turnbull, 2006). We believe that the comments and observations presented in this chapter have the potential to contribute to the discussion on the design and provision of optimal support to children and adolescents with disabilities on the path to autonomy, but also on the important role and significance of points of view in this process. Once again, we emphasise in this publication the vital importance of focusing on resources and skills, rather than on deficiencies. This has, strictly speaking material significance, in terms of the content. The child gains awareness of specific resources. It also has functional significance, in a sense. The adolescent learns and internalises certain coping strategies presented by the parent, which may prove particularly important, especially in the development of self-determination.

References

Bakiera, L. (2008). Rozwojowe współoddziaływanie pokoleń w rodzinie. Rodzice w wieku średnim i dorastające dzieci [Developmental Interaction Between Generations Within the Family. Middle-Aged Parents and Adolescent Children]. *Psychologia Rozwojowa* [*Developmental Psychology*], *13*, 25–37.

Bakiera, L., & Stelter, Z. (2010). Rodzicielstwo z perspektywy rodziców dziecka pełnosprawnego i niepełnosprawnego intelektualnie. Zalety i wady życia w rodzinie i poza rodziną. [Parenting from the Point of View of Parents of an Intellectually Able and Disabled Child]. *Roczniki Socjologii Rodziny* [*Annals of Family Sociology*], *20*, 131–151.

Bauman, Z. (2006). *Płynna nowoczesność. Kunz* [*Liquid Modernity, translated by Kunz, T.*]. Wydawnictwo Literackie.

Biernat, T. (2014). Czy istnieje rodzina ponowoczesna? [Does a Post-Modern Family Exist?]. *Pedagogia Christiana*, *2*(34), 183–195.

Brzezińska, A. (2000). *Społeczna psychologia rozwoju* [*Social Psychology of Development*]. Wydawnictwo Naukowe Scholar.

Brzezińska, A. , & Krzywicki, P. (2001). Właściwościsamowiedzy na przełomie późnejadolescencji i wczesnej dorosłości [Characteristics of self-knowledge duringtransitional period between late adolescence and early childhood]. *CzasopismoPsychologiczne [Psychological Journal]*, *7*(1), 87–94.

Brzezińska, A.I., & Piotrowski, K. (2009). Diagnoza statusów tożsamości w okresie adolescencji, wyłaniającej się dorosłości i wczesnej dorosłości za pomocą Skali Wymiarów Rozwoju Tożsamości (DIDS) [Diagnosis of Identity Statuses in the Period of Adolescence, Emerging Adulthood and Early Adulthood Using the Dimensions of Identity Development Scale (DIDS)]. *Studia Psychologiczne* [*Psychological Studies*], *47*, 93–109.

Brzezińska, A.I., Kaczan, R., Piotrowski, K., & Rękosiewicz, M. (2011). Odroczona dorosłość: fakt czy artefakt? [Deferred Adulthood: Fact or Artefact?]. *Nauka* [*Science*], *4*, 67–107.

Bülow, A., Neubauer, A.B., & Soenens, B. (2022). Universal ingredients to parenting teens: Parental and autonomy support promote adolescent well-being in most families. *Scientific Report*, *12*, 16836. 10.1038/s41598-022-21071-0

Byra S. (2017). Wielowymiarowa Skala Akceptacji Utraty Sprawności (WSAUS) – Polska adaptacja Multidimensional Acceptance of Loss Scale Jamesa M. Ferrina, Fonga Chana, Julie Chronister i Chung-Yi Chiu [WSAUS: Polish Adaptation of the

Multidimensional Acceptance of Loss Scale by James M. Ferrin, Fong Chan, Julie Chronister, and Chung-Yi Chiu], *Człowiek – Niepełnosprawność – Społeczeństwo* [*Humans – Disability – Society*], *1*(35), 29–50.

Gąsior, K. (2014). Prężność rodzinna – nowe wyzwanie dla profilaktyki [Family Resiliency – A New Challenge for Prevention]. *Resocjalizacja Polska* [*Polish Resocialisation*], *6*, 79–88.

Gurba, E. (2006). Relacje: rodzice – dorastające dzieci w ocenie rodziców i ich dorastających dzieci [Relationships Between Parents and Adolescents from the Point of View of the Former and of the Latter]. *Psychologia Rozwojowa* [*Developmental Psychology*], *11*, 81–90.

Gurba, E. (2009). Uwarunkowania relacji rodzice – dorastające dzieci [Determinants of the Relationship Between Parents and Their Adolescent Children]. In M. Kielar-Turska (ed.), *Studia nad rozwojem i wychowaniem: w osiemdziesiątą rocznicę powstania Zakładu Psychologii Rozwojowej i Wychowawczej na Uniwersytecie Jagiellońskim* [*Studies on Development and Education: on the Eightieth Anniversary of the Department of Developmental Psychology at the Jagiellonian University*] (153–170). Wydawnictwo Uniwersytetu Jagiellońskiego.

Hilberink, S.R., Grootoonk, A., Ketelaar, M., Vos, I., Cornet, L., & Roebroeck, M.E. (2020). Focus on autonomy: Using 'Skills for Growing Up' in pediatric rehabilitation care. *Journal of Pediatric Rehabilitation Medicine*, *13*, 161–167. 10.3233/PRM-190618

Hodapp, R.M., Burack, J.A., & Zigler, E. (1998). Developmental approaches to mental retardation: A short introduction. In J. Burack, R.M. Hodapp & E. Zigler (eds.), *Handbook of mental retardation and development* (3–19). Cambridge University Press.

Kiang, L., & Bhattacharjee, K. (2019). Developmental change and correlates of autonomy in asian american *adolescents. Journal of Youth and Adolescence*, *48*, 410–421. 10.1007/s10964-018-0909-3

Kudlińska-Chróścicka, I. (2019). Stawanie się osobą dorosłą w czasach płynnej nowoczesności w doświadczeniu wielkomiejskich młodych dorosłych [Becoming an Adult Person in Times of Liquid Modernity in the Experience of Young Adults from Big Cities]. *Przegląd Socjologii Jakościowej* [*Qualitative Sociology Review*], *15*, 34–60. 10.18778/1733-8069.15.4.03

Li, J-B., Delvecchio, E., Lis, A., Nie, Y-G., Di, & Riso, D. (2015), Parental attachment, self-control, and depressive symptoms in Chinese and Italian adolescents: Test of a mediation model. *Adolescence*, *43*, 159–170. 10.1016/j.adolescence.2015.06.006

Liberska, H., Głogowska, K., & Deja, M. (2016). Attachment to parents and peers as a predictor of self-evaluation in the period of adolescence. *Psychological Journal*, *22*, 219–227.

Macdonald, E., Lee, E., Geraghty, K., McCann, K., Mohay, H., & O'Brien, T. (2007). Towards a developmental framework of consumer and carer participation in child and adolescent mental health services. *Australasian Psychiatry*, *15*(6), 504–508. 10.1080/10398560701458228

Nomaguchi, K.M. (2008). Gender, family structure, and adolescents' primary confi dants. *Journal of Marriage and Family*, *70*, 1213–1227.

Obuchowska, I. (2006), Adolescencja [Adolescence]. In B. Harwas-Napierała & J. Trempała (eds.), *Psychologia rozwoju człowieka* [*Human Development Psychology*] (163–210). Wydawnictwo Naukowe PWN.

Olearczyk, T. (2009). Psychopedagogiczne aspekty sytuacji konfliktowych w okresie adolescencji [Psychopedagogical Aspects of Conflict Situations in the Period of Adolescence]. In M. Leśniak (ed.), *Mediation in resolving the conflicts of adolescence* (97–112). Krakowska Akademia im. A.F.Modrzewskiego.

Oleszkowicz, A., & Misztela, A. (2010). Strategie konstruowania przyszłości a style tożsamości w późnej adolescencji [Future Construction Strategies vs Identity Styles in Late Adolescence]. *Psychologia Rozwojowa* [*Developmental Psychology*], *15*, 65–77.

Palisano, R. J., Di Rezze, B., Stewart, D., Freeman, M., Rosenbaum, P.L., Hlyva, O., Wolfe, L., & Gorter, J.W. (2020). Promoting capacities for future adult roles and healthy living using a lifecourse health development approach. *Disability and Rehabilitation*, *42*, 2002–2011. 10.1080/09638288.2018.1544670

Perlberg, M., Katz, I., Loewenthal, N., Kahil, N., Haim, A., Chechik, T., & Hershkovitz, E. (2021). The role of autonomy-supportive parenting in the competence, adherence and glycemic control of adolescents with type 1 diabetes. *Diabetes Research and Clinical Practice*, *173*, 10.1016/j.diabres.2021.108679

Shogren, K.A., & Turnbull, A.P. (2006). Promoting self-determination in young children with disabilities: The critical role of families. *Infants & Young Children*, *19*(4), 338–352.

Sicilia,A., Águila,C., Posse, M., & Alcaraz-Ibáñez, M. (2020). Parents' and peers' autonomy support and exercise intention for adolescents: Integrating social factors from the self-determination theory and the theory of planned behaviour. *International Journal of Environmental Research and Public Health*, *17*, 5365. 10.3390/ijerph17155365

Sikorski, W. (2021). *Psychologia relacji wewnątrzrodzinnych* [*Psychology of Intra-Family Relationships*]. Difin.

Szymańska, J. (2015). *Programy profilaktyczne. Podstawy profesjonalnej psychoprofilaktyki* [*Prevention Programmes. Foundations of Professional Psychoprevention*]. Ośrodek Rozwoju Edukacji.

Chapter 6

Personal and social resources of adolescents with a disability and of their parents

Similarities and differences

In line with the conceptual framework underlying our research, the analysis of health-related quality of life in adolescents with disabilities and FASD is performed in the context of resources, both inherent to the individual and those inherent to their environment (family, relations with peers). In the case of personal resources, we focused on those constituting dispositional traits (ego-resiliency), shaped in the form of a specific habit (health-promoting lifestyle) and directly linked to beliefs related to health and disability, and to the limitations related to the latter. In turn, within social resources, the characteristics of the family were taken into account, as aspects particularly significant during the child's adolescence, considered in terms of the family's resources: cohesion and flexibility, as well as the financial situation perceived subjectively. Contacts with friends (both direct and using social media) were identified as compatible in this group of resources.

This chapter juxtaposes two points of view: that of adolescents with disabilities, and that of their parents. The theoretical context justifying the value of juxtaposing the personal and social resources of adolescents with disabilities and their parents is provided by assumptions from the area of intergenerational transmission (or social inheritance). According to these assumptions, parents, through their attitude towards their children, transmit a certain set of personality traits to them, including beliefs, values, norms, views, rules of behaviour, goals of action, and perception of social phenomena (Sitarczyk, 1993). Regardless of the specific theoretical approach explaining intergenerational transmission in the family of origin (systems theory, attachment theory, social learning theory, ecopsychology, psychoanalytic concept), the parent-child relationship and the experiences acquired within it are assumed to have certain developmental implications for children later in life (Branje et al., 2020).

We used the paired t-test in order to compare adolescent-parent dyads in terms of personal and social resources. We compared the personal and social resources of adolescents with the personal and social resources of their parents. We verified the differences between adolescents and parents 1) in dyads within the entire study group, 2) in dyads divided into subgroups due

DOI: 10.4324/9781003367772-6

Table 6.1 Differences in the assessment of personal and social resources in adolescent-parent dyads: Results of paired *t*-test in all surveyed dyads

All adolescent-parent dyads surveyed (n = 98 adolescents with intellectual, physical disability, and FASD, and n = 98 parents)					
HRQoL	*Groups*	M(SD)DS	M(SD)	t(df)	p
Self-rated health	adolescents	17.66(3.09)	**−2.47(4.07)**	**−6.00(97)**	**<.001**
	parents	20.13(2.95)			
Disability acceptance	adolescents	8.19(2.47)	.03(2.45)	.12(97)	.902
	parents	8.16(2.14)			
Physical activity	adolescents	9.65(3.22)	**−.99(4.23)**	**−2.13(97)**	**.023**
	parents	10.64(3.26)			
Nutrition	adolescents	21.58(6.12)	**−1.78(5.32)**	**−.3.32(97)**	**<.001**
	parents	23.37(6.32)			
Social support	adolescents	26.30(3.74)	.28(4.18)	.68(97)	.500
	parents	26.02(4.16)			
Stress management	adolescents	12.06(2.47)	**−1.15(2.91)**	**−3.92(97)**	**<.001**
	parents	13.21(2.52)			
Identity	adolescents	35.05(5.74)	**−2.64(5.89)**	**−4.44(97)**	**<.001**
	parents	37.69(4.71)			
General health practices	adolescents	10.42(2.69)	**−1.32(3.27)**	**−3.98(97)**	**<.001**
	parents	11.73(3.03)			
Safety	adolescents	29.29(5.06)	**−1.85(4.79)**	**−3.84(97)**	**<.001**
	parents	31.15(3.71)			
Lifestyle – general score	adolescents	144.37(17.43)	**−9.46(19.71)**	**−4.75(97)**	**<.001**
	parents	153.83(17.49)			
Ego-resiliency	adolescents	45.19(5.08)	**−1.37(5.87)**	**−2.31(97)**	**.023**
	parents	46.56(4.92)			
Family cohesion	adolescents	27.06(4.46)	**−1.19(3.62)**	**−3.25(97)**	**.002**
	parents	28.25(4.20)			
Family flexibility	adolescents	26.36(4.43)	−.65(3.72)	−1.74(97)	.086
	parents	27.01(3.98)			
Financial situation	adolescents	3.60(.65)	.05(.65)	.78(97)	.438
	parents	3.55(.61)			
Frequency of meetings with friends	adolescents	3.50(.91)	**1.24(1.14)**	**10.81(97)**	**<.001**
	parents	2.25(.71)			
Frequency of social media use	adolescents	4.73(.82)	**1.91(1.78)**	**10.62(97)**	**<.001**
	parents	2.83(1.46)			
	parents	4.09(1.45)			

Note: M(SD)DS – Means and standard deviations (descriptive statistics).

to the type of disability of adolescents: intellectual disability, physical disability, and FASD. The results of the analyses are presented in Tables 6.1–6.4.

Comparisons of the adolescent-parent dyads carried out in the whole group showed that the parents had a higher level of ego-resiliency, higher self-rated health, and a higher score on almost all lifestyle factors, except

Table 6.2 Differences in the assessment of personal and social resources in adolescent with intellectual disability-parent dyads: Results of paired *t*-test

Adolescent with intellectual disability-parent dyads (n = 26 adolescents with intellectual disability and n = 26 parents)

HRQoL	*Groups*	M(SD)$_{DS}$	M(SD)	t(df)	p
Self-rated health	adolescents	19.00(3.19)	−.84(3.53)	−1.22(25)	.233
	parents	19.85(2.34)			
Disability acceptance	adolescents	9.31(3.23)	−1.23(3.16)	−1.98(25)	.059
	parents	10.54(2.00)			
Physical activity	adolescents	12.38(3.87)	1.46(5.53)	1.35(25)	.190
	parents	10.92(4.38)			
Nutrition	adolescents	26.92(7.58)	**−2.38(5.04)**	**−2.41(25)**	**.023**
	parents	29.31(6.13)			
Social support	adolescents	27.96(4.63)	54(3.51)	.78(25	.442
	parents	27.42(4.93)			
Stress management	adolescents	11.92(3.42)	−1.53(3.31)	−1.78(25)	.087
	parents	13.08(2.78)			
Identity	adolescents	33.35(7.73)	**−3.77(6.69)**	**−2.87(25)**	**.008**
	parents	37.11(5.29)			
General health practices	adolescents	12.15(3.23)	−.88(3.73)	−1.21(25)	.238
	parents	13.04(2.89)			
Safety	adolescents	29.19(6.25)	−.46(4.67)	−.05(25)	.618
	parents	29.65(4.77)			
Lifestyle – general score	adolescents	153.88(22.68)	−6.65(17.82)	−1.90(25)	.069
	parents	160.53(20.98)			
Ego-resiliency	adolescents	45.73(7.40)	−2.15(7.31)	−1.47(25)	.153
	parents	47.85(5.76)			
Family cohesion	adolescents	29.92(4.81)	**−1.54(3.52)**	**−2.23(25)**	**.035**
	parents	31.46(4.31)			
Family flexibility	adolescents	28.92(4.54)	−.38(3.70)	−.53(25)	.601
	parents	29.31(4.06)			
Financial situation	adolescents	3.54(.76)	.00(.63)	.00(25)	1.00
	parents	3.54(.65)			
Frequency of meetings with friends	adolescents	3.65(.68)	**1.50(.81)**	**9.41(25)**	**<.001**
	parents	2.15(.61)			
Frequency of social media use	adolescents	4.81(.63)	**2.00(1.79)**	**5.71(25)**	**<.001**
	parents	2.81(1.50)			

Note: M(SD)$_{DS}$ – Means and standard deviations (descriptive statistics).

social support (see Table 6.1). In the area of social resources, parents assess their family as more cohesive than adolescents. However, adolescents meet more frequently with their friends and use social media more often than their parents. It also seems important that dyads of all surveyed adolescents and

Table 6.3 Differences in the assessment of personal and social resources in adolescent with physical disability-parent dyads: Results of paired *t*-test

Adolescent with physical disability-parent dyads (n = 61 adolescents with physical disability and n = 61 parents)

HRQoL	*Groups*	$M(SD)_{DS}$	M(SD)	t(df)	p
Self-rated health	adolescents	17.26(2.25)	**−3.52(2.87)**	**−9.60(60)**	**<.001**
	parents	20.79(2.24)			
Disability acceptance	adolescents	7.65(1.49)	.38(1.74)	1.69(60)	.096
	parents	7.28(1.27)			
Physical activity	adolescents	8.21(1.86)	**−1.98(2.86)**	**−5.41(60)**	**<.001**
	parents	10.20(2.23)			
Nutrition	adolescents	19.49(3.62)	−.75(4.01)	−1.47	.147
	parents	20.24(3.64)			
Social support	adolescents	26.16(2.32)	.59(3.39)	1.36(60)	.179
	parents	25.57(2.83)			
Stress management	adolescents	12.24(1.95)	**−1.05(2.13)**	**−3.53(60)**	**<.001**
	parents	13.29(1.92)			
Identity	adolescents	36.82(3.11)	**−1.93(3.71)**	**−4.06(60)**	**<.001**
	parents	38.75(2.59)			
General health practices	adolescents	9.72(1.82)	**−1.05(2.30)**	**−3.55(60)**	**<.001**
	parents	10.77(2.51)			
Safety	adolescents	30.24(3.71)	**−1.92(4.23)**	**−3.60(60)**	**<.001**
	parents	32.20(1.89)			
Lifestyle – general score	adolescents	142.90(9.86)	**−8.13(12.80)**	**−4.96(60)**	**<.001**
	parents	151.03(8.41)			
Ego-resiliency	adolescents	45.59(2.95)	−.70(3.82)	−1.44(60)	.155
	parents	46.29(4.16)			
Family cohesion	adolescents	26.39(3.01)	**−.85(3.04)**	**−2.22(60)**	**.030**
	parents	27.26(2.58)			
Family flexibility	adolescents	25.84(3.55)	−.70(3.41)	−1.61(60)	.112
	parents	26.54(2.80)			
Financial situation	adolescents	3.63(.58)	.08(.64)	1.00(60)	.321
	parents	3.56(.61)			
Frequency of meetings with friends	adolescents	3.44(.90)	**1.26(1.01)**	**9.71(60)**	**<.001**
	parents	2.18(.53)			
Frequency of social media use	adolescents	4.77(.80)	**2.16(1.55)**	**10.89(60)**	**<.001**
	parents	2.61(1.36)			

Note: $M(SD)_{DS}$ *– Means and standard deviations (descriptive statistics).*

their parents do not differ in terms of disability acceptance, social support, financial situation, or family flexibility.

Analyses conducted by subgroups of dyads due to the type of disability of the adolescents indicated that among the teenagers with intellectual disabilities-parent dyads, differences were revealed in two lifestyle factors and in the assessment of family cohesion. Parents scored higher in nutrition

Table 6.4 Differences in the assessment of personal and social resources in adolescent with FASD-parent dyads: Results of paired *t*-test

Adolescent with FASD-parent dyads (n = 11 adolescents with FASD and n = 11 parents)					
HRQoL	*Groups*	$M(SD)_{DS}$	M(SD)	t(df)	p
Self-rated health	adolescents	16.73(5.78)	−.45(7.89)	−.19(10)	.852
	parents	17.18(5.31)			
Disability acceptance	adolescents	8.54(3.80)	3.01(3.01)	1.20(10)	.258
	parents	7.45(2.21)			
Physical activity	adolescents	11.18(2.82)	−1.27(5.14)	−.82(10)	.431
	parents	12.45(4.48)			
Nutrition	adolescents	20.54(6.27)	−6.09(9.31)	−2.17(10)	.055
	parents	26.64(7.13)			
Social support	adolescents	23.18(5.65)	−2.00(7.96)	−.83(10)	.424
	parents	25.18(7.24)			
Stress management	adolescents	11.36(2.54)	−1.73(4.69)	−1.22(10)	.250
	parents	13.09(4.50)			
Identity	adolescents	29.27(7.00)	−3.91(11.56)	−1.12(10)	.288
	parents	33.18(8.65)			
General health practices	adolescents	10.18(2.92)	**−3.82(5.42)**	**−2.34(10)**	**.042**
	parents	14.00(3.79)			
Safety	adolescents	24.27(5.93)	**−4.64(6.84)**	**−2.24(10)**	**.048**
	parents	28.91(6.04)			
Lifestyle – general score	adolescents	130.00(24.59)	−23.45(41.80)	−1.86(10)	.092
	parents	153.45(35.76)			
Ego-resiliency	adolescents	41.73(6.77)	−3.27(10.24)	−1.06(10)	.314
	parents	45.00(6.36)			
Family cohesion	adolescents	24.00(6.81)	−2.18(6.19)	−1.17(10)	.270
	parents	26.18(6.86)			
Family flexibility	adolescents	23.18(5.79)	−1.00(5.48)	−.606	.558
	parents	24.18(6.46)			
Financial situation	adolescents	3.54(.82)	.00(.77)	.00(10)	1.00
	parents	3.54(.52)			
Frequency of meetings with friends	adolescents	3.45(1.37)	.54(2.02)	.90(10)	.391
	parents	2.91(1.30)			
Frequency of social media use	adolescents	4.36(1.21)	.27(2.19)	.41(10)	.689
	parents	4.09(1.45)			

Note: $M(SD)_{DS}$ *– Means and standard deviations (descriptive statistics).*

and identity than adolescents (see Table 6.2). There are similarities with the results obtained in the totality of dyads surveyed. In these dyads, parents also assess their family as more cohesive than adolescents. Another similarity is that adolescents with intellectual disabilities more frequently meet with their friends and use social media more often than their parents. In these dyads, the adolescent and the parent do not differ in terms of disability acceptance, ego-resiliency, family flexibility, and financial situation.

In the case of the adolescent with physical disability-parent dyads, the results are similar, but we observed more statistically significant differences between the teenagers and their parents. Adolescents with physical disability assess their family as less cohesive than their parents. This is similar. In these dyads, the adolescent and the parent do not differ in terms of disability acceptance, ego-resiliency, family flexibility, or financial situation either. Moreover, adolescents with physical disability also meet with their friends more often than their parents, and have a higher level of social media use. The results indicated that parents of teenagers with physical disability have higher self-rated health in comparison with adolescents, a higher level of physical activity, and score higher on almost all lifestyle factors (except nutrition and social support) (see Table 6.3).

In the area of the personal and social resources analysed, almost none of the variables turned out to be statistically significant for the adolescents with FASD-parent dyads. The results only showed that adolescents with FASD had lower scores on such lifestyle factors as safety and general health practices (see Table 6.4).

The results obtained in our research point to a number of interesting aspects. On the basis of the differences and similarities found in the intensity of the personal and social resources of the adolescents with disabilities and their parents surveyed, possible aspects of intergenerational transmission can be formulated, but one can also see the clearly separate nature of the young people, reflecting the aspirations to maintain autonomy, specific to the period of adolescence. Statistically significant differences were found in three of the four personal resources taken into account: ego-resiliency, health-promoting lifestyle, and self-rated health. Similar levels of acceptance of disability were recorded in both study groups: in adolescents assessing their own disability and in parents expressing the degree of acceptance of disability in their adolescent child.

The differences found in terms of ego-resiliency and the higher level of this personality trait in the parents seem obvious and in line with previous findings by researchers, pointing to its increasing intensity with age. In fact, the research shows that, although ego-resiliency is relatively stable throughout adolescence, it can already show an upward trend during emerging adulthood (Alessandri et al., 2016). Arguably, the parents' more extensive life experiences may have predicted higher levels of this favourable personality trait in them. This corresponds with previous findings showing different factors predicting ego-resiliency trajectory during adolescence and at later developmental stages. Whereas during adolescence, ego-resiliency was predicted by beliefs about one's self-efficacy in dealing with negative emotions, at a later stage earlier experience of family support and self-efficacy beliefs in expressing positive emotions were more important (Alessandri et al., 2016). On top of that, it can be assumed that the protective function of ego-resiliency becomes stronger with age as a result of the individual confronting various stressful and volatile circumstances. Importantly, regardless of the type of disability experienced by the adolescents and the psychosocial consequences characterising it, the difference found between the parents and their adolescent children in the intensity of ego-resiliency persisted.

It is concluded on the basis of our study that health-promoting lifestyle, as a resource including specific health-promoting beliefs, behaviours, and activities, differed significantly between the adolescents with disabilities and their parents surveyed. Significantly higher physical activity, better eating habits, more effective coping with difficult situations, greater attention to strengthening one's identity, more frequent engagement in a variety of general development practices, and higher daily concern for one's own safety were found in the parents. Admittedly, within this personal resource, one could expect a relatively high intergenerational compatibility, given the expected effects of imitation and the habits formed with regard to behaviour within the family ties. However, the difference found in almost all health-promoting practices (except activity aimed at seeking and providing support) in the parents' favour may suggest two possibilities.

Firstly, it may reflect a developmentally determined difference in the awareness of the consequences of preferred lifestyle for health and general wellbeing. On the basis of greater life experience, the parents can undertake specific health-promoting activities with greater awareness and responsibility. Secondly, due to the adolescents' disabilities and the associated limitations, they may implement some of the activities making up a health-promoting lifestyle to a smaller extent. This would include for instance less physical activity in the case of adolescents with physical disabilities, or the smaller set of effective coping strategies for dealing with stress in adolescents with intellectual disabilities. The conjecture put forward here is consistent with the differentiation found in the preference for a health-promoting lifestyle related to the type of disability of the adolescents surveyed. Previous research showed that parents of adolescent children with physical disabilities were highly motivated to undertake activities making up a health-promoting lifestyle: proper nutrition, physical activity, refraining from consuming stimulants, or nurturing social contacts. They expressed a high awareness of the importance of health promotion and put a lot of effort into daily activities and observance of various commitments in order to transmit appropriate role models to the adolescents (Antle et al., 2008). High motivation in the parents of children with disabilities, dictated by the concern for their psychophysical wellbeing, is furthermore associated with the use of various strategies to encourage young people to adopt healthy habits, which results in the performance of a wide range of diverse health-promoting activities (Peña & Payne, 2022).

Our research revealed that parents scored significantly higher on self-rated health compared to their adolescent children with disabilities. The difference found between the two studied groups reflects previous findings, suggesting a relatively weak effect of family transmission within health ratings (Breidablik et al., 2010). Nevertheless, it should be noted that the self-assessment of health made by the parents and the adolescents refers to objectively different health conditions. Although the sole fact of having a disability does not translate directly into the overall health rating, the consequences of the disability and the resulting health complications may be relevant for the assessment expressed. The research by Breidablik et al. (2008) suggests for instance that self-rated health in adolescents is relatively stable, but may deteriorate with the lack of general wellbeing and the experience of disability. It is important to emphasise that, when taking into account the type of disability of the adolescent, a significant difference in self-rated health was only found between parents and adolescents with physical disabilities. The parents of these adolescents rated their health significantly higher.

Acceptance of disability proved not to be a differentiating factor between the parents and their adolescent children surveyed. Regardless of the type of disability, adolescents scored low on acceptance of their disability, similarly to the parents, expressing low acceptance of their child's disability. The consistent and low assessment of disability is most likely dictated by the perception of the significant impact of the disability on the adolescent's life and of the fact that it limits their developmental opportunities. The particular nature of the period of adolescence, expressed in dynamic changes, taking on new challenges and social roles, makes it a time when the child and parents may be confronted once again with the consequences of disability, problems they previously did not know (Hamilton et al., 2015).

In the case of social resources, family cohesion and family flexibility, assessment of the family's financial situation, as well as contacts with friends (directly and via social media), our research findings point to some differences, but also similarities.

It is particularly interesting that the adolescents with disabilities and their parents surveyed differed significantly in terms of their rating of family cohesion, but perceived family flexibility in a similar way. Characteristically, parents rate significantly higher the emotional ties between the individual family members, reporting a sense of greater mutual closeness, spending time together developing interests, and paying more attention to the fact that decisions in the family are made taking into account the needs of its members. As pointed out by previous research (Mitchell et al., 2016), families of adolescents with disabilities are particularly vulnerable to disruption of cohesion, due to the changes taking place during adolescence and possible adaptive problems, including ones related to adolescents' behaviour. At the same time, while certain factors such as marital satisfaction may predict a higher rating of family cohesion in the parents, in the case of the adolescents, there may be increased difficulty in perceiving certain areas of family relationships positively, due to the adaptive problems experienced.

Our research also revealed the differing points of view of parents and adolescents with disabilities in terms of rating their direct and social media contacts with friends. Adolescents with disabilities scored significantly higher with regard to both forms of contact with friends. The results obtained most likely reflect the particular need for contact with peers during adolescence, a time when peer group relationships become a platform for building identity, autonomy, and self-esteem, as well as for satisfying the need to be accepted by someone with similar interests and expectations. Satisfactory relations with peers found in young people with disabilities are perceived as a special resource through which the adolescents define themselves. Earlier research revealed that adolescents with physical disabilities valued relationships with their peers and saw themselves as regular members of their peer group, at the same time emphasising the awareness of others perceiving them through the lens of their limitations (Skär, 2003). It should be noted, therefore, that frequent and satisfactory contacts between young people with disabilities and their friends can be important because of the growing awareness during adolescence of the differences dictated by the limitations and of the increased risk of rejection and stigmatising reactions. As pointed out by Mackey and Beckert (2017), the experience of disability has relatively little impact on how adolescents define themselves, but it becomes a decisive factor in how others perceive them. Importantly, the satisfactory and frequent contacts with others reported by the adolescents not infrequently involve other persons with disabilities, with whom they have friendly and mutually supportive relationships. They may also involve peers without a disability but who have, for example, a family member experiencing one (Bossaert et al., 2011). In addition, shared interests and hobbies and the amount of free time spent together can enhance contacts and their quality in young people with disabilities (Kalymon et al., 2010).

The difference in frequency of contacts with friends (directly and through social media) captured in our study reflects real generational differences in the demand for contacts outside the family, undertaken to a much greater extent at earlier developmental stages. This may actually not only show that adolescents consciously allocate an increasing amount of free time to relationships with their peers, but also point to the more limited scope of daily activities and responsibilities that characterise them, which increases as they take on more life roles. Moreover, as the research indicates, parents of adolescents with disabilities are characterised by higher levels of stress, fatigue, tension, and strain in relation to various parenting issues and challenges (Mackey & Beckert, 2017). During this period, the demands related to being a parent of an adolescent child with a disability accumulate, which may be significant in reducing the time dedicated to contacts with friends (Migerode et al., 2012).

The similarities revealed in our study between parents and adolescents with disabilities in their assessment of the family's financial resources and the use of the latter to meet individual needs may reflect the adoption of similar criteria for judging the financial situation, becoming more objective in the context of other elements of the family's functioning.

Contrary to certain expectations, the similarities and differences in the adolescents with disabilities-parents dyads captured in our research can confirm the importance of intergenerational transmission mechanisms only to a limited extent. The differences found in the self-rating of health, lifestyle, or contacts with friends clearly reveal the differences in opinion, as well as the needs that make up the personal and social resources of the two groups of respondents.

References

Alessandri, G., Eisenberg, N., Vecchione, M., Caprara, G.V., & Milioni, M. (2016). Ego resiliency development from late adolescence toemerging adulthood: A ten-year longitudinal study. *Journal of Adolescence*, *50*, 91–102. 10.1016/j.adolescence.2016.05.004

Antle, B.J., Mills, W., Steele, C., Kalnins, I., & Rossen, B. (2008). An exploratory study of parents' approaches to health promotion in families of adolescents with physical disabilities. *Child Care Health & Development*, *34*, 185–193. 10.1111/j.1365-2214.2007.00782.x

Bossaert, G., Colpin, H., Pijl, S. J., & Petry, K. (2011). The attitudes of Belgian adolescents towards peers with disabilities. *Research of Developemental Disabilities*, *32*, 504–509. 10.1016/j.ridd.2010.12.033

Branje, S., Geeraerts, S., de Zeeuw, E.L., Oerlemans, A.M., Koopman-Verhoeff, M.E., Schulz, S., Nelemans, S., Meeus, W., Hartman, C.A., Hillegers, M.H.J., Oldehinkel, A.J., & Boomsma, D.I. (2020). Intergenerational transmission: Theoretical and methodological issues and an introduction to four Dutch cohorts. *Developmental Cognitive Neuroscience*, *45*, 1–12. 10.1016/j.dcn.2020.100835.

Breidablik, H.J., Meland, E., Holmen, T. L., & Lydersen, S. (2010). Role of parents in adolescent self-rated health: Norwegian Nord-Trondelag Health Study. *Adolescent Health Medicine and Therapuetics*, *1*, 97–104. 10.2147/AHMT.S12877

Breidablik, H-J., Meland, E., & Lydersen, S. (2008). Self-rated health in adolescence: A multifactorial composite. *Scandinavian Journal of Public Health*, *36*, 12–20.

Hamilton, A., Mazzucchelli, T.G., & Sanders, M.R. (2015). Parental and practicioners perspectives on raising an adolescent with a disability: A focus group study. *Disability & Rehabilitation*, *37*, 1664–1673. 10.3109/09638288.2014.973969

Kalymon, K., Gettinger, M., & Hanley-Maxwell, Ch. (2010). Middle school boys' perspectives on social relationships with peers with disabilities. *Remedial and Special Education*, *31*, 41–50. 10.1177/07419325083274

Mackey, M., & Beckert, T.E. (2017). Adolescent with disability. *Adolescent Research Review*, *2*, 59–75. DOI 10.1007/s40894-016-0043-y

Migerode, F., Maes, B., Buysse, A., & Brondeel, R. (2012). Quality of life in adolescents with a disability and their parents: The mediating role of social support and resilience. *Journal of Developmental and Physical Disabilities*, *24*, 487–503.

Mitchell, D.B., Szczerepa, A., & Hauser-Cram, P. (2016). Spilling over: Partner parenting stress as a predictor of family cohesion in parents of adolescents with developmental disabilities. *Research in Developemental Disabilities*, *49*, 258–267. 10.1016/j.ridd.2015.12.007

Peña, C.M., & Payne, A. (2022). Parental experiences of adopting healthy lifestyles for children with disabilities living with overweight and obesity. *Disability & Health Journal*, *15*. 10.1016/j.dhjo.2021.101215

Sitarczyk, M. (1993). Międzypokoleniowa transmisja postaw rodzicielskich. Doniesienie z badań, [Intergenerational transmission of parental attitudes. Research Report]. *Problemy Rodziny [Family Problems]*, 6, 13–25.

Skär, R.N.L. (2003). Peer and adult relationship of adolescents with disabilities. *Journal of Adolescence*, *26*, 635–649. 10.1016/s0140-1971(03)00061-7.

Chapter 7

Meaning of personal and social resources in maintaining a health-related quality of life of adolescents with a disability

Health and health-related quality of life as well as disability are categories that, according to the ICF, are separate, but, through a variety of contextual and personal factors, can also be related (McDougall et al., 2010). While research has not proven a direct relationship between disability and health, study findings have shown that disability can be associated with a reduction (at least temporary) in quality of life (Bishop, 2005). Experiencing satisfactory quality of life is to a greater extent determined by factors unrelated to the disability as such, but to psychosocial resources, both among adults (Kagan et al., 2018) and young people (Edwards et al., 2003).

Analyses of health-related quality of life among children and adolescents with disabilities have provided inconclusive results, revealing both their lower and relatively high self-rated health. Moreover, research conducted among children and adolescents with various disabilities (intellectual, physical, hearing, and autism spectrum) has shown that, although the type of disability did not matter for the overall assessment of health, it did make the sense of health-related quality of life differ. Adolescents with physical or intellectual disabilities and on the autism spectrum reported more unsatisfactory elements compared to young people in the general population (Domellöf et al., 2014).

Health-related quality of life in adolescents is determined by multiple factors, categorised in various ways in the literature. The role of external (including environmental, social, and interpersonal) and internal (individual and intrapsychic) factors is indicated (Solera-Sanchez et al., 2021). Even more complex explanations involving diversified factors determined by resources concern the health and quality of life of young people with disabilities and chronic diseases (Petersson et al., 2013). Research has revealed that a disability or chronic illness do not translate in a simple and direct manner into quality of life, including health-related quality of life (Lin et al., 2009; Murray et al., 2015). Importantly, adolescents with disabilities report a relatively high subjective health-related quality of life, which clearly points to the operation of additional factors, but also to their perceived distinction between disability and health. Compared to their peers without disabilities, adolescents with physical disability scored lower on objective quality of life,

DOI: 10.4324/9781003367772-7

but the two groups did not differ in subjective terms (Chow et al., 2005). In relation to the globally increasing numbers of children and adolescents with disabilities in recent years, researchers have been focusing increasingly strongly not so much on the factors leading to disrupted health and reduced quality of life, but rather on factors making it possible to maintain the former and strengthen the latter (Cieza et al., 2021). The analyses performed have concerned, therefore, not so much the deficiencies and the pathogens, but rather the resources that make it possible to preserve/protect health and a satisfactory quality of life, and promote recovery after health disruption, e.g. due to an existing or developing disability. Particular emphasis is placed on the group of resources available to the individual, representing their individual potential, either innate or shaped by a variety of life experiences. These are referred to as personal resources (physical, mental, and social/interpersonal), not infrequently equated with individual coping resources (Mayeri et al., 2017).

This chapter contains an analysis of the role of selected personal resources in maintaining a satisfactory quality of life in adolescents with a disability. The following personal resources will be analysed: ego-resiliency, health-promoting lifestyle, self-rated health, and acceptance of disability. Further on in the chapter, the relations between personal and social resources will be presented, together with research findings pointing to the role of social resources in health-related quality of life among the adolescents surveyed. Particular attention will be focused here on the family and peer contexts. We will examine the resources important in these areas and their relevance for health-related quality of life, experienced within the family or among peers.

The role of personal resources for health-related quality of life

Ego-resiliency is a multidimensional construct, in terms both of its structure and of its functions. It is treated as a personal resource in the form of a trait, as the individual capacity for dynamic and situationally appropriate self-regulation (Kołodziej-Zaleska & Przybyła-Basista, 2018). It is the ability to flexibly adjust to difficult and stressful conditions (Block, 2002; Farkas & Orosz, 2015). The resource has permanent properties but constantly evolves, which has been verified in different countries and cultures (Alessandri et al., 2012). It involves adaptive flexibility and creative response to external demands. Individuals with high ego-resiliency are characterised by better psychological adaptation in difficult situations, they display more flexible and dynamic coping with stressors, as well as a better ability to recover from negative emotional experiences. They are more resilient to the impact of stressful circumstances. Such individuals are capable of making use of resources, adjusting quickly to environmental changes, and dealing in an effective manner with a variety of stressors (Willson & Hughes, 2006). In turn, individuals with low ego-resiliency find it difficult to modulate self-control, have little adaptive flexibility, and display a stronger tendency towards anxiety reactions faced with stressful situations; they also have difficulty recovering from traumatic life events (Alessandri et al., 2020; Farkas & Orosz, 2015). Ego-resiliency is ascribed the status of a meta-resource, particularly important in circumstances requiring a flexible and dynamic response, and an adequate choice of remedies according to what the situation requires. This meta-resource creates favourable conditions for experiencing positive emotions despite difficult situations, resulting in the achievement of emotional balance (Ziarko et al., 2019). Some researchers (e.g. Armstrong et al., 2005) even emphasise that ego-resiliency is a protective trait, making it possible to predict adaptive functioning regardless of risk. Since ego-resiliency is responsible for flexible and adaptive thinking and self-regulation of emotions fostering pro-adaptive behaviours, this resource correlates positively with many beneficial outcomes in health, wellbeing, and quality of life. Research so far has shown a negative correlation between ego-resiliency and depression, anxiety, and stress, and a positive correlation with life satisfaction (Nemati & Maralani, 2016).

Research into the link between ego-resiliency and age has demonstrated the key role of the resource in psychosocial functioning during adolescence, which is a transitional developmental stage associated with numerous dynamic changes. Alessandri and colleagues (2012) demonstrated a relative stability of ego-resiliency in adolescents up to the age of 19, and the resource has also been recognised as essential in processes of self-regulation of behaviour, or the development of social competence in adolescents (Alessandri et al., 2017; Hofer et al., 2010). The links of ego-resiliency with various health indicators in adolescents have been examined. Ego-resiliency has been revealed to potentially constitute a long-term negative predictor of depression (Taylor & Jones, 2020), and to negatively correlate with anxiety symptoms, distress, and dissatisfaction (Alessandri et al., 2017; Kim et al., 2015). However, the importance of ego-resiliency in explaining health and health-related quality of life in adolescents with a disability has so far been studied to a limited extent.

In this context, it is important to cite the findings obtained among adolescents with physical disabilities, indicating that increased life stress related to the challenges of adolescence and the limitations resulting from a disability were associated with poorer quality of life, within both objective and subjective indices. The achievement of a higher quality of life, in turn, was identified as a consequence of a number of factors at play, among which resilience also performed an important role. Importantly, these studies revealed that resilience alone without other resources might not be sufficient to improve quality of life in adolescents with physical disabilities (Alriksson-Schmidt et al., 2007). It was found, for example, that resilience, together with the social support obtained, played an important role in improving quality of life, despite the growing problems indicated by adolescents (Migerode et al., 2012). Resilience also acted as a moderator of the relationship between emotional disorders and health-related quality of life in adolescents with physical disabilities. A negative relationship between these variables could be noticed in adolescents with high resilience. Thus, the level of this resource appeared to be of key importance for mitigating emotional disorders and enhancing the sense of health-related quality of life (Rainone et al., 2017). The supportive function of resilience has also been established among adolescents with intellectual disabilities. Using qualitative research, the conditions were identified under which resilience in adolescents was reflected in a sense of greater satisfaction with their daily life. Their relatively successful coping with everyday challenges is the result of a favourable social context. It means, therefore, that the beneficial role of resilience is revealed when the individual receives the right support from significant others. Support, in turn, facilitates emotional and behavioural regulation (Hall & Theron, 2016).

Lifestyle is also taken into account in the category of resources relevant for health and health-related quality of life. It is defined in different ways; generally, it includes certain reactions and behavioural patterns formed in the process of socialisation, and is related to the daily individual choices of specific activities and actions (Dębska & Bielawska, 2002). It is divided, among other things, into health-promoting and health-harming lifestyles. A health-promoting lifestyle is a multidimensional construct that involves voluntary, everyday actions and attitudes towards life that can have easily observable health consequences. It includes areas relatively most conducive to maintaining health, such as pro-health behaviours. Health-promoting behaviours that define a lifestyle positively contributing to overall wellbeing include physical activity, balanced nutrition, attention to personal hygiene, coping with stress, appropriate interpersonal contacts, and regularly undergoing preventive examinations. In turn, health-harming behaviours indicate a lifestyle leading to health disruption/risk include smoking, use of alcohol and other drugs, as well as casual sex (Ponczek & Olszowy, 2012). Health-promoting and health-harming lifestyles are described using at least five categories related to human activity: diet, physical activity, being overweight/underweight, substance use, and sexual health (Emerson & Baines, 2010).

Adolescence is a key stage during which lifestyle choices (more or less informed) determine long-term outcomes in health, wellbeing, and quality of life (including health-related quality of life) (Patton et al., 2016). While some lifestyle changes in adolescents are temporary, others persist into adulthood, shaping health habits (Bottolfs et al., 2020). Health-related lifestyle is treated as a determinant of health-related quality of life. Analyses performed among adolescents show that a healthy lifestyle in the form of physical activity, appropriate sleep hygiene, proper eating habits, preventing excessive workload, and avoiding stimulants can significantly contribute to the improvement of health-related quality of life (da Costa et al., 2020; Muros et al., 2017). At the same time, research reveals that an unhealthy lifestyle adopted/pursued by adolescents can negatively affect their health, consequently threatening health-related quality of life (Boberska et al., 2018). Findings based on data from 37 countries (167,021 children and adolescents) demonstrated relatively unambiguously that individuals engaging in physical activity on a daily basis, spending less than two hours a day in front of screens, not drinking alcohol, and not smoking cigarettes were characterised by a smaller degree of subjective health complaints. A healthy lifestyle in adolescents was significantly related to fewer health complaints in general (Marques et al., 2019).

Although the link between a healthy/unhealthy lifestyle and health or quality of life has been documented among adolescents, the greater number of health problems and a less active lifestyle in adolescents with a disability provides an additional interpretative context and calls for an extension of the existing analyses. In fact, promoting a healthy lifestyle in this group of young people involves not only developing and maintaining health, but also facilitating measures to prevent secondary health complications characterising persons with disabilities. These secondary health complications may lead to the development of a preference for a health-harming lifestyle, manifesting itself, among other things, in a lower capacity for physical activity, and only occasional participation in physical exercise (Sutherland et al., 2002). Significantly increased rates of secondary health complications are particularly evident among adolescents with FASD, and this is usually accompanied by behaviours making up a health-harming lifestyle (addiction to alcohol and other drugs, including narcotics) (Petrenko et al., 2014). Few analyses exist explaining the relationship between the lifestyle of such young people, which can often represent a linear effect of the symptoms of FASD itself on health and sense of wellbeing. Previous research in this group of adolescents revealed significant deficits in adaptive behaviours, and low physical activity levels, translating to a significant extent into reduced overall psychosocial wellbeing. It has been shown that modifiable lifestyle elements such as improved sleep and increased participation in sporting activities in children with FASD can be used to improve health-promoting behaviours, including adaptive behaviours and those related to wellbeing (Hammond et al., 2020).

Persons with an intellectual disability have been shown to understand the importance of certain habits for staying healthy and maintaining wellbeing. They would emphasise the importance of a healthy diet, the benefits of physical activity, and the dangers of abusing certain substances. Respondents would highlight opportunities to engage in healthy behaviours, and the need for moderation in certain activities to maintain health. They would also distinguish the barriers and drivers of a healthy lifestyle (Caton et al., 2012). Young adults with a history of developmental disability were less inclined to engage in risky behaviours not conducive to health, compared to their peers in the general population. The type and extent of disability was found to be a factor differentiating the health-promoting behaviours. The greatest differences were noticeable between young adults with complex disabilities and their peers without disabilities, both in terms of the lower likelihood to engage in health-threatening behaviours (smoking, use of alcohol and other drugs, irresponsible sexual behaviours), and of experiencing greater difficulties in using preventive measures (sex education, preventive health care for adolescent women). The lower intensity of health-threatening behaviours in young people with disabilities may result from the absence of exposure or from weaker exposure to social situations that could potentially influence their decision to engage in health-harming activities (Rurangirwa et al., 2006).

An aspect relevant for the discussion on the importance of lifestyle for health and the sense of health-related quality of life is the higher prevalence of overweight and obesity found in children and adolescents with intellectual and physical disabilities, compared to non-disabled peers. At the same time, adolescents with intellectual disabilities experiencing overweight and obesity were demonstrated to have a significantly higher range of secondary health complications, predisposing them to more severe health problems as they enter adulthood (Rimmer et al., 2007). Overweight and obesity and their secondary consequences (e.g. fatigue, pain, social isolation, difficulties in performing everyday tasks) are associated with a significant deterioration of the psychophysical condition, mobilising greater expenditure of personal and family resources, including financial resources (Rimmer et al., 2007). Health-harming lifestyle identified in young people with intellectual disabilities, manifesting itself mainly in poor diet and low physical activity, constituting a risk factor for overweight and obesity, was linked to poorer health (Robertson et al., 2000). Overweight and obesity were also found among adolescents with FASD, with the highest rates of weight problems in persons with partial FASD and among adolescent women. In this context, it was pointed out that a lifestyle involving bad eating habits or lack of exercise in adolescents with FASD might be insufficient in explaining adverse health consequences, most likely dictated by the interaction of genetic, social, and intra-individual factors (Fuglestad et al., 2014).

Another area of lifestyle considered in the context of health and quality of life, alongside eating habits leading to overweight and obesity, is physical activity, including sports. Due to its recreational and therapeutic properties, and by mobilising the body to make an effort, it promotes the development and maintenance of physical and psychological wellbeing. The beneficial effects of sports and physical activity on quality of life and life satisfaction in children and adolescents have been proven many times in research (Boberska et al., 2018; Marker et al., 2018). The association between practising sports and favourable physical and mental functioning, improved life satisfaction, and health-related quality of life has also been found among persons with physical disabilities (Yazicioglu et al., 2012). Individuals with a physical disability who engaged in sport experienced less severe secondary health complications, improved wellbeing, higher levels of positive mood, development of physical skills, as well as a positive perception of physical competences (Shapiro & Martin, 2010), better relationships with peers and higher quality of social life in a variety of contexts (Groff, 2009), and overall enjoyment of life. Exercise in its multiple forms results in the improvement of various elements considered as indicators of health-related quality of life, contributing to the reduction of negative affect, psychological stress, depression, anxiety, and fatigue, and increasing the positive perception of wellbeing. It was found that a positive reappraisal of oneself and of one's health as a beneficial outcome of practising sports could mitigate any negative impact of disability on health-related quality of life (Edwards et al., 2003). Findings from the study by Shapiro and Malone (2016) indicate that children and adolescents with physical disabilities who practise sports have a positive perception of health-related quality of life in all dimensions. Adolescents with disabilities who train in a variety of sports (in a way that matches their capabilities) are found to record improvements in endurance, performance, gross motor skills, psychological wellbeing and overall satisfaction (Johnson, 2009). A meta-analysis of findings concerning the health benefits of physical activity among children and adolescents with intellectual disabilities showed that systematic physical exercise had a very high influence on physical health and a moderately high impact on psychosocial health. These relationships were in turn moderated by other factors: in the case of the relationship between physical activity and physical health, significant moderators proved to be age, the degree of intellectual disability, and additional disabilities, while the association between physical activity and psychophysical health was moderated among other things by the presence of additional disabilities. Greater improvement in physical health was recorded among adolescents (vs children), having more severe intellectual disabilities and additional disabilities. Higher rates of psychosocial health were found, on the other hand, among adolescents with combined disabilities (Kapsal et al., 2019).

Lifestyle as an important determinant of health and health-related quality of life in adolescents with disabilities is affected by contextual factors, such as the COVID-19 pandemic. Modification under its influence turned out to be bi-directional: health-promoting (devoting more time to activity, healthy eating, interactions with family members) and health-harming (abandoning activity, sitting around for hours using digital devices, social isolation, etc.). By eliminating or reducing certain activities, the pandemic has drastically impoverished lifestyle. This is alarming, especially since the lifestyles of young people that are currently being established will most likely determine their way of functioning in adulthood. In the case of adolescents with disabilities, this is all the more important since they experience delayed acquisition of life skills, including the shaping of a health-promoting lifestyle, due to their limitations (Donkervoort et al., 2007). Consequently, the lifestyle of adolescents with disabilities was taken into account in the research presented here. It is treated as an important factor in explaining health-related quality of life.

Resources considered in the context of health-related quality of life linked to health and disability also include self-rated health and acceptance of disability. Self-rated health is a subjective indicator of health status, integrating biological, psychological, social, and functional aspects, including individual health beliefs and behaviours (Stanojević Jerković et al., 2017). This rating is not infrequently treated as one of the decisive predictors of health-related quality of life, as it directly reflects the individual's assessment of their ability to function on a daily basis (Gładczuk et al., 2017). Research among adolescents revealed that these two constructs, namely self-rated health and health-related quality of life, would be understood as having distinct meaning, with an emphasis on the greater importance in self-rated health of elements linked to mental health, as opposed to physical and social health (Zullig et al., 2005). Lower self-rated health, both in physical and mental terms, is correlated with lower self-rated quality of life in adolescents (Sawatzky et al., 2010). In the context of the discussion on the relationship between health and disability, it has been demonstrated that persons with disabilities may construct their definition of health and self-rated health differently. This justifies the possible occurrence of the phenomenon of the disability paradox, manifesting itself, among other things, in high self-rated health with the simultaneous significant, severe damage to body structure and function (Drum et al., 2008). In adolescents with visible disabilities, self-rated health was a factor changing the relationship between the consequences of disability and quality of life (Edwards, Patrick, & Topolski).

Acceptance of disability is a key element in psychosocial adaptation. The most popular term for acceptance of disability introduced by Wright (1983) involves integrating the disability in the individual's self-concept without lowering their self-esteem. It is also treated as being able to minimise the losses experienced as a result of having a disability, as well as to see the value of the developmental potential kept (Keany & Glueckauf, 1993). It is one of the most important indicators of successful psychosocial adaptation to life with a disability, expressing the acceptance of the latter as one of the traits characterising the individual. Consequently, it is not tantamount to resignation, passivity, or surrendering to the situation, nor does it express the individual's acceptance of all the implications of having a disability. Instead, it involves the acceptance of the fact of having permanent limitations, and acknowledgement of their effects on psychosocial functioning, while being aware of retaining strengths, capabilities, and opportunities for development (Byra, 2012). As emphasised by Kowalik (2007), acceptance of disability means acknowledging the possibility of considering oneself in an expanded perspective of new values. Research among adolescents showed that acceptance of disability was crucial for wellbeing (Berntsson et al., 2007), as well as for higher self-rated quality of life. Recognising the value of one's capabilities and making use of them in the pursuit of life goals, accompanied by the belief that one would cope with the obstacles encountered, were linked to higher self-rated quality of life in adolescents with physical disabilities (Davis et al., 2009).

Concluding the review of the existing research on the relationship between selected resources (ego-resiliency, lifestyle, self-rated health, and acceptance of disability) and health-related quality of life in adolescents with disabilities, it can be pointed out that the scope of analyses in this area continues to be insufficient. So far, no tests have been performed concerning the associations of all these resources with health-related quality of life in that group of young people, whose already different functioning (due to their impairments) has been further altered by pandemic conditions.

Consequently, the research presented here fills the knowledge gap that was found, and is oriented towards testing the importance of ego-resiliency, health-promoting lifestyles, self-rated health, and acceptance of disability for the overall assessment of health-related quality of life in adolescents with physical disabilities, intellectual disabilities, and FASD. Our analyses sought to establish not only the links between these variables, but also to test the direct and indirect effects in the relationship between the personal resources of adolescents with disabilities taken into account and listed above. The analyses were designed to include the following stages: correlation analysis of variables (Table 7.1), regression model (Table 7.2), and mediation analysis (Figure 7.1).

We conducted linear regression to verify the significance of personal resources for maintaining health-related quality of life among the surveyed adolescents. Stepwise regression was used to see how the variance explained changes by adding predictors to the model separately. The results of stepwise regression are presented in Table 7.2.

In the first step of regression analysis, it was checked whether two self-rated health and disability acceptance indicators were predictors of health-related quality of life among the surveyed adolescents. Both variables turned out to be statistically significant in explaining the health-related quality of life of adolescents (see Table 7.2). The model explained over 48% of the variance of the dependent variable in the first step of the analysis. In the second step, lifestyle and ego-resiliency were also taken into account in the regression analysis. The percentage of explained variance increased to 57. Self-rated health and disability acceptance continued to be significant predictors of health-related quality of life. In addition, lifestyle turned out to be a statistically significant predictor for HRQoL, while ego-resiliency was devoid of statistical significance. In order to explain the role of ego-resiliency

Table 7.1 Correlation between personal and social resources and health-related quality of life in the group of surveyed adolescents

	Self-rated health	*Disability acceptance*	*Lifestyle*	*Ego-resiliency*	*Financial situation*	*Frequency of meetings with friends*	*Frequency of social media use*	*Family cohesion*	*Family flexibility*
self-rated health	–	–	–	–	–	–	–	–	–
disability acceptance	.32***	–	–	–	–	–	–	–	–
lifestyle	.42***	.39***	–	–	–	–	–	–	–
ego-resiliency	.54***	.26***	.56***	–	–	–	–	–	–
financial situation	.46***	.13	.11	.21*	–	–	–	--	–
frequency of meetings with friends	.20	.12	.09	.32***	.18	–	–	–	–
frequency of social media use	.07	−.12	−.006	.23*	.07	.28**	–	–	–
family cohesion	.43***	.14	.41***	.29**	.32***	-.008	.07	–	–
family flexibility	.31**	.11	.37***	.24*	.34***	.01	.02	.80***	–
health-related quality of life	.66***	.45***	.59***	.56***	.45***	.31**	–.003	.52***	.51***

Notes. *r-Pearson's correlation.*

* $p < .05$;

** $p < .01$;

*** $p < .001$

Table 7.2 Results of two steps of linear regression for health-related quality of life

Personal resources	B	SE	β	t	p
Step 1 self-rated health	2.27	.31	.57	7.39	**<.001**
disability acceptance	1.32	.38	.26	3.42	**<.001**
Step 2 self-rated health	1.61	.33	.41	4.94	**<.001**
disability acceptance	.88	.37	.18	2.39	**<.001**
lifestyle	.19	.06	.27	3.12	**.002**
ego-resiliency	.36	.21	.15	.1.71	.091

Step 1: *adj.*R^2 = .482, F = 46.17, df_1 = 2, df_2 = 95, p < .001
Step 2: adj.R^2 = .568, F = 32.80 ,df_1 = 2, df_2 = 93, p < .001, *F-change* = 10.35, p < .001

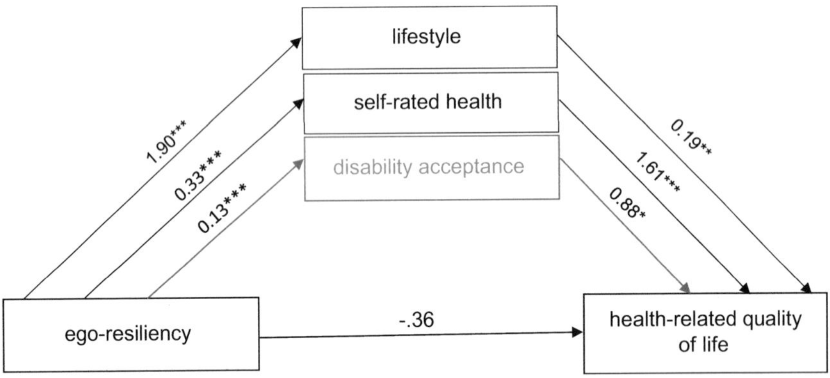

Note. * p < .05; ** p < .01; *** p < .001.
There are unstandardized b-coefficients above the lines.

Figure 7.1 Lifestyle and self-rated health as mediators of relationship between ego-resiliency and health-related quality of life in group of surveyed adolescents: results of mediation.

in maintaining health-related quality of life, we decided to verify the model of indirect dependencies: mediation.

We verified the assumption concerning the mediating role of three variables: lifestyle, self-rated health and disability acceptance in the relationship between ego-resiliency and health-related quality of life.

The adopted mediation model proved statistically significant. It explains 59% of the variance (F = 32.80; df_1 = 4; df_2 = 93; *adj.* R^2 = .59.; p < .001). The correlation between ego-resiliency and lifestyle proved statistically significant (b = 1.90; CI = <1.33; 2.48>; p < .001). The correlation between lifestyle and health-related quality of life also proved significant (b = 0.19; CI = <0.07; 0.31>; p = .024). The correlation between ego-resiliency and self-rated health proved statistically significant (b = 0.33; CI = <0.23; 0.43>; p < .001).

The correlation between self-rated health and health-related quality of life also proved significant ($b = 1.61$; $CI = <0.96; 2.26>$; $p < .001$). The correlation between ego-resiliency and disability acceptance proved statistically significant ($b = 0.13$; $CI = <0.03; 0.22>$; $p < .001$). The correlation between disability acceptance and health-related quality of life also proved significant ($b = 0.88$; $CI = <0.15; 1.61>$; $p = .019$).

The indirect effect of lifestyle on health-related quality of life was statistically significant, with $b = 0.36$ $CI = <0.90; 0.67>$; $p < .05$. The indirect effect of self-rated health on health-related quality of life was also statistically significant, with $b = 0.53$ $CI = <0.21; 0.91>$; $p < .05$. However, the indirect effect of disability acceptance on health-related quality of life was not statistically significant ($b = 0.11$ $CI = <-0.02; 0.30>$; $p > .05$). The results also show the direct impact of ego-resiliency on health-related quality of life with controlled indirect effect not being significant: $b = 0.36$; $CI = <-0.06; 0.79>$; $p > .05$. Lifestyle and self-rated health can be considered full mediators for the relationship between ego-resiliency and health-related quality of life in the surveyed group of adolescents. Among the three indirect effects analysed, only disability acceptance turned out not to be a mediator. The model of mediation is presented in Figure 7.1.

On the basis of the research results presented, positive associations are found between all the personal resources considered (ego-resiliency, health-promoting lifestyle, self-rated health, and acceptance of disability) and the overall assessment of health-related quality of life in the adolescents studied. The links established here are therefore consistent with the earlier research findings, presented in the introductory section of this chapter. The positive correlation between these variables thus confirms the conjectures that strong aspects of individual functioning defined by resources would be associated with higher quality-of-life assessments in areas influenced by health. Importantly, the contribution of these resources to explaining the assessment of health-related quality of life is neither uniform nor direct.

Our research indicates that the link between ego-resiliency and health-related quality of life in the adolescents with disabilities who were studied occurs with the involvement of two mediators: self-rated health and health-promoting lifestyle. Consequently, ego-resiliency, as a personality disposition promoting greater resilience to the impact of stressors, including those resulting from disability, can facilitate the perception of the strengths of one's health condition and the formation of a positive health assessment.

According to the findings by Bąk et al. (2021), individuals with higher ego-resiliency may be more accurate in the assessment of their health, taking into account a wider range of its elements, and pay attention to those confirmed by objective parameters. Due to their overall higher self-esteem, they may also be more likely to emphasise their stronger health-related aspects and to appreciate their remedial dispositions with regard to the weaker aspects of their functioning (Liu et al., 2021). Thus, ego-resiliency, being responsible for the accuracy of health assessment, higher self-esteem, and buffering of the effects of daily stressors leading to exhaustion and health disruption (Alessandri et al., 2020), may constitute an important psychological resource determining positive self-rated health in adolescents with disabilities. Higher self-ratings in adolescents with higher ego-resiliency may also be a consequence of the fact that this resource promotes health maintenance and supports recovery after temporary health disruption. Research indicates relatively clearly that higher levels of resiliency are associated with fewer health problems in adolescents (Mesman et al., 2021). Thus, it can be predicted that adolescents with disabilities and higher ego-resiliency, experiencing better health, will rate the latter more positively.

The research we present here revealed the mediating function of self-rated health in the relationship between ego-resiliency and health-related quality of life. In this manner, higher self-rated health in the adolescents with disabilities surveyed is associated with their higher rating of health-related quality of life. Self-rated health includes information about one's capability to function efficiently. The expression of this belief can therefore be associated with a positive assessment of those planes of life that are influenced by one's health. Previous research (Edwards et al., 2003) showed that while adolescents with disabilities reported lower quality of life compared to their peers without disabilities, self-rated health appeared nevertheless to buffer the impact of the disability on quality of life ratings. This may confirm that adolescents with disabilities clearly distinguish between limitations due to the disability and aspects of health, which they can rate positively, and as a result also rate their health-related quality of life higher.

According to our findings, ego-resiliency is linked to health-related quality of life through a health-promoting lifestyle in the adolescents with disabilities surveyed. As a meta-resource, being responsible for self-regulation and flexible adaptation to different conditions and external demands, ego-resiliency can foster actions and activities oriented towards maintaining psychophysical balance. Thus, it may shape a tendency to favour a health-promoting lifestyle manifesting itself in greater attention to fitness in various aspects of functioning. Ego-resiliency as a pro-adaptive and protective resource can also create favourable conditions for a style of action expressed in seeking support when needed, looking after one's safety, health and life, effectively coping with difficult situations encountered, and constructively building one's identity as a strong person focused on self-actualisation. Due to its characteristic capacity for flexible self-regulation, it can also foster higher readiness to engage in activities that modulate health indicators, such as physical activity, developing health-promoting eating habits, and undertaking a variety of actions aimed at maintaining wellbeing. Ego-resiliency is a personality trait providing the individual with the cognitive, emotional, and motivational resources necessary to self-regulate their behaviour and to successfully adapt to dynamically changing circumstances (Letzring et al., 2005).

It can be particularly important during adolescence, a period that requires people to adapt to changes in their environment and respond to social demands. The results of research by Shi et al. (2021) showed that children and adolescents with high resilience displayed very low severity of behavioural problems as well as high social-emotional functioning. Growing up with a disability involves a number of dynamic challenges, resulting not only from developmental transformations, but also from individual limitations. High ego-resiliency in adolescents with disabilities may, through a greater capacity to self-regulate behaviour, contribute to choosing adaptive and health-promoting activities. As ego-resiliency also supports recovery from extremely stressful situations, it can be a resource helping such adolescents develop new ways of coping when confronting the numerous challenges of adolescence.

Ego-resiliency as a resource that fosters flexible adaptation to dynamically changing circumstances could prove particularly significant in regulating the lifestyle of adolescents with disabilities in the pandemic and post-pandemic periods. It should be noted that the lifestyle of this group of adolescents (including their families), being generally a personal resource, may have been subject to the determining influences of pandemic conditions during that time. Studies have shown that adolescents with cerebral palsy would report reduced opportunities for socialisation, including reduced interactions with family and friends, less physical activity, reduced need to do anything, and predominance of communication using technology, while also highlighting the presence of increased depressive symptoms, a sense of isolation from others, feelings of depression and lack of enjoyment of the activities undertaken (Lai et al., 2022). A study by Theis and colleagues (2021) found negative effects of pandemic-induced restrictions on lifestyle and, consequently, on health outcomes among children and adolescents with intellectual and physical disabilities. A vast majority of the respondents reported a reduction in physical activity and more than 90% reported negative health impacts: lowered mood, worse behaviour, lower fitness, and increased feelings of isolation. Although, as the researchers highlighted, there are no definitive recommendations concerning required physical activity in disability, nevertheless the significant reduction in exercise induced by isolation has been shown to be a significant barrier to maintaining optimal physical and mental wellbeing in adolescents (Theis et al., 2021). Our research reveals that ego-resiliency can be an important resource that fosters choosing health-promoting lifestyle by adolescents with disabilities, even in pandemic conditions when the possibilities of action are limited.

The findings presented here suggest an indirect way ego-resiliency can impact health-related quality of life through health-promoting lifestyles in adolescents with disabilities. A preference for a health-promoting lifestyle as a consequence of higher ego-resiliency is linked to higher health-related quality of life. Desirable aspects of functioning, i.e. taking up physical activity, pursuing a healthy diet, taking care of one's own safety, effectively coping with problems, and performing various health-promoting activities, can consequently shape a more positive evaluation of various areas of life influenced by health. Our research results are consistent with previous findings, indicating higher health-related quality of life in adolescents with a health-promoting lifestyle (Marques et al., 2019; Sigvarsten et al., 2016). Taking up activities that lead to the development or enhancement of psychophysical fitness through exercise, an appropriate diet, high-quality relationships with others, achieving one's life goals, overcoming difficult situations, and acquiring coping competences can shape adolescents' sense of higher self-efficacy, responsibility, and control over their own lives and its individual areas. These beliefs, in turn, are a significant predictor of adolescents' rating of their health-related quality of life (Mikkelsen et al., 2020). In the case of adolescents with disabilities, adopting a health-promoting lifestyle is particularly important in relation to prevention or mitigation of the severity of secondary health complications being a consequence of the disability experienced. Recognising the beneficial effects of a health-promoting lifestyle in this area may lead to a higher rating of health-related quality of life in this group of adolescents.

Interdependence between personal and social resources from a sociological point of view

Social resources can be considered from different points of view. Firstly, that of the individual and their own resources resulting from who they are, from their mental and physical predispositions, which could also be referred to as innate or acquired competences, or personal resources. Secondly, from the point of view of the individual in their environment, i.e. their relationships with loved ones and the broader milieu (relations with neighbours, at school, with friends and acquaintances, while in the case of adults, also workplace relations). Thirdly, from the point of view of relations and the capability of using the available infrastructure (i.e. the access the individual has to tools ensuring proper communication with the environment or availability of that communication as such). These resources can also be considered to include access to service outlets (shops, post office, etc.) but also to means of transport. Fourthly, from the point of view of access to institutions, entities, organisations, and individuals who help to achieve life goals or provide support. Nowadays, this access to services and institutions is often provided without having to physically change one's location, via modern online technologies.

A decisive role in the fulfilment of life plans is also played by financial resources allowing one to gain better access to various types of institutions or to obtain support. Financial resources often also influence, and sometimes even determine, lifestyle and ways of coping. Social standing/status, i.e. the social class and milieu the individual identifies with, can also be a determinant factor. One can also talk about health resources, which will also have an impact on how and to what extent the above-mentioned resources related to the individual's functioning in their environment can be used. Similarly, personal competences can boost or limit one's skills in terms of seeking support and using the help of institutions, etc. When defining resources in this manner, it is impossible not to refer to the concept of social capital as defined by key figures such as Bourdieu, Coleman, and Putman (after: Bourdieu & Passeron, 2006; Bourdieu, 1986; Coleman, 1999; Putman & Goss, 2004; Putnam et al., 1993). They perceive social capital as a network of broadly defined resources available to the individual. The place of a person with a disability in their social environment from a social capital point of view is described by Masłyk (2019), among others. Following Field (2008), he assumes that the most relevant relationships from the point of view of persons with disabilities are relations with other people, being the initiating and causative force behind many events. At the same time, he points out that this concept has been used to study quality of life and health (Kawachi & Berkman, 2001; Kawachi et al., 1997; Kawachi et al., 1999, see also: Masłyk, 2019).

From the point of view of our research, the most important aspect in terms of social capital is the relationships in which adolescents with disabilities and FASD participate. This is linked to the extent to which relationship networks support or hinder the adolescents' sense of wellbeing and coping with the environment, and to which they improve their self-rated health and wellbeing. In the context of the study of persons with disabilities, it can therefore be assumed that an indisputable advantage of social capital theory is above all the fact that it brings together in a coherent way aspects related to the nature of social relations, social networks, and social structure (Lin, 2008; Masłyk, 2019). These elements are the foundation underlying the actions of individuals seeking to defend or multiply their existing resources. Lin (2008; see also: Masłyk, 2019) does not ignore the sociocultural context either, so important in shaping the relationships listed above, making a clear distinction between structural and cultural aspects, such as trust and social norms. The researcher places the latter within collective resources which, together with socioeconomic and sociocultural forces on the macro level (economy, technology, history, etc.), and sociodemographic ones, i.e. individual traits on the micro level, form a complex spectrum of factors responsible for inequalities in the process of building and maintaining social capital (after: Masłyk, 2019).

What seems particularly important from the point of view of our research, which focuses on adolescents' relationships on the micro rather than the macro level, are considerations concerning relationships and relationship networks, addressing relationship bridges and networks of strong and weak ties. The sociologist Granovetter (1973), in his classic publication *The*

Strength of Weak Ties, demonstrates that often weak ties, i.e. those which the individual establishes outside their immediate environment, i.e. their nearest and dearest with whom they function most often, are the relationships that actually help to build social capital, change, and seek new solutions. Granovetter (1973) believes weak rather than strong links to be the most useful and beneficial in interpersonal communication. The sociologist explains that through strong ties (due to information redundancy), people exchange a limited amount of data or resources, in a sense locking us in a hermetically sealed box with the same information reproduced all over again. Meanwhile, really important information is exchanged precisely through weak links. Strong interpersonal relationships are a channel for transmitting information that is not much different from that the individual already has. Social networks provide a good modern-day example of how weak ties, as it is there that where we often seek help or solutions through people completely unknown to us. As rightly pointed out by Szpunar (2012), following Wellman (Boase & Wellman, 2006), networked individualism is characterised by a large number of weak ties, a loosely knit structure, ease of entering into relationships (but also ending them), as well as the simultaneously local and global nature of ties.

This networked individualism becomes the base around which the individual builds their contacts with others, customizing their social life according to their own needs. The individual is no longer determined by their social standing and milieu. The ease of networking online facilitates access to other social circles. Learning about the group's rules and norms first from the position of an observer, and only later as a member, reduces the likelihood of the individual being excluded from the group already at the start. Szpunar (2012), investigating functioning within a virtual network, recognises that even functioning in a network of weak ties brings many profits, such as gaining new experiences, improving communication skills, and encountering different problems, which does not mean that such presence satisfies all our needs. Consequently, depending on the needs, but also on the type of problem the individual faces, they often make use of strong ties in the network (Szpunar, 2012). In this context, one might ask the question whether, for persons with disabilities, strong ties are always the most helpful, or whether perhaps they may sometimes be the most limiting ones. The lack of access to weak ties resulting from one's place of residence or social position may be an element that excludes such people. The group of persons with disabilities is particularly vulnerable to social exclusion.

In the context of social capital, Masłyk and colleagues (2016) provide very interesting insights on the use of resources, as well as on the self-rated psychological wellbeing in persons with disabilities. The researchers review the components of social capital, including how people with disabilities participate in different activities as part of public life (participation in organisations, having friends), to show their similarities to non-disabled citizens and their differences from the latter. These investigations are based on the 2013 Social Diagnosis study (Czapiński & Panek, 2014) and show the differences in access to the above resources. In nearly every category of those mentioned, differences can be seen in the perception and use of resources by persons with and without disabilities. Results in the following categories: activity for a community organisation, engagement in the local community, membership of organisations, performing functions within an organisation, and participation in public meetings show that even if sometimes the groups being compared differ only slightly, the comparisons almost always work to the disadvantage of persons with disabilities. The differences concern both involvement and participation in public life through activities performed for different organisations, as well as holding positions within the latter. However, it should be mentioned that the degree of involvement of non-disabled persons in such activities is not high either. The two groups compared also differ, albeit slightly, in terms of their feelings of trust and the number of regular contacts with friends they have and maintain. Significant differences are found in self-rated quality of life, sense of happiness, and positive evaluation of their life so far, in favour of non-disabled people. It is significant that a higher share of people with disabilities have suicidal thoughts, and these individuals also have higher levels of depressive symptoms (Masłyk et al., 2016).

It can be assumed that persons with disabilities will participate better and more efficiently in public life if they have access to resources and networks, including a wide network of weak ties. This is more likely to be the case in large urban areas, while it can be substantively more difficult for people living in small towns and rural areas, where one is much more determined by the exclusive functioning in a network of strong ties. However, it can be assumed that since that time, i.e. since the 2013 Social Diagnosis, the Internet has become, at least for some people with disabilities, a convenient and accessible place of building weak ties significant for finding new solutions. The COVID-19 pandemic forced everyone to make greater and deeper use of the Internet, not only to maintain relationships, but also for work and education, as well as for the seeking of new solutions to function efficiently in society.

The broad social context in the understanding of disability and the resources which are important for it prompts us to refer to the concept of resilience understood not only in terms of our own personal internal capital helping us to cope with difficult situations, and resulting from our personal traits or resources, but also in sociological terms, as social resources, i.e. networks of relationships or behaviours that the individual activates in a situation of crisis caused by a life event or external circumstances, such as war, economic crisis, or the COVID-19 pandemic. Wódz et al. (2020), citing extensive literature, define resilience from a sociologist's point of view as the ability of people, households and communities to survive, highly dependent on resources that can be used to cope with difficult situations. It is also understood as resourcefulness, coping strategies, remedial strategies or life strategies, as well as the ability of social actors to access various forms of capital and make use of such resources, not only to cope and adapt to adverse conditions, but also to search for and create options, thus building competences to deal with threats or difficulties. Resilience is not only what we learn in dealing with a difficult situation once it arises, but also the capability to draw on previous experiences stored in collective memory. An important element of social resilience is the strength of internal relationships, trust, and reciprocity, which we could refer to as social capital of the group, but also economic and human capital, or natural capital (Revilla et al., 2018).

In recent years, as societies, we have often used our resilience resources in the face of a pandemic situation, the current economic crisis, or the war in Ukraine. In Poland, we have recently seen the mobilisation of such resources in Ukrainian war refugees. The wave of refugees from Ukraine is an example of how internal resources are activated in people fleeing and struggling for survival, but also as a social response and the building up of an ad hoc non-institutional support network to help people to cope with the crisis and the traumatic situation by the general public welcoming the refugees (NGOs that changed the focus of their aid efforts virtually overnight; mobilisation of huge, completely non-institutionalised support from private individuals). The war in Ukraine mobilised enormous resources of support among Poles and demonstrated the vastness of the social capital represented by human solidarity, in spite of the initial historically determined distrust, which has been overcome to a large extent in society due to the situation that emerged.

Even micro-scale research such as ours shows that our resilience strategies, similarly to the potential for building and using social capital resources, depend on how we are positioned in relation to larger social structures, the economic environment, and various types of institutions. In relation to the group of people with disabilities, regardless of age and type of disability, it is important to highlight that in Poland, the institutional determinants related to assistance, health, education, and protection of such people have undergone a huge transformation since the 1990s. However, the outcomes of these changes seem insufficient, or simply not always well functioning, and consequently there is a huge non-institutional sector, including for instance NGOs, operating alongside them, perhaps as part of a resilience strategy, but also in the process of building separate support networks. According to the Central Statistical Office of Poland (GUS, 2021), there were 95,200 registered non-profit organisations operating in 2020. They had 150,300 full-time employees, accounting for 1.4% of average workforce in the national economy. These organisations reached 5 million people with their additional activities related to the COVID-19 pandemic, and provided financial and in-kind support worth 850 million Polish zlotys. The number of third-sector organisations increased by 18% between 2010 and 2020. Of them, 12.2%

work in the field of health protection and broadly understood social and humanitarian help. More than half of the organisations were active in sports, tourism, recreation, hobbies, rescue services, and arts and culture: these could be referred to as soft resources, but closely related to cultural capital (GUS, 2021). However, alongside these documented activities, there is a whole spectrum of grassroots activities that have found their place in the virtual space, bringing together parents, carers, and disabled persons in informal support networks.

In this study involving two general groups (adolescents and their parents), and actually six specific groups of respondents (if we take into account three groups of adolescents: with intellectual disabilities, physical disabilities, and FASD, and the parents/carers of each group who, after all, constitute the first network of resources for the adolescents surveyed), different problems can be observed resulting from the specific nature of disability of the adolescents studied in terms of accessing and using resources, but also different problems of the parents/carers in accessing resources and supporting institutions due to the respective disabilities. To illustrate how topical these problems are, one can cite the fact that currently in Poland, carers of people with disabilities who receive carer's allowance are fighting for the right to take up additional gainful employment, as the benefits granted to them are insufficient to meet the basic needs of the person with disability and of the carers themselves (RynekZdrowia.pl, 15 Nov 2022). In addition, it is worth mentioning that the people with FASD we studied represent a group that does not have the status of disabled in Poland; the disorder is not treated as a separate entity for the purposes of providing formal institutional assistance, and the specific nature of FASD burdens it with an additional social taboo.

Social resources from a psychological point of view and their role for health-related quality of life

When defining social resources from a psychological point of view and referring them to how adolescents function in their relationships with their immediate environment and how these affect their sense of quality of life, self-rated health, and health-promoting behaviours, it is important to look at the family system in which the adolescent lives. In this context, the rather broad concept of David Olson's Circumplex Model, based on a systemic understanding of the family, can be adopted (Margasiński, 2003; Margasiński, 2009; Olson & Gorall, 2003). The concept proposed by Olson and colleagues distinguishes three basic dimensions describing the family: cohesion, flexibility, and communication. Family cohesion is understood as the emotional ties that bind the family members together, indicators of which are their closeness, spending free time together, and having shared interests. Cohesion can span a continuum from disengagement, through balanced cohesion, to enmeshment. Flexibility is the capacity to change, to adapt to change, and to the amount of changes in the family. Flexibility manifests itself in leadership, in the roles assumed by family members, and in the rules they set among themselves, as well as in the ability to negotiate roles. The scale of flexibility extends from rigidity, through balanced flexibility, to chaos (Margasiński, 2009). Communication is the ability to communicate, listen to each other, and express feelings. Communication skills affect both flexibility and family cohesion. They can be defined on a scale ranging from weak to effective. All these dimensions can influence one another, and so the ability to communicate can affect both cohesion and flexibility (Mróz & Kaleta, 2013).

Numerous studies indicate that closeness, communication, and flexibility within the family influence various aspects in the development of adolescents (Henry & Lovelace, 1995; Smets & Hartup, 1988). It has been noted that if a family tends to be found on the extreme ends of the scales of cohesion and flexibility, this is usually correlated with its dysfunctional nature (Zabriskie & McCormick, 2001). According to the research, the optimal state for a family is when it functions between connection and separation in the cohesion dimension (Margasiński, 2011), while in the flexibility dimension it reaches a balance between stability and change (Olson, 2000). Research into the influence of family relationships on identity formation in adolescents and young adults (Luyckx et al., 2008) indicates significant relationships between identity dimensions and only selected elements of the family system, i.e. balanced cohesion, balanced flexibility, chaos, the indicator of cohesion and flexibility, and the indicator of the overall level of functioning of the given family system. With regard to the other characteristics of family functioning (disengagement, enmeshment, rigidity, communication), the analyses performed did not reveal significant relationships between them and identity processes. It can therefore be conjectured that only certain aspects of family functioning have a regulating function with regard to activity manifested by adolescents and young adults in relation to exploration in breadth, exploration in depth, commitment making, and identification with commitments, as well as in relation to the severity of the concerns and problems experienced by the individual in the process of engaging in areas important for identity development. Wysota et al. (2014) note that although the family is certainly important in the development and building of identity in adolescents, it is not the only place where their identity is formed. The social environment, relationships with peers, and with other people that adolescents meet are very important. The results of another study (Mróz & Kaleta, 2013) show that the structure of relationships in the family influences the health-promoting behaviours of adolescents, but balanced family cohesion had an impact only on some of their health-promoting behaviours. Family cohesion in this research did not correlate with preventive and health-promoting behaviours, or with positive psychological attitude, usually associated with life satisfaction and with experiencing a larger number of positive emotions. The research by Mróz and Kaleta (2013) also shows the importance of balanced flexibility for health-promoting behaviours and the lack of correlation between communication in the family and preventive and health-promoting behaviours. In other studies (Marta, 1997; Ornelas, Perreira, & Ayala, 2007), the lack of good communication correlated positively in adolescents with engaging in risky behaviours, while when communication in the family was positive, this had a positive effect on children's physical activity. Referring once again to the research by Mróz and Kaleta (2013), it is worth mentioning that families characterised by balanced cohesion and optimal flexibility (more than other family types) would avoid negative emotions (depression, anger, anxiety, and depression) as well as stress, and displayed positive thinking. The weak connection between family members with the simultaneous confusion of rules, roles and power is less likely to shape desirable mental health behaviours. Similarly, in the research by De Bourdeaudhuij and Van Oost (1998), adolescents and young adults displaying the largest number of health-promoting behaviours described their families as having more cohesion and balanced flexibility, while the group with the most unhealthy behavioural pattern experienced less cohesion and more flexibility. Family flexibility and cohesion as a resource is important for families that include persons with disabilities, as family cohesion ensures the family's survival, while flexibility gives it resilience in the face of difficult events and obstacles (Masłyk, 2020).

Interesting from the point of view of our work is the research carried out by Karwowska (2008) on coping with everyday problems by parents of a child with a disability, demonstrating how the arrival of such a child affects the family relationships, its cohesion, and flexibility. When a child with a disability appears in the family, it can affect the latter's cohesion and communication, as the problem forces changes in the parents' roles, such as different role burdens, different degrees of responsibility, or different sharing of responsibilities. It places the parents and the whole family in a difficult, crisis situation and requires a number of changes and transformations. Stress and strain can contribute to burnout in parental roles (Sekułowicz & Kwiatkowski, 2013) and even cause the atrophy of family functions, which may cause the family to break apart. It can lead to burnout when performing the self-imposed tasks related to caring roles, or to the adoption of a strategy of excessive rehabilitation and treatment, which, if there are no clear signs of improvement, can lead to depression (of the carer) and can also involve the parents or other family members not coming to terms with their child's disability (Karwowska & Albrecht, 2008). Key aspects in this situation, therefore, seem to be on the one hand the family's flexibility in coping, and on the other hand cohesion and closeness within the family. The family's financial situation and access to social support in the form of external institutional and non-institutional help (Karwowska, 2008) will also be important, but so will be the support of relatives, friends, and other family members, which might prove crucial for the mental health of the parents and, at the same time, for the mental health and health-related quality of life of adolescents with disabilities and FASD. These are the personal resources that we took into account in our analyses aimed at verifying which social resources were important for health-related quality of life in adolescents with intellectual and physical disabilities and FASD, and for its individual dimensions related to physical wellbeing, psychological well-being, and relationships with parents, peers, and school.

We conducted linear regression to verify the significance of social resources for maintaining health-related quality of life among the adolescents surveyed. Stepwise regression was used to see how the variance explained changes by adding predictors to the model separately. The results of stepwise regression are presented in Table 7.3–7.6. In the first step of regression analysis, it was checked whether a sociodemographic variable such as financial situation was a predictor of health-related quality of life among the surveyed adolescents. In the second step, we added two variables linked to relations with friends: frequency of meetings with friends and frequency of social media use, and in the last step, family variables (family cohesion and family flexibility) were analysed. We conducted analyses for each dimension of health-related quality of life and for general HRQoL.

Table 7.3 Results of three steps of linear regression for health-related quality of life: General score

	Health-related quality of life				
Social resources	B	SE	β	t	p
Step 1 financial situation	8.37	1.72	**.45**	**4.88**	**<.001**
Step 2 financial situation	7.59	1.69	**.40**	**4.49**	**<.001**
frequency of meetings with friends	3.63	1.26	**.27**	**2.88**	**.005**
frequency of social media use	−1.59	1.38	−.11	−1.15	.254
Step 3 financial situation	4.46	1.58	**.24**	**2.83**	**.006**
frequency of meetings with friends	4.13	1.10	**.31**	**3.75**	**<.001**
frequency of social media use	−1.94	1.21	−.13	−1.61	.111
family cohesion	.83	.35	**.30**	**2.34**	**.021**
family flexibility	.53	.36	.19	1.47	.145

Step 1: $adj.R^2 = .190$, $F = 23.78$, $df_1 = 1$, $df_2 = 96$, $p < .001$
Step 2: $adj.R^2 = .240$, $F = 11.28$, $df_1 = 3$, $df_2 = 94$, $p < .001$; F-change = 4.23, $p = .017$
Step 3: $adj.R^2 = .424$, $F = 15.31$, $df_1 = 5$, $df_2 = 92$, $p < .001$; F-change = 15.96, $p < .001$

Table 7.4 Results of three steps of linear regression for dimensions of health-related quality of life: Autonomy and parent relation

	HRQoL: Autonomy and parent relation				
Social resources	B	SE	β	t	p
Step 1 financial situation	3.237	4.68	**.44**	**4.73**	**<.001**
Step 2 financial situation	3.02	.67	**.41**	**4.54**	**<.001**
frequency of meetings with friends	1.27	.50	**.24**	**2.56**	**.012**
frequency of social media use	−1.22	.54	**−.21**	**−2.25**	**.027**
Step 3 financial situation	1.51	.57	**.20**	**2.67**	**.009**
frequency of meetings with friends	1.47	.39	**.28**	**3.72**	**<.001**
frequency of social media use	−1.32	.43	**−.22**	**−3.05**	**.003**
family cohesion	.17	.13	.15	1.33	.188
family flexibility	.48	.13	**.44**	**3.72**	**<.001**

Step 1: $adj.R^2 = .183$, $F = 22.78$, $df_1 = 1$, $df_2 = 96$, $p < .001$
Step 2: $adj.R^2 = .240$, $F = 11.23$, $df_1 = 3$, $df_2 = 94$, $p < .001$; F-change = 4.59, $p = .0512$
Step 3: **$adj.R^2 = .521$, $F = 22.09$, $df_1 = 5$, $df_2 = 92$, $p < .001$; F-change = 28.54, $p < .001$**

Social resources as predictors of health-related quality of life

Financial situation turned out to be statistically significant in explaining the health-related quality of life of adolescents in each step of the analyses (see Table 7.3). The model explained only 19% of variance in the first step of the analysis. After adding, in the second step, frequency of meetings with friends and frequency of social media use, the percentage of explained variance increased to 24%. The frequency of social media use is not significant, but frequency of meetings with friends turned out to be a positive predictor of HRQoL. In the third step, family cohesion and family flexibility were also taken into account in the regression analysis. A model with five variables (financial situation, frequency of meetings with friends, frequency of social media use, family cohesion, and family flexibility) explained 42% of the variance of the dependent variable. Financial situation and frequency of meetings with friends continued to be significant positive predictors of health-related quality of life. Frequency of social media use remained insignificant for HRQoL. In addition, family cohesion turned out to be a

Table 7.5 Results of three steps of linear regression for two dimensions of health-related quality of life: Physical wellbeing and psychological wellbeing

	HRQoL: Physical wellbeing					*HRQoL: Psychological wellbeing*				
Social resources	B	SE	β	t	p	B	SE	β	t	p
Step 1 financial situation	1.69	.59	**.28**	**2.88**	**.005**	.60	.36	.17	1.65	.102
Step 2 financial situation	1.66	.59	**.28**	**2.84**	**.006**	.46	.36	.13	1.27	.209
frequency of meetings with friends	.51	.44	.12	1.17	.245	.63	.27	**.24**	**2.33**	**.022**
frequency of social media use	−1.13	.48	**−.24**	**−2.36**	**.020**	−.21	.30	−.07	−.7	.483
Step 3 financial situation	1.28	.61	**.21**	**2.10**	**.038**	.18	.38	.05	.47	.639
frequency of meetings with friends	.61	.43	.14	1.43	.157	.66	.27	**.255**	**2.46**	**.016**
frequency of social media use	−1.24	.47	**−.26**	**−2.65**	**.009**	−.22	.29	−.07	−.73	.464
family cohesion	.33	.14	**.37**	**2.38**	**.020**	−.01	.96	−.01	−.07	.940
family flexibility	−.15	.14	−.17	−1.11	.269	.12	.09	.23	1.43	.157
	Step 1: *adj.*R^2 = .070, F = 8.29, df_1 = 1, df_2 = 96,p = .005 Step 2: *adj.*R^2 = .106, F = 4.84, df_1 = 3, df_2 = 94, p = 004; F-change = 2.94, p = .058 Step 3: **adj.R^2 = .151, F = 4.44, df_1 = 5, df_2 = 92, p < .001**; **F-change = 3.46, p < .036**					Step 1: *adj.*R^2 = .018. F = 2.73, df_1 = 1, df_2 = 96, p = 102 Step 2: *adj.*R^2 = .051, F = 2.75, df_1 = 3, df_2 = 94, p = 0.47; F-change = 2.71, p = .072 Step 3: **adj.R^2 = .077, F = 2.63, df_1 = 5, df_2 = 92, p < .029**; F-change = 2.31, p = .105				

Table 7.6 Results of three steps of linear regression for two dimensions of health-related quality of life: Peer and social support and school environment

	HRQoL: Peer and social support					*HRQoL: School environment*				
Social resources	B	SE	β	t	p	B	SE	β	t	p
Step 1 financial situation	1.55	.41	**.36**	**3.81**	**<.001**	1.29	.43	**.29**	**3.01**	**.003**
Step 2 financial situation	1.24	.38	**.29**	**3.28**	**.001**	1.21	.43	**.27**	**2.79**	**.006**
frequency of meetings with friends	1.10	.28	**.36**	**3.91**	**<.001**	.12	.32	.04	.37	.715
frequency of social media use	.35	.31	.11	1.24	.216	.59	.35	.17	1.68	.097
Step3 financial situation	.82	.39	**.19**	**2.10**	**.038**	.67	.44	.15	1.52	.131
frequency of meetings with friends	1.18	.27	**.38**	**4.34**	**<.001**	.21	.31	.07	.69	.492
frequency of social media use	.32	.29	.09	1.08	.281	.52	.33	.15	1.54	.126
family cohesion	.16	.09	.25	1.80	.074	.18	.09	.28	1.87	.065
family flexibility	.027	.088	.043	.312	.756	.05	.09	.08	.52	.605
	Step 1: $adj.R^2 = .123$, $F = 14.55$, $df_1 = 1$, $df_2 = 96$, $p < .001$ Step 2: $adj.R^2 = .267$, $F = 12.79$, $df_1 = 3$, $df_2 = 94$, $p < .001$; F-change = 10.47, $p < .001$ Step 3: **$adj.R^2 = .323$, $F = 10.43$, $df_1 = 5$, $df_2 = 92$, $p < .001$; F-change = 5.19, $p = .007$**					Step 1: $adj.R^2 = .077$, $F = 9.06$, $df_1 = 1$, $df_2 = 96$, $p = .003$ Step 2: $adj.R^2 = .091$, $F = 4.25$, $df_1 = 3$, $df_2 = 94$, $p = .007$, F-change = 1.77, $p = .176$ Step 3: **$adj.R^2 = .186$, $F = 5.43$, $df_1 = 5$, $df_2 = 92$, $p < .001$; F-change = 6.46, $p = .002$**				

statistically significant positive predictor for HRQoL, while family flexibility was devoid of statistical significance. On the basis of the results obtained, it can be concluded that the better the respondents' self-rated financial situation, the more often they met with friends and the higher they rated family cohesion, the higher their health-related quality of life.

Social resources as predictors of HRQoL: Autonomy and parent relations

In the case of HRQoL: autonomy and parent relations, the arrangement and meaning of the independent variables in the model is similar (see Table 7.4). A similar increase in variance can be observed, but the significance of the change in the explained variance can only be seen in the third step of the analysis, after including family context variables. A big change is visible precisely in the area of these variables: it turned out that an important positive predictor of HRQoL; autonomy and parent relations was not family cohesion, but family flexibility. A model with five variables (financial situation, frequency of meetings with friends, frequency of social media use, family cohesion, and family flexibility) explained 52% of the variance of the dependent variable. Referring to the results obtained, it can be said that the better the respondents' self-rated financial situation, the more often they met friends, the less often they used social media, and the higher they rated family flexibility, the higher their health-related quality of life in autonomy and parent relations.

Social resources as predictors of HRQoL: Physical wellbeing

For the HRQoL dimension: physical wellbeing, financial situation, and family cohesion, as well as frequency of social media use turned out to be statistically significant, but the last one was a negative predictor (see Table 7.5). The significance of the change in the explained variance can only be seen in the third step of the analysis, after including family context variables. However, a model with five variables (financial situation, frequency of meetings with friends, frequency of social media use, family cohesion, and family flexibility) explained only 15% of the variance of the dependent variable. Based on the obtained results, it can be concluded that the better the respondents' self-rated financial situation, and the higher they assessed family cohesion and the less often they used social media, the higher their health-related quality of life in the physical wellbeing dimension.

Social resources as predictors of HRQoL: Psychological wellbeing

In the case of HRQoL, psychological wellbeing, the only statistically significant variable among the analysed variables, turned out to be frequency of meetings with friends. This was a positive predictor for the dependent variable. The variance explained did not change significantly after adding variables in next steps of analyses, and the adopted model with five variables (financial situation, frequency of meetings with friends, frequency of social media use, family cohesion, and family flexibility) explained only 7% of the variance. Based on the results obtained, it can be concluded that the more often adolescents met with their peers, the higher their quality of life in terms of psychological wellbeing (see Table 7.5).

Social resources as predictors of HRQoL: Peers and social support

Financial situation and frequency of meetings with friends turned out to be positive predictors for HRQoL: peers and social support. Family cohesion and family flexibility were statistically insignificant (see Table 7.6). In each step of the analysis, a significant increase in the explained variance can be seen, and the generally accepted model with five variables (financial situation, frequency of meetings with friends, frequency of social media use, family cohesion, and family flexibility) explained 32% of the variance of the dependent variable. Based on the obtained results, it can be concluded that the better the respondents' self-rated financial situation and the more often they met with friends, the higher their quality of life related to health in the dimension of peers and social support.

Social resources as predictors of HRQoL: School environment

For HRQoL: school environment, none of the variables among the social resources adopted in the model turned out to be statistically significant predictors (see Table 7.6).

In the case of our respondents, the aspects key for the assessment of health-related quality of life turned out to be the assessment of financial situation, the frequency of contacts with friends, and rating of the family as having balanced cohesion, but also as flexible, especially for the experience of autonomy. The higher the respondents rated these aspects, the better their health-related quality of life was. For the two HRQoL dimensions in the adolescents surveyed, the frequency of contacts with peers was found to be significant, but not directly, as it was mediated by social media. The more frequent such contacts were, the worse physical wellbeing and autonomy the adolescents experienced.

The result regarding financial situation is not surprising, as it is mainly that aspect that determines how effectively and positively the family is capable of coping with problems resulting from the disability by ensuring additional activities, rehabilitation, or treatment. Many studies highlight the relationship between HRQoL and financial situation (e.g. von Rueden et al., 2006; Xiang et al., 2019). Furthermore, during adolescence, financial situation becomes a measurable element used for comparisons in the peer group and, as one can infer, it influences the young person, allowing them manifest their social position.

The adolescents' high rating of family cohesion, i.e. the quality of bonds and relations between the family members, turned out to be a strong social resource significant for many HRQoL dimensions. It can be conjectured that the assessment of family relationships as normal, based on the one hand on closeness and cooperation between the family members, and on the other hand on respect of the autonomy and independence of each of the persons constituting the family system, is crucial for health-related quality of life in adolescents with disabilities and FASD. The third social resource, i.e. the assessment of the frequency of contacts with friends, also fits within the developmental stage in which young people separate themselves increasingly strongly from the family relationships, and their contacts with peers often begin to play an even more important role in the construction of the self than their contacts with parents. This explanation may also prove important in understanding why rating the family as cohesive is not significant for the autonomy and parent relations dimension of HRQoL. Family cohesion loses its importance in the understanding of health-related quality of life in the areas of independence, autonomy, and relations with parents. The family, as viewed by adolescents, is a permanent foundation; closeness, cohesion, warm, and trust-based relations between its members do not affect the formation of one's autonomy. Family flexibility gains importance in this dimension. It is more important for the family to be capable of change and transformation, especially during a period of developmental and situational transitions and crises it experiences throughout its development cycle, as well as not to become rigid, but not chaotic either. This is particularly important during adolescence, which represents a significant developmental crisis for the family (Bee, 2004). The parents' capacity to adapt to this new situation, i.e. to accept the fact that their child is becoming an independent adult person, is undoubtedly a difficult task and, as the findings indicate, it is important for higher health-related quality of life in adolescents experienced precisely in the area of autonomy. Flexibility in the case of the families studied could also refer to the family's capabilities to change and transform related to the child's disability or FASD. However, our research findings do not show this family resource to be important for other dimensions of HRQoL. Family flexibility is only important for the transforming relationships between the parents and the adolescent, who starts to become an increasingly separate and independent entity as they reach the stage of adulthood. In this case, flexibility will therefore be related to a larger extent to the acceptance of the changes taking place in the developmental process by the whole family, which is difficult in any family, not only in those struggling with a disability. However, it is perhaps particularly difficult precisely in these families due to, among other things, the child's lower self-reliance, and the parent's stronger caring attitude.

Rating the family as cohesive and flexible is insignificant for the adolescent's psychological wellbeing, for quality of life related to social support and contact with peers, or for the assessment of the school environment. Higher psychological wellbeing is determined by maintaining frequent contact with friends, and this seems to confirm the importance of the peer group at this age, becoming crucial for the formation of the adolescent's identity. For the same reason, in the assessment of peer and social support, frequency of contacts with friends and financial situation are important, the latter being an element of social visibility and wellbeing, but also providing an opportunity to participate in life and pastimes typical of one's peers.

Good financial situation is important alongside the rating of one's family as cohesive for the adolescents' physical wellbeing. One might believe that these two resources support the family in overcoming problems caused by disability, by looking after health-promoting behaviours, such as physical activity and practising sports, accessing rehabilitation, or pursuing a healthy diet. This, in turn, is possible provided that the family has adequate financial resources (Tabak et al., 2013).

The findings indicate that social media activity can be considered a risk factor for HRQoL in adolescents with physical disabilities, intellectual disabilities, and FASD for dimensions related to physical wellbeing and autonomy. Especially during the COVID-19 pandemic, social media became increasingly important for maintaining relationships with peers. Our study findings show that the frequency of this form of contact is not a social resource, but it is not without an impact on HRQoL either. It can be referred to as an anti-resource. The result indicating its negative association with physical wellbeing of adolescents may seem unsurprising, as time spent online is itself antithetical to development in the physical area and to physical wellbeing. On the other hand, the result indicating that the frequency of social media use is associated with lower quality of life related to autonomy and becoming independent from one's parents may come as a surprise. These aspects undoubtedly require further investigation.

Neither building relationships, nor acquiring friendships and skills in virtual social networks worked well, considering the health-related quality of life of the adolescents surveyed. This may be due to parents controlling their online presence and the lack of trust in the young people, especially those with disabilities or FASD. Parental overprotection can limit the development of autonomy in this area. From the point of view functioning of persons with disabilities, various social networks might seem of key importance in the search for ways to achieve independence, and also the most easily attainable one. Perhaps it must involve permission to build relations outside of parental control. It is there that parents themselves look for support and solutions too. On the other hand, the Internet is a place where apparent weaker relationships are established; online communities are often characterised by more radical social ostracism, cyberbullying, to which those who are "different," and distinct are more vulnerable. The ambivalent impact of social media activity or online activity in general on adolescents with disabilities has been indicated out by various researchers (Caton & Chapman, 2016; Ellis & Kent, 2017). On the one hand, the use of social media provides positive experiences in the form of friendships, social identity development, self-esteem, or entertainment. On the other hand, in the case of intellectual disability, access is hindered due to difficulties with reading and writing, communication difficulties, cyber-language, and cyber-etiquette (for a review, see Caton & Chapman, 2016). Social media provide persons with disabilities the opportunity to participate socially and to interact, share services and things, and engage in social and political activism. The darker flipside, however, is that they can create yet another space of exclusion (Kent, 2019).

Researchers always consider young people's Internet use in terms of benefits and risks (O'Keeffe & Clarke-Pearson, 2011; Reid & Weigle, 2014). However, access to social media communities by the most socially isolated people involves the additional burden of double exclusion or rejection. This outcome may be related to reasons other than the lack of ability to participate online, exclusion, or excessive parental control. As noted by Masłyk (2020), people with disabilities compared to those without disabilities have much less developed and less dense friendship networks. In general, their networks are based on strong ties, and other contacts are also mediated through them. It can therefore be assumed that they find it more difficult to form relationships also online, compared to their non-disabled peers. Family could consequently be seen as performing a supportive role and providing a sense of security for the disabled person, but on the other hand, it can be one of the factors hindering the establishment of weak ties, relations beyond those resulting from care, rehabilitation, school, and a close circle of friends.

Another explanation for the negative attitude towards online participation and networking in addition to those mentioned above may be provided by the results of research conducted among adolescents during the COVID-19 pandemic, which, although they indicated an intensified and extended presence of young people online, at the same time suggested that the relationships maintained there were not satisfying to them, were significantly limited, and did not reduce the adolescents' negative feelings about isolation (Brudzińska & Godawa, 2021). The density of the network and, probably, the number of contacts have decreased, at least in the case of those that were actually important for the adolescents.

From the point of view of social capital, it can be pointed out that financial situation has a large impact on the quality of functioning of the family and within the family, and influences the way in which the adolescent functions socially. It determines one's social standing. The family's financial situation makes it possible to activate resilience strategies that help to find and use external support. For a young person with a disability or FASD, the financial situation of their family is an important aspect in maintaining HRQoL in most of the latter's dimensions.

At the same time, the important role of family cohesion, but also that of flexibility for health-related quality of life of the adolescents studied may point to the high resilience capacity of families of adolescents with disabilities and FASD. Both the surveyed adolescents' perception of their own family as one based on closeness and trust, nurturing family relationships, but respecting the independence of each family member, and the assessment of the family as being capable of adaptive change, are important for the young respondents' high quality of life. A strong, cohesive, and flexible family constitutes a social resource important for the adolescents' health and development. However, the family is not always of key importance, and other social resources beyond the family become more important for peer or school areas in the adolescents' rating of health-related quality of life.

The broader social context in which families of persons with disabilities are perceived shows their significant effectiveness in dealing with the challenges of everyday life. The effects they see and are affected by include limited access to external help and a problem with the amount of money available to continue rehabilitation or pay for additional activities. It can be asserted that the disability of a family member reduces the family to using only certain social and support networks, in a sense forcing them into certain established patterns of behaviour and coping methods, at the same time restricting their participation in or completely eliminating them from other networks. Lack of institutional support or low trust in such support may contribute to the development of other methods of coping, taking the problem into one's own hands and engaging other networks, such as community activation and involvement, etc. Looking after the health and health-related quality of life of adolescents is the result of work done primarily by the family. It is the family that can activate resilience resources, it is the first most important circle in the relationship network of the person with a disability, building the latter's sense of identity and self-acceptance, but also their resourcefulness. It is the family that forms the fundamental social capital of a person with a disability. Therefore, it should open up rather than just close itself in the circle of support issues and activities focused on dealing with its young member's disability. The family must teach them to cope outside to the greatest extent possible. This is the only way to allow them to achieve autonomy and take independent steps during the subsequent stages of their life.

References

Alessandri, G., De Longis, E., Eisenberg, N., & Hobfoll, S.E. (2020). A multilevel moderated mediational model of the daily relationships between hassles, exhaustion, ego-resiliency and resulting emotional inertia. *Journal of Research in Personality*, *85*, 103913. 10.1016/j.jrp.2020.103913.

Alessandri, G., Vecchione, M., Caprara, G.V., & Letzring, T.D. (2012). The Ego Resiliency Scale revised: A crosscultural study in Italy, Spain, and the United States. *European Journal of Psychological Assessment*, *28*, 139–146. 10.1027/1015-5759/a000102.

Alessandri, G., Zuffianò, A., Eisenberg, N., & Pastorelli, C. (2017). The role of ego-resiliency as mediator of the longitudinal relationship between family socio-economic status and school grades. *Journal of Youth and Adolescence*, *46*, 2157–2168. 10.1007/s10964-017-0691-7

Alriksson-Schmidt, A.J., Wallander, J., & Biasini, F. (2007). Quality of life and resilience in adolescents with a mobility disability. *Journal of Pediatric Psychology*, *32*, 370–379.

Armstrong, J.M., Birnie-Lefcovitch, S., & Ungar, M.T. (2005). Pathways between social support, family well-being, quality of parenting, and child resilience: What we know. *Journal of Child and Family Studies*, *14*, 269–281.

Bąk, W., Dutkiewicz, D., & Brudek, P. (2021). Relationship between self-assessed health and life satisfaction in older adults: The moderating role of ego-resiliency. *Ageing & Society*, 1–12. 10.1017/S0144686X21001689

Bee, H. (2004). *Psychologia rozwoju człowieka [Human Development Psychology]*. Wydawnictwo Zyska i S-ka.

Berntsson, L., Berg, M., Brydolf, M., & Hellstróm, A-L. (2007). Adolescents' experiences of well-being when living with a long-term illness and disability. *Scandinavian Journal of Caring Sciences*, *21*, 419–425. 10.1111/j.1471-6712.2006.00490.x

Bishop, M. (2005). Quality of life and psychosocial adaptation tochronic illness and acquired disability: preliminary analysis of a conceptual and theoretical synthesis. *Rehabilitation Counseling Bulletin*, *48*, 219–232.

Block, J. (2002). *Personality as an affect-processing system: Toward an integrative theory*. Lawrence Erlbaum Associates Publishers. 10.4324/9781410602466.

Boase, J., & Wellman, B. (2006). Personal relationships: On and off the internet, In A.L. Vangelisti, & D. Perlman (eds.), *The Cambridge handbook of personal relationships* (709–723). Cambridge University Press.

Boberska, M., Szczuka, Z., Kruk, M., Knoll, N., Keller, J., Hohl, D.H., & Luszczyńska, A. (2018). Sedentary behaviours and health-related quality of life. A systematic review and meta-analysis. *Health Psychology Review*, *12*, 195–210. 10.1080/17437199.2017.1396191

Bottolfs, M., Støa, E.M., Reinboth, M.S., Svendsen, M.V., Schmidt, S.K., Oellingrath, I.M., & Gratland-Sanda, S. (2020). Resilience and lifestyle-related factors as predictors for health-related quality of life among early adolescents: A cross-sectional study. *Journal of International Medical Research*, *48*, 1–15. 10.1177/0300060520903656

Bourdieu, P. (1986). The forms of capital. In: I. Szeman & T. Kaposy (eds.) (2010). *Cultural theory: An anthology* (81–93). Willey-Blackwell.

Bourdieu, P., & Passeron, J.C. (2006). *Reprodukcja. Element teorii systemu nauczania* [*Reproduction in Education, Society and Culture*]. Wydawnictwo Naukowe PWN.

Brudzińska, P., & Godawa, S. (2021). Sytuacja psychospołeczna uczniów podczas pandemii Covid-19 - Przegląd Badań 2020–2021 [Psychosocial Situation of

Students During the COVID-19 Pandemic - 2020–2021 Research Review]. *Acta Universitatis Nicolai Copernici Pedagogika*, *41*, 123–146. 10.12775/AUNC_PED.2021.006.

Byra S. (2012). *Przystosowanie do życia z niepełnosprawnością ruchową i chorobą przewlekłą. Struktura i uwarunkowanie* [*Adaptation to Life with Physical Disability and Chronic Disease. Structure and Determinants*]. Wydawnictwo Uniwersytetu Marie Curie-Skłodowskiej.

Caton, S., & Chapman, M. (2016). The use of social media and people with intellectual disability: A systematic review and thematic analysis. *Journal of Intellectual & Developmental Disability*, *41*, 125–139. 10.3109/13668250.2016.1153052

Caton, S., Chadwick, D., Chapman, M., Turnbull ,S., Mitchell, D., & Stansfield, J. (2012). Healthy lifestyles for adults with intellectual disability: Knowledge, barriers, and facilitators. *Journal of Intellectual & Developmental Disability*, *37*, 248–259. 10.3109/13668250.2012.703645

Chow, S.M.K., Lao, K.L., & Cummins, R.A. (2005). Self-perceived quality of life of children and adolescents with physical disabilities in Hong Kong. *Quality Life Research*, *14*, 415–423.

Cieza, A., Kemenov, K., Sanchez, M.G., Chatterji, S., Balasegaram, M., Lincetto, O., Servilli, Ch., Bermejo, R., & Ross, D.A. (2021). Disability in children and adolescents must be integrated into the global health agenda. *BMJ*, *372*, 1–4. 10.1136/bmj.n9

Coleman, J.S. (1999). Social capital in the creation of human capital. In P. Daspagupta, & I. Serageldin (eds.), *Social theory for a changing society* (1–14). Boulder: Westview Press.

Czapiński, J., & Panek, T. (2014). *Diagnoza Społeczna 2013* [*2013 Social Diagnosis*]. Centrum Rozwoju Zasobów Ludzkich https://www.researchgate.net/publication/273316975_Diagnoza_spoleczna_2013_Warunki_i_jakosc_zycia_Polakow [access: 06 Dec 2022].

Da Costa, B.G.G., Chaput, J-P., Lopes, M.V.V., da Costa, R.M., Malheiros, L.E.A., & Silva, K.S. (2020). Association between lifestyle behaviors and health-related quality of life in a sample of Brazilian adolescents. *International Journal of Environmental Research and Public Health*, 1717,2-11.10.3390/ijerph17197133

Davis, E., Shelly, A., Waters, E., MacKinnon, A., Reddihough, D., Boyd, R., & Graham, H.K. (2009). Quality of life of adolescents with cerebral palsy: Perspectives of adolescents and parents. *Developmental Medicine & Child Neurology*, *51*, 193–199. 10.1111/j.1469-8749.2008.03194.x.

De Bourdeaudhuij, I., & Van Oost, P. (1998). Family characteristics and healthbehaviours of adolescents and families. *Psychology Health*, *13*, 785–803.

Dębska, U., & Bielawska, I. (2002). Ku prozdrowotnemu stylowi życia w kontekście zagrożeń cywilizacyjnych [Towards a Health-Promoting Lifestyle in the Context of Civilisational Threats]. *Advances in Clinical and Experimental Medicine*, *11* (suppl. 1), 11–24.

Domellöf, E., Hedlund, L. & Odman, P. (2014). Health-related quality of life of children and adolescents with functional disabilities in a northern Swedish county. *Quality of life research: anAn international journal of quality of life aspects of treatment, care and rehabilitation*, 23, 1877–1882. 10.1007/s11136-013-0613-4.

Donkervoort, M., Roebroeck, M., Wiegerink, D.J., van der Heijden-Maessen, H., & Stam, H. (2007). Transition Research Group South West Netherlands. Determinants of functioning of adolescents and young adults with cerebral palsy. *Disability & Rehabilitation*, *29*, 453–463. 10.1080/09638

Drum, Ch. E., Horner-Johnson, W., & Krahn, G.L. (2008). Self-rated health and healthy days: examining the "disability paradox". *Disability & Health Journal*, 1, 71–78. 10.1016/j.dhjo.2008.01.002

Edwards, T., Patrick, D.L., & Topolski, T.D. (2003). Quality of life in adolescents with perceived disabilities. *Journal of Pediatric Psychology*, *28*, 233–241.

Ellis, K., & Kent, M. (2017). *Disability and social media-global perspectives*. Routledge.

Emerson, E., & Baines, S. (2010). *Health inequalities and people with learning disabilities in the UK: 2010*. Improving Health and Lives: Learning Disabilities - Department of Health. https://pureportal.strath.ac.uk/filesasset/7402206/vid_7479_IHaL2010_3HealthInequality200pdfObservatory.

Farkas, D., & Orosz, G. (2015). Ego-resiliency reloaded: A three-component model of general resiliency. *PLoS* One, 10. 10.1371/journal.pone.0120883

Field, J. (2008). *Social capital*. Routledge.

Fuglestad, A.J., Boys, Ch. J., Chang, P.N., Miller, B.S., Eckerle, J.K., Deling, L., Fink, B.A., Hoecker, H.L., Hickey ,M.K., Jimenez-Vega, J.M., & Wozniak, J.R. (2014). Overweight and obesity among children and adolescents with fetal alcohol spectrum disorders. *Alcoholism Clinical & Experimental Research*, *38*, 2502–2508. 10.1111/acer.12516

Gładczuk, J., Kleszczewska, E., & Święcicki, A. (2017). Współczesne poglądy dotyczące zdrowia oraz ich ewolucja w czasie. [Contemporary views on health and their evolution over time]. *Medical & Health Sciences Review*, *3*, 3–10.

Granovetter, M. (1973). The strength of Weak links. *American Journal of Psychology*, *78*, 1360–1380.

Groff, D.G., Lundberg, N.R., & Zabriskie, R.B. (2009). Influence of adapted sport on quality of life: Perceptions of athletes with cerebral palsy. *Disability & Rehabilitation*, *31*, 318–326.

GUS: Działalność stowarzyszeń i podobnych organizacji społecznych, fundacji, społecznych podmiotów wyznaniowych oraz samorządu gospodarczego i zawodowego w 2020 r. – wyniki wstępne [Central Statistical Office of Poland: Activity of Associations and Similar Social Organisations, Foundations, Social Religious Entities and Economic and Professional Self-Government Bodies in 2020 – Preliminary Results] (2021). GUS https://stat.gov.pl/wyszukiwarka/?query=tag:organizacje+pozarz%C4%85dowe

Hall, A-M., & Theron, L.C. (2016). Resilience processes supporting adolescents with intellectual disability: A multiple case study. *Intellectual and Developmental Disabilities*, *54*, 45–62.

Hammond, L., Joly, V., Kapasi, A., Kryska, K., Andrew, G., Oberlander, T.F., Pei, J., & Rasmussen, C. (2020). Adaptive behavior, sleep, and physical activity in adolescents with fetal alcohol spectrum disorder. *Research in Developmental Disabilities*, *131*. 10.1016/j.ridd.2022.104366

Henry, C.S., & Lovelace, S.G. (1995). Family resources and adolescent family life satisfaction in remarried family households. *Journal of Family Issues*, *16*, 765–786.

Hofer, C., Eisenberg, N., & Reiser M. (2010). The role of socialization, effortful control, and ego resiliency in French adolescents' social functioning. *Journal of Research on Adolescence*, *20*, 555–582. 10.1111/j.1532-7795.2010.00650.x.

Johson, C.C. (2009). The benefits of physical activity for youth with developmental disabilities: A systematic review. *The Science of Health Promotion*, *23*, 157–167. 10.4278/ajhp.070930103

Kagan, M., Itzick, M., & Tai-Katz, P. (2018). Demographic, psychosocial, and health- and disability-related factors associated with psychological distress among people with physical disabilities. *Rehabilitation Psychology*, *63*, 392–399. 10.1037/rep0000206

Kapsal, N.J., Dicke, T.D., Morin, A.J.S., Vasconcellos, D., Maïano, C.M., Lee, J., & Lonsdale, C. (2019). Effects of physical activity on the physical and psychosocial health of youth with intellectual disabilities – A systematic review and meta-analyses. *Journal of Physical Activity and Health*, *16*. 10.1123/jpah.2018-0675

Karwowska, M. (2008). Zmaganie się z problemami dnia codziennego rodziców wychowujących dziecko z niepełnosprawnością umysłową: w świetle badań własnych [Struggling with Everyday Problems in Parents Raising a Child with Mental Disability in Light of Own Research]. *Transdyscyplinarne Studia o Kulturze (i) Edukacji* [*Transdisciplinary Studies on Culture and/of Education*], *3*, 93–109. http://bazhum.muzhp.pl

Karwowska, M., & Albrecht, M. (2008). Niepełnosprawność dziecka przyczyną rozpadu czy spójności rodziny? [The Child's Disability as a Reason for Family Disintegration or Cohesion?], *Transdyscyplinarne Studia o Kulturze (i) Edukacji* [*Transdisciplinary Studies on Culture and/of Education*], *3*, 13–26. http://bazhum.muzhp.pl

Kawachi, I., & Berkman, L.F. (2001). Social ties and mental health. *Journal of Urban Health, Bulletin of the New York Academy of Medicine*, 3, 458–467.

Kawachi, I., Kenendy, B.P., Lochner, K., & Prothrow-Sith, D. (1997). Social capital, income inequality, and morality. *American Journal of Public Health*, *9*, 1491–1498.

Kawachi, I., Kennedy, B.P., & Glass, R. (1999). Social capital and self-rated health: Contextual analysis. *American Journal of Public Health*, *8*, 11187–11193.

Keany, K.C., & Glueckauf, R.L. (1993). Disability and value changes: An overview and analysis of acceptance of loss theory. *Rehabilitation Psychology*, *38*, 199–210.

Kent, M. (2019). Social media and Disability. In K. Ellis, G. Goggin, B. Haller, & R. Curtis (eds.), *The Routledge companion to disability and media*. Routledge, Ch.24. 10.4324/9781315716008

Kim, Y.J., Cho, Y.-A., & Kim, H.A. (2015). A mediation effect of ego resiliency between stresses and mental health of North Korean refugee youth in South Korea. *Child and Adolescent Social Work Journal*, *32*, 481–490. 10.1007/s10560-015-0385-5

Kołodziej-Zaleska, A., & Przybyła-Basista, H. (2018). Ego-resiliency jako zasób osobisty – narzędzie pomiaru i jego wykorzystanie w badaniach interdyscyplinarnych [Ego-Resiliency as a Personal Resource – Measurement Tool and Its Use in Interdisciplinary Research]. *Czasopismo Psychologiczne* [*Psychology Periodical*], *24*, 159–170.

Kowalik, S. (2007). *Psychologia rehabilitacji* [*Psychology of Rehabilitation*]. WAiP.

Lai, B., Wen, H., Sinha, T., Davis, D., Swanson-Kimani, E., Wozow, C., Young, R., Powell, D., &, Rimmer, J.H. (2022). The impact of COVID-19 on the lifestyles of adolescents with celebral palsy in the Southeast United States. *Disability & Health Journal*, *15*, 10.1016/j.dhjo.2021.101263

Letzring, T.D., Block, J., & Funder, D.C. (2005). Ego-control and ego-resiliency: Generalization of self-report scales based on personality descriptions from acquaintances, clinicians, and the self. *Journal of Research in Personality*, *39*, 395–422. 10.1016/j.jrp.2004.06.003

Lin, J-H., Ju, Y-H., Lee, S-J., Lee, Ch-H., Wang, H-Y., Teng, Y-L., & Lo, K.L. (2009). Do physical disabilities affect self-perceived quality of life in adolescents?. *Disability and Rehabilitation*, *31*, 181–188. 10.1080/09638280801942854.

Lin, N. (2008). A network theory of social capital. In D. Castiglione, J.W. van Deth, & G. Wolleb (eds.), *New York: The handbook of social capital* (50–59). Oxford University Press Inc.

Liu Q., Jiang M., Li S., & Yang Y. (2021). Social support, resilience, and self-esteem protect against common mental health problems in early adolescence. A nonrecursive analysis from a two-year longitudinal study. *Medicine*, 100, 10.1097/MD.0000000000024334.

Luyckx, K., Schwartz, S.J., Berzonsky, M.D., Soenens, B., Vansteenkiste, M., Smits, I., & Goossens, L. (2008). Capturing ruminative exploration: Extending the four-dimensional model of identity formation in late adolescence. *Journal of Research in Personality*, *42*, 58–82.

Margasiński, A. (2003). Rodzina w Modelu Kołowym i FACES IV Davida H. Olsona [The Family in David H. Olson's FACES IV and Circumplex Model]. *Nowiny Psychologiczne* [*Psychology News*], 44, 69–89.

Margasiński, A. (2009). *Skale Oceny Rodziny. Polska adaptacja FACES IV Davida Olsona. Podręcznik* [*Family Rating Scales. Polish Adaptation of David Olson's FACES IV. A Textbook*]. Pracownia Testów Psychologicznych.

Margasiński, A. (2011). *Model kołowy i skale FACES jako narzędzie badania rodziny. Historia, rozwój i zastosowanie* [*Circumplex Model and FACES Scales as a Family Study Tool. History, Development and Application*]. Wydawnictwo Akademii im. J. Długosza.

Marker, A.M., Steele, R.G., & Noser, A.E. (2018). Physical activity and health related quality of life in children and adolescents: A systematic review and meta - analysis. *Health Psychology*, *37*, 893–903. 10.1037/hea0000653

Marques, A., Demetriou, Y., Tesler, R., Gouveia, E.R., Peralta, M., & de Matos, M.G. (2019). Healthy lifestyle in children and adolescents and its associations with subjective health complaints: Findings from 37 countries and regions from the HBSC Study. *International Journal of Environmental Research and Public Health*, *16*, 3292. 10.3390/ijerph16183292

Marta, E. (1997). Parent-adolescent interactions and psychosocial risk in adolescents: An analysis of communication, support and gender. *Journal of Adolescence*, *20*, 473–487. 10.1006/jado.1997.0103

Masłyk, T. (2019). *Po pierwsze człowiek - Kapitał społeczny osób niepełnosprawnych w Polsce* [*Humans First – Social Capital of Disabled Persons in Poland*]. Wydawnictwo Naukowe Scholar.

Masłyk, T. (2020). Deficyt wsparcia społecznego – osoby niepełnosprawne w nieformalnych sieciach społecznych [Social Support Deficit – Disabled Persons in Informal Social Networks]. In G. Całka, J. Niedbalski, & D. Żuchwska-Skiba (eds.), *Jak badać zjawisko niepełnosprawności - szanse i zagrożenia założeń teoretycznych i metodologicznych studiów nad niepełnosprawnością* [*How to Study the Phenomenon of Disability – Opportunities and Threats of Theoretical and Methodological Studies on Disability*] (178–194), Wydawnictwo Uniwersytetu Łódzkiego.

Masłyk, T., Migaczewska, E., Stojkow, M., & Żuchowska-Skiba, D. (2016). *Aktywni niepełnosprawni? Obywatelski i społeczny potencjał środowiska osób niepełnosprawnych* [*Disabled and Active? Civic and Social Potential of the Disabled Persons Milieu*]. Wydawnictwo AGH.

Mayeri, H., Stolz, E., Großschädl, F., Rásky, E., & Freidl, W. (2017). The moderating role of personal resources in the relationship between psychosocial job demands and health: A cross-sectional study. *BMJ Open*, 7, 1–10. 10.1136/bmjopen-2016-015710

McDougall, J., Wright, V., & Rosenbaum, P. (2010). The ICF model of functioning and disability: Incorporating quality of life and human development. *Developmental Neurorehabilitation*, *13*, 204–211.

Mesman, E., Vreeker, A., & Hillegers, M. (2021). Resilience and mental health and adolescents: An update of the recent literature and future directions. *Current Opinion in Psychiatry*, *34*, 586–592. 10.1097/YCO.0000000000000741

Migerode, F., Maes, B., Buysse, A., & Brondeel, R. (2012). Quality of life in adolescents with a disability and their parents: The mediating role of social support and resilience. *Journal of Developmental and Physical Disabilities*, *24*, 487–503.

Mikkelsen, H.T., Haraldstad, K., Helseth, S., Skarstein, S., Cvancarova Smastuen, M., & Rohde, G. (2020). Health related quality of life is strongly associated with self efficacy, self esteem. *Health and Quality of Life*, *18*. 10.1186/s12955-020-01585-9

Mróz, J., & Kaleta, K. (2013). Struktura relacji w rodzinie pochodzenia a zachowania prozdrowotne dorosłych [The structure of relations in the family of origin and positive health behaviors of adults]. *Problemy Higieny i Epidemiologii* [*Problems of Hygiene and Epidemiology*], *94*, 239–246.

Muros, J.J., Pérez, F.S., Ortega, F.Z., Gámez Sánchez, V.M., & Knox, E. (2017). The association between healthy quality of life among adolescents. *Journal de Pediatria*, *93*, 406–412. 10.1016/j.jped.2016.10.005

Murray, C.B., Holmbeck, G.N., Ros, A.M., Flores, D.M., Mir, S.A., & Varni, J.W. (2015). A longitudinal examination of health-related quality of life in children and adolescents with spina bifida. *Journal of Pediatric Psychology*, *40*, 419–430.

Nemati, S., & Maralani, F.M. (2016). The relationship between life satisfaction and happiness: The mediating role of resiliency. *International Journal of Psychological Studies*, *8*, 194–201.

O'Keeffe, G., Sch., & Clarke-Pearson, K. (2011). The impact of social media on children, adolescents, and families. *Pediatrics*, *127*, 800–804. 10.1542/peds.2011-0054

Olson, D.H. (2000). Circumplex model of marital and family systems. *Journal of Family Therapy*, *22*, 144–167.

Olson, D.H., & Gorall, D.M. (2003). Circumplex model of marital and family systems. In F. Walsh (ed.), *Normal family processes* (514–547). Guilford.

Ornelas, I.J., Perreira, K.M., & Ayala, G.X. (2007). Parental influences on adolescent physical activity: A longitudinal study. *International Journal of Behavioral Nutrition and Physical Activity*, *4*, 3–10.

Patton, G.C., Sawyer, S.M., Santelli, J.S., Ross, D.A., Afifi, R., Allen, N.B., Arora, M., Azzopardi, P., Baldwin, W., Bonell, Ch., Kukuma, R., Kennedy, E., Mahon, J., McGovern, T., Mokdad, A.H., Patel, V., Petroni, S., Reavley, N., Taiwo, K., Waldfogel, J., Wickremarathne, D., Barroso, C., Bhutta, Z., Fatusi, A.O., Mattoo, A., Diers, J., Fang, J., Ferguson, J., Ssewamala, F., & Viner, R.M. (2016). Our future: A Lancet commission on adolescent health and wellbeing. *Lancet*, *387*, 2423–2478. 10.1016/S0140-6736(16)00579-1.

Petersson, Ch., Simeonsson, R.J., Enskar, K., & Huus, K. (2013). Comparing children's self-report instruments for health-related quality of life using the International Classification of Functioning, Disability and Health for children and youth. *Health and Quality of Life Outcomes*, *11*, 1–10. 10.1186/1477-7525-11-75

Petrenko, Ch. L. M., Tahir, N., Mahoney, E.C., & Chin, N.P. (2014). Prevention of secondary conditions in fetal alcohol spectrum disorders: Identification of systems level barriers. *Maternal & Child Health Journal*, *18*, 1496–1505. 10.1007/s10995-013-1390-y

Ponczek, D., & Olszowy, I. (2012). Styl życia młodzieży i jego wpływ na zdrowie [Adolescents' Lifestyle and Its Impact on Health]. *Problemy Higieny i Epidemiologii* [*Problems of Hygiene and Epidemiology*], *93*, 260–268.

Putman, R.D., & Goss, K.A. (2004). Introduction. In R. Putman (ed.), *Democracie in Flux: The evolution of social capital in contemporary socjety* (13–18). Oxford University Press.

Putnam, R.D., Leonardi, R., & Nonetti, R. (1993). *Cicvic traditions in modern Italy*. Princeton University Press.

Rainone, N., Chiodi, A., Lanzillo, R., Magr,i V., Napolitano, A., Morra, V.B., Valerio, P., & Freda, M.F. (2017). Affective disorders and Health-Related Quality of Life (HRQoL), On adolescents and young adults with Multiple Sclerosis (MS): The moderating role of resilience. *Quality of Life Research*, *26*, 727–736.

Reid, D., & Weigle, P. (2014). Social media use among adolescents: Benefits and risks. *Adolescent Psychiatry*, *4*, 78–80.

Revilla, J.C., Martin, P., & de Castro, C. (2018). The reconstruction of resilience as a social and collective phenomenon: Poverty and coping capacity during the economic crisis. *European Societies*, *20*, 92–93. 10.1080/14616696.2017.1346195

Rimmer, R.H., Rowland, J.L., & Yamaki, K. (2007). Obesity and secondary conditions in adolescents with disabilities: Addressing the needs of an underserved population. *Journal of Adolescent Health*, *41*, 224–229. 10.1016/j.jadohealth.2007.05.005

Robertson, J., Emerson, E., Gregory, N., Hatton, Ch., Turner, S., Kessissoglou, S., & Hallam, A. (2000). Lifestyle related risk factors for poor health in residential settings for people with intellectual disabilities. *Research in Developmental Disabilities*, *21*, 469–486. 10.1016/s0891-4222(00)00053-6

Rurangirwa, J., Braun, K.V.N., Schendel, D., & Yeargin-Allsopp, M. (2006). Healthy behaviors and lifestyles in young adults with a history of developmental disabilities. *Research in Developmental Disabilities*, 27, 381–399. 10.1016/j.ridd.2005.01.003

Sawatzky, R., Ratner, P.A., Johnson, J.L., Kopec, J.A., & Zumbo, B.D. (2010). Self-reported physical and mental health status and quality of life in adolescents: A latent variable mediation model. *Health & Quality of Life Outcomes*, *8*. 10.1186/1477-7525-8-17

Sekułowicz, M., & Kwiatkowski, P. (2013). Wypalenie się sił u rodziców dzieci z niepełnosprawnością [Burnout in Parents of Children with Disabilities]. *Studia edukacyjne* [*Educational Studies*], *25*, 29–49.

Shapiro, D.R., & Malone, L.A. (2016). Quality of life and psychological affect related to sport participation in children and youth athletes with physical disabilities: A parent and athlete perspective. *Disability and Health Journal*, *9*, 385–391.

Shapiro, D.R., & Martin, J.J. (2010). Athletic identity, affect, and peer relations in youth athletes with physical disabilities. *Disability and Health Journal*, *3*, 79–85.

Shi, Q., Liew, J., Ettekal, I., & Woltering, S. (2021). Childhood resilient personality trajectories and associations with developmental trajectories of behavioral, social-emotional, and academic outcomes across childhood and adolescence: A longitudinal study across 12 years. *Personality & Individual Differences*, *177*. 10.1016/j.paid.2021.110789

Sigvarsten, J., Gabrielsen, L.E., Abildsnes, E., Stea, T.H., Omfjord, Ch.S., & Rohde, G. (2016). Exploring the relationship between physical activity, life goals and health-related quality of life among high school students: A cross-sectional study. *BMC Public Health*, *16*, 1–9. 10.1186/s12889-016-3407-0

Solera-Sanchez, A., Adelantado-Renau, M., Moliner-Urdiales, D., & Reyes Beltran-Valls, M. (2021). Health-related quality of life in adolescents: Individual and combined impact of health-related behaviors (DADOS-study). *Quality of Life Research*, *30*, 1093–1101. 10.1007/s11136-020-02699-9

Stanojević, Jerković, O., Sauliūnė, S., Šumskas, L., Birt, Ch. A., & Kersnik, J. (2017). Determinants of self-rated health in elderly populations in urban areas in Slovenia, Lithuania and UK: Findings of the EURO-URHIS 2 survey. *European Journal of Public Health*, *27* (Suppl 2), 74–79. 10.1093/eurpub/ckv097280600836018

Sutherland, G., Couchm, M.A., & Iaconom, T. (2002). Health issues for adults with developmental disability. *Research in Developmental Disabilities*, *23*, 422–445. 10.1016/s0891-4222(02)00143-9

Szpunar, M. (2012). *Nowe-stare medium - Internet między tworzeniem nowych modeli komunikacyjnych a reprodukowaniem schematów komunikowania masowego* [*New/Old Medium – The Internet Between Creating New Communication Models and Reproducing Mass Communication Patterns*]. IFIS PAN.

Tabak, I., Jodkowska, M., & Oblacińska, A. (2013). Spożywanie wspólnych posiłków, wsparcie i komunikacja w rodzinie jako predyktory zdrowia subiektywnego i zadowolenia z życia nastolatków /Family meals, support and communication within the family as predictors of teenagers' subjective health and life satisfaction. *Pediatria Polska* [*Polish Journal of Paediatrics*], *88*, 533–539. 10.1016/j.pepo.2013.09.006

Taylor, Z., & Jones, B. (2020). Cultural contributions to ego-resiliency and associations with depressive problems in midwestern Latino youth. *Journal of Research on Adolescence*, 2, 349–361. 10.1111/jora.12481

Theis, N., Campbell, N., de Leeuw, J., Owen, M., & Schenke, K.C. (2021). The effects of COVID-19 restrictions on physical activity and mental health of children and young adults with physical and/or intellectual disabilities. *Disability and Health Journal*, *14*. 10.1016/j.dhjo.2021.101064

von Rueden, U., Gosch, A., Rajmil, L., Bisegger, C., & Ravens-Sieberer, U. (2006). Socioeconomic determinants of health related quality of life in childhood and adolescence: Results from a European study. *Journal of Epidemiology and Community Health*, *60*, 130–135. 10.1136/jech.2005.039792.

Willson, V.L., & Hughes, J.N. (2006). Retention of Hispanic/Latino students in first grade: Child, parent, teacher, school, and peer predictions. *Journal of School Psychology*, *44*, 31–49.

Wódz, K., Mandrysz, W., & Klimek, M. (2020). Potyczki z codziennością - Społeczność lokalna jako źródło rezyliencji. Z badań w województwie śląskim [Squabbles with Daily Life – Local Community as a Source of Resilience. From Research in the Silesian Province] (15–19). Wydawnictwo Uniwersytetu Śląskiego.

Wright, B. (1983). *Physicaldisability – A Psychosocial Approach*. Harper & Row.

Wysota, M.,Pilarska, A., & Adamczyk, K. (2014). Specyfika funkcjonowania rodziny w percepcji adolescentów i młodych dorosłych a formowanie się ich tożsamości [Specificity of Family Functioning in the Perception of Adolescents and Young Adults vs the Formation of Their Identity], *Psychologia Rozwojowa [Developmental Psychology]*, *19*, 103–120. 10.4467/20843879PR.14.014.2292

Xiang, L., Su, Z., Liu, Y., Huang, Y., Zhang, X., Li, S., & Zhang, H. (2019). Impact of family socioeconomic status on health-related quality of life in children with critical congenital heart disease. *Journal of the American Heart Association: Cardiovascular and Cerebrovascular Disease*, *8*. 10.1161/JAHA.118.010616.

Yazicioglu, K., Yavuz, F., Goktepe, A.S., & Tan, A.T. (2012). Influence of adapted sports on quality of life and life satisfaction in sport participants and non-sport participants with physical disabilities. *Disability and Health Journal*, *5*, 249–253. 10.1016/j.dhjo.2012.05.003

Zabriskie, R.B., & McCormick, B.P. (2001). The influences of family leisure patterns on perceptions of family functioning. *Family Relations*, *50*, 281–289.

Ziarko, M., Mojs, E., Sikorska, D., & Samborski, W. (2019). Coping and life satisfaction: Mediating role of ego-resiliency in patients with rheumatoid arthritis. *Medical Principles and Practice*, *29*, 160–165. 10.1159/000503708

Zullig, K.J., Valois, R.F., & Drane, J.W. (2005). Adolescent distinctions between quality of life and self-rated health in quality of life research. *Health & Quality of Life Outcomes*, *3*. 10.1186/1477-7525-3-64

Chapter 8

Conclusion

The leading inspiration to write this book was provided by the positive perspective in thinking about the individual and about the family. Acknowledging the difficult circumstances affecting people, the authors focused on the dynamic coping process of the individual aimed at maintaining health-related quality of life. Important assumptions involved searching for resources for an optimal and successful adaptation process and the belief in the possibility of minimising the costs of disorders and of simultaneously strengthening developmental potential to maintain a high level of health-related quality of life.

The study was prepared by an interdisciplinary team of psychologists, special educators, and sociologists. The starting point for the design of the research concept and for the discussion of the data collected was provided, therefore, by an interdisciplinary approach to the aspects covered. The underlying intention was to look at disability in line with the ICF assumptions in terms of body/mind functions and structures, rather than in terms of the dysfunctions described by ICD or DSM classification categories. We treat the ICF interactionist model as central since our investigations concern the broadly perceived individual and social resources that determine the quality of life and mental health of young people with individual development limitations. The research presented in the book addresses a relatively broad context of health-related quality of life, and it was extended by reflections from the fields of education, psychology, and sociology, synergistically intertwined in an attempt to offer another perspective on the quality of life of persons with disabilities.

Ninety-eight parent-adolescent dyads took part in the research presented in the book. They included 26 adolescents with an intellectual disability-parent dyads, 61 adolescents with a physical disability-parent dyads, and 11 adolescents with FASD-parent dyads. In our research, we focused on health-related quality of life in adolescents, both self-rated and as rated by their parents. Particular attention paid to each dimension of health-related quality of life: physical and psychological wellbeing, autonomy and parents, as well as school, and social support and peer contexts. The results of comparative

DOI: 10.4324/9781003367772-8

analyses concerning adolescents with an intellectual disability, a physical disability, and FASD, and their parents in their evaluation of the adolescents' health-related quality of life generally pointed to similarities between the ratings. At the same time, the different ratings coming from parents and children were found to be significant for areas of HRQoL related, firstly, to the emerging autonomy and the relationships with the parents, and secondly, to social support and the importance of peers.

In the subsequent chapters of the book, we extended our presentation of the health-related quality of life of the adolescents studied by seeking its determinants. We investigated personal resources such as self-rated health, disability acceptance, lifestyle, and ego-resiliency, as well as social resources related to family functioning (its financial situation, cohesion and flexibility) and social relationships, including those taking place through social media.

We found it interesting how both the adolescents and their parents rated their own health and assessed their own resources. The results of our research indicate that adolescents define health similarly to their parents. However, they rate their own health lower compared to their parents. Moreover, the surveyed parents had higher self-rated health, a higher level of ego-resiliency, and a higher score on almost all lifestyle factors except social support compared to their children. In our study results, the parents also assess their family as more cohesive compared to the adolescents. However, adolescents meet more frequently with their friends and use social media more often than their parents.

More in-depth statistical analyses indicated a direct and an indirect role of the examined resources in maintaining health-related quality of life in the surveyed adolescents. Personal resources such as self-rated health, disability acceptance, lifestyle, and ego-resiliency were significant for health-related quality of life. Interestingly, the study results pointed to more complex relationships between the variables studied. In turn, social resources such as financial situation, perceived family cohesion, family flexibility, meeting with friends, and using social media turned out to vary in importance depending on the HRQoL area analysed.

The main research findings indicate the key role of personal and social resources in maintaining health-related quality of life in adolescents with intellectual disability, physical disability, and FASD, and in particular the importance of different resources for different areas of HRQoL. In addition, the interesting detailed results presented in the book concern the similarities and differences in the areas of health, resources, and HRQoL between the adolescents and their parents and between the three different groups of adolescents surveyed and the three different groups of the adolescent-parent dyads surveyed.

We took particular care to maintain high methodological and statistical standards in the collection and discussion of data. However, we realise that the research has its limitations. We present them in the first part of this chapter. Furthermore, the data presented and discussed encouraged us to discuss the practical implications. They constitute an important, practical continuation of the analyses carried out. The implications are presented in the second part of this chapter and provide a conclusion of sorts to the book.

We worked on the research concept and implementation with a view to ensuring the highest possible standards of reliability and validity. Respecting good scientific research practice and ethical principles, we applied validated measurement tools during the studies, we took care to apply inclusion and exclusion criteria for the study group and the subgroups of adolescents and parents, and we used adequate statistical analyses. However, although the research presented in the book carried out using the dyadic approach and provided a lot of valuable information, it is not free of limitations. These can be formulated in relation to several aspects.

1 Firstly, the study sample, although relatively large considering the parent-adolescent with a disability pairs, is still insufficiently large to perform more advanced and multidimensional analyses. We realise that there is inequality and underrepresentation in the sample when it comes to parents and adolescents with FASD, which makes it impossible to draw binding conclusions, but rather preliminary findings, which can be used to continue the research.

   Despite our intense efforts, we were unable to gain access to the group of adolescents with FASD and their parents. This may be due to several reasons. First of all, there are few people with a diagnosis of FASD in this age category. This results from the fact that there are only a few centres in Poland that have the appropriate qualifications and tools to diagnose the disorder (Stopikowska, 2016.) At the same time, the issue of FASD has only been the subject of broader public discussion in Poland for a few years now, and thus the general public has only recently become aware of it. The first and so far the only study attempting to identify the population of children (aged 7–9) with FASD was carried out in 2014, commissioned by the Polish National Agency for Solving Alcohol-Related Problems (PARPA), and named "Projekt Alicja". However, due to difficulties in recruiting respondents, that study did not make it possible to accurately estimate the prevalence of FASD in Poland. Of the random sample of 2,500 pupils, 2,091 children refused to participate in the survey. This demonstrates perfectly clearly the social taboo associated with the spectrum of disorders related to FASD, with fears that the parents' bad habits would be exposed, and that the parents would consequently be held to account for the children's disorder. A majority of children and adolescents diagnosed with the disorder live in adoptive or foster families, sometimes in orphanages or care and education centres. Unfortunately, education or rehabilitation facilities where people with FASD often reside do not carry out such diagnoses. Often, social workers in assistance facilities such as community centres are able to identify people with FASD, but this does not mean that they refer them for a diagnosis, as this would require the consent of the parents or legal guardians. In turn, in the case of children with suspected FASD, access to the parents can be difficult.

With regard to the size of the group we studied, we also need to point out that the group of parents we surveyed was composed predominantly of the mothers. It would be interesting, both in terms of the knowledge-gaining potential and practice, to capture differences or similarities between the mothers and fathers of adolescents with disabilities in the context of mental health and health-related quality of life, as well as of personal and social resources. At the same time, our study group was quite homogeneous in terms of marital status and family type. The parents were mostly married, and the families were complete. There was a small percentage of divorced, widowed or single parents. A small share was represented by foster families. This is undoubtedly a limitation of the research in terms of the possibility of generalising the results. In future research projects, it would be worth ensuring a more diverse group of parents and families of children with disabilities.

2 Another limitation of the study was related to the research design presented in the book, assuming the significance of the type of disability the adolescent has as a potential variable differentiating mental health and health-related quality of life in the adolescents and their parents. Although this assumption finds justification in the literature to date, in future research it would nevertheless be worth analysing, in line with for instance with the ICF propositions, the role of the degree of daily functioning of adolescents with different types of physical or mental impairment.
3 The cross-sectional nature of the quantitative research used, supplemented by qualitative data elements, enables only limited inferences, with the awareness of the potential variability of health-related quality of life assessments in time. At the same time, a strength of this research involves the comparisons in adolescent-parent pairs, providing opportunities to trace variability. Admittedly, this variability is not temporal, but concerns the broader here and now, with the acknowledgement of different points of view in assessing the same phenomena: the dimensions of HRQoL or personal and social resources.
4 Although the topic of sibling relationships was not addressed in the research plan, we nevertheless recognise their importance, also in the context of health-related quality of life. Relationships between siblings are special in that they last over their entire lives, and take into account a shared genetic and psychosocial heritage (Pisula & Danielewicz, 2007). Alongside the relations with parents/guardians, these are the closest relationships. Their quality and development, therefore, also determines

how the individual functions (not infrequently also by way of imitation or modelling) in wider social groups, in other relationships. Although the relations between the parents and parent-child relationships are key for the family's functioning, relations between siblings constitute an important adaptive resource from childhood onwards (Jurkiewicz, 2017). This is particularly evident during adolescence, a period of separation and individuation. Siblings can be an important source of support for each other (Goetting, 1986). If there is a child with a disability in the family, the wide spectrum of emotions in sister-brother relationships is even greater. The non-disabled/healthy siblings may find it difficult to understand and accept the disease/disorder, they may feel lonely, ashamed, angry about the possible relational difficulties of the child with the disability/disease (inability to talk or play) or, finally, there may be tension resulting from anger directed at the parents, who are less available to the other children due to the need to look after the child with special needs. There may also be a desire to help, a greater sensitivity to the special needs of others, but also a sense of guilt, a need to compensate for the family constraints, or the risk of parentification (Jurkiewicz, 2017). It also creates particular contexts for the functioning of the child with a disability or FASD. We are aware of the importance of such a relationship and, with a view to further research, we will consider including verification of this aspect too.

5 The definitions or health models cited in the previous chapters do not capture the context of adolescents' sexual functioning. Meanwhile, the holistic approach emphasises that sexuality is an important part of being human. It is inextricably linked to other aspects of the individual's functioning. Sexual health is wellbeing in relation to sexuality and is particularly significant for physical and mental wellbeing in general. It is treated as a determinant of subjective health perceived as holistic wellbeing (WHO, 2014). It corresponds to the global sense of quality of life in the psychophysical area (Nomejko et al. 2012). Hence, sexuality should be discussed in the context of human psychological development, of the subjective sphere, but also more broadly – taking into account aspects of nature, civilisation, culture, and society (Dymowska, 2019). When discussing sexual health, it is worth highlighting its relationship with reproductive health, meaning the individual's ability to engage in sexual life and to live it in a satisfying and safe manner; in fact, it includes not only the possibility of conceiving offspring, but also the ability to make informed decisions and choices related to procreative plans (Izdebski & Wąż, 2014). Adolescence is the period of most dynamic psychosexual development, as one passes from childhood sexuality to adult sexuality, learning how to function in a future intimate relationship and how to play an assumed role. Naturally, medical categories are key to understanding and diagnosing phenomena from this area. This period

(late adolescence) is often associated with sexual initiation, engaging in various sexual behaviours (sometimes also risky ones), and curiosity leading to risk-related areas (for example, pornography). It also brings about the need to confront in a particular manner the emerging sexual needs and sexual expression with specific cultural demands, but also social, legal, or political boundaries (Beisert, 2006; Dymowska 2019; Izdebski & Wąż, 2014; Jewtuch, 2020). Importantly, from the point of view of this book, it is also the period when one learns to build close relationships (combining emotionality with sexuality), and at the same time when a key process for autonomy takes place, namely that of becoming independent from one's parents (Beisert, 2006).

Changes in morals, the modern-day sexualisation phenomenon, and at the same time the specific nature of adolescence, the different dynamics of sexual behaviour and attitudes towards sexuality all mean that young people sometimes feel lost in this area. Another important aspect is the quality and specific nature of sexual education within the family, differentiating between interventions dedicated to girls (raised more restrictively in this aspect; with their upbringing additionally influenced by environmental factors) and boys (Churska-Nowak et al., 2018). The above and many other factors result in a diversified picture of adolescents' sexual health. This book does not address these issues. Nevertheless, we acknowledge the legitimacy of addressing this topic in future research on health-related quality of life, since the sexual health of children and adolescents is a variable that has growth potential relatively to positive values of health determinants; moreover, it is linked to the aspect of building adolescents' autonomy.

6 We conducted our research online, including both the questionnaire stage. The time of the pandemic, with the impossibility of conducting the surveys in direct contact with the respondents, amplified the trend of doing so. Online surveys were also often the only way for the researcher to come into contact with the study subjects, especially in the lockdown period. We designed our research plan during the successive waves of COVID-19. The research started in turn almost simultaneously with the lifting of the major pandemic restrictions in Poland. However, a state of pandemic emergency continued to be (and still is) in force in Poland. Despite the changes taking place, we kept our online survey design. There are probably both advantages and disadvantages to this. The virtual space has certainly become more accessible and available for today's generations, both younger and older, potentially allowing a relatively broad sample to be invited to participate in the research. This research form made it possible to invite a relatively diverse group of people from all over Poland to participate. Thus, it was possible to survey individuals who, due to numerous responsibilities, logistical difficulties and other constraints, would not have been able to come to a designated physical

> location at the same time. The online space definitely also made it easier for us to reach the parents and the children with the questionnaires, and thus made the dyadic study possible. We assume that the possibility of answering the questions at any time allowed the respondents to complete the questionnaires at their convenience, which is very important in the case of persons with disabilities and their relatives/carers. The online formula was also more time-saving, both for the respondents and for the researchers. However, we are aware that the group of Internet users may differ from the general population.

Only volunteers participated in the study, which certainly makes our research model distant from the desirable random model. Participation in such surveys (especially if they are relatively long, as was the case of our study) requires motivation on the part of the respondents, efficiently operating computer hardware and proficiency in its use, as well as good-quality Internet access. Respondents completing questionnaires online have no opportunity to ask about anything that is unclear to them, and they might not be sufficiently motivated to complete the entire questionnaire, which leads to phenomena such as dropout or abandoning the survey (also occurring in the course of our research). These variables are examples of factors beyond our control. During online surveys, we have no way of verifying the respondents' identity either (Chlipała, 2020; Daszkiewicz-Wrona, 2014; Miller, 2012).

While aware of the aforementioned limitations of our research, we believe that it contributes to the understanding of health-related quality of life in adolescents with disabilities and FASD and their parents, especially in the context of the importance of personal and social resources for the adolescents' HRQoL and of the difference between the adolescent and parental perspectives in their assessment.

The research presented in the book provides many reasons for continuing to analyse health-related quality of life in adolescents with disabilities. However, the results obtained, despite certain limitations, also reveal important areas of practical intervention. We situate these practical implications in two mutually compatible areas: prevention and health promotion, with the outlining of specific recommendations for interventions targeted at adolescents with disabilities and FASD and their families.

The basis for such application developments is provided by a sound diagnosis of a specific fragment of reality. "Learning about the specific nature of functioning of the family of a child with a disability is an important topic both from the point of view of holistic support for the child's development and in the areas of reflection on the integration of persons with disabilities and normalisation of the social environment" (Doroszuk, 2017, p. 51). Diagnosis accompanied by this intention should be carried out above all with a view to recognising resources, rather than focusing on pathology and dysfunction.

This is a key assumption underlying our work and the considerations presented here regarding the application-related aspects of the research.

Children and adolescents with disabilities and FASD, their parents (carers), and siblings should be covered by systemic solutions comprising medical support, care, welfare, spiritual, legal, and economic assistance, as well as educational and psychological support, including preferential access to psychotherapy (Jurkiewicz, 2017). Access to a multidimensional support system, with professionals working together between sectors, seems to be a valid response to the need to think about the human being in holistic terms.

In Poland, the system of assistance to people with disabilities is transforming from an institutional (medical, functional) model, interested in the person with a disability as a patient (who "requires" health compensation), through a rehabilitation model focused on the client-consumer, to a civic (social) model. The starting point for this model involves treating persons with disabilities as members of the respective community (Firkowska-Mankiewicz, 2006). This also implies the need to change the assistance dedicated to their families, in particular with regard to children and adolescents with disabilities. Help should be organised in line with the principle of subsidiarity. It should therefore involve measures that respect the right to autonomy of the child and of the family, and do not restrict their own initiatives. Assistance is supposed to have a subsidiary, accompanying role, as an invitation to work with professionals as partners, opening up new perspectives (Szczupał, 2010; Żyta & Ćwirynkało, 2015). This collaboration is also crucial in designing and implementing health-related quality of life measures for adolescents with disabilities and their families.

Understanding individual health not so much in a static, but rather in a dynamic way requires optimal comprehensive and coordinated support in different areas of functioning (family, school, medical care), but also in different scopes:

- prevention, to protect health;
- health promotion, aimed at improving health;
- treatment and rehabilitation, to restore health in general or in specific areas (Bielski & Blada, 2014).

Prevention, health promotion, and health education, which fit within these areas, are key pathways to improve the level of health within society, in line with the assumptions of evidence-based medicine. At the same time, they optimise the expenditures incurred by state/organisations' budgets to protect health (Rezner et al., 2013; Woolf, 2009). "Prevention and promotion of a healthy lifestyle among the youngest have an impact on the health of the future working-age population, for the health of future generations depends on the health of today's children" (NIK, 2020, p. 5). In line with the recommendation of the Polish Supreme Audit Office (NIK), and above all due to the nature of our study, we will devote most attention to the potential inherent in prevention and health promotion. At the same time, we are fully aware that a child with a disability or FASD (and their family) should first and foremost have comprehensive access to treatment and rehabilitation procedures.

"Prevention is the process of assisting an individual in coping with difficulties that threaten proper and correct development and healthy life, as well as reducing and eliminating the factors that disrupt correct development and disorganise healthy life, and initiating and strengthening protective factors" (Gaś, 2006, p. 14). Prevention, therefore, is the creation of opportunities for the accumulation of experiences within which the individual creatively constructs, develops, realises, and strengthens the various resources required in the process of optimal coping with challenges. It is a certain training process, in which adaptive individual and social systems are consolidated. Prevention organisers create the opportunity for this to happen, for instance by developing the family guidance system, organising various pro-social activities, spaces for the activation of specific community groups, etc. (Śliwa, 2016).

The following three key types of prevention are currently enumerated:

- universal prevention – addressed to everyone (the undiagnosed population, the general public, regardless of risk potential); it is oriented towards providing extensive knowledge and developing the psychosocial competences essentially constituting what we nowadays call the protective factor;
- selective prevention – dedicated to individuals who, due to biological, family, or environmental determinants, are exposed to specific risk factors/behaviours; the scope of selective prevention is similar to that of universal prevention, the difference, however, being that these activities are dedicated to a group of people with diagnosed problems, and therefore having specific needs;
- indicated prevention – recommended to individuals who display early symptoms of specific dysfunctions, engage in problem behaviours/situations; activities in this area fit within broadly understood intervention addressed to the individual and to their immediate environment, above all the family; according to the former classification system, selective and indicated prevention correspond to secondary prevention (Szymańska, 2015).

What used to be referred to as tertiary prevention, in turn, is primarily treatment, rehabilitation, revalidation, re-education, or resocialisation. These are usually activities addressed to people with an experience of disease or disability (Borzucka-Sitkiewicz & Kowalczewska-Grabowska, 2013; Szymańska, 2015).

In the course of prevention activities, it is also important to engage other people and environments, including above all the family. In general, prevention covers five specific areas with its interventions: the individual, the peer group, the school environment, the local community, and the family (Gaś, 2006).

The first and last of these areas are particularly interesting from the point of view of the topic of our work. An analysis of the results of our research shows the need for intervention and long-term preventive actions dedicated to children and parents. However, we are aware that during adolescence, the peer group, school, but also the local community play an important role too. "Working with the child separately from the family results, in the best case scenario, in neutralising the changes developed. The young person, as a weaker element in the system, has little chance of adapting the family system to their needs. It is rather the system that forces them to return to old habits. Hence, a preventive intervention without the family's engagement is doomed in advance to failure or limited, deferred success" (Poleszak, 2017, p. 11). The family can therefore become a target for preventive actions. The climate present within it can be a risk factor (e.g. lack of parental support, chaotic family environment) or a protective factor (e.g. positive bonds, secure attachment, the parents cooperating with representatives of other education environments important for the child). However, the family can essentially function in two ways: as a subject and as an object of prevention. Two approaches are derived from this:

- prevention within the family, i.e. actions taken by the family in response to self-diagnosis; therefore, intrinsic motivation, reflection, awareness of needs, and readiness for directional change predominate here;
- family within prevention, i.e. an imposed form of action, not consulted with the family; established institutionally in response to a diagnosis justified by social grounds. A parent/guardian engaged in prevention activities can be the recipient, but also an actor implementing the prevention activities. Regardless of the parent's role, their participation alone increases the effectiveness of prevention (Śliwa, 2016). This effectiveness furthermore increases as the number and variety of strategies implemented grow (Gaś, 2006; Poleszak, 2017).

Various strategies are mentioned in the literature:

- information activities, primarily intended to provide basic knowledge in a given area, since it is the lack of knowledge about phenomena, mechanisms, regularities, and possible consequences that induces unconstructive, negative behaviours, e.g. health-harming ones; what is referred to as "teaching facts", i.e. various lectures and presentations are, however, essentially not very effective strategies; in order to improve their effectiveness, it is worth making sure that the content provided is adapted to the age, the cognitive abilities of the individual, and the amount of knowledge they already have; the message should be reliable, interesting, and motivating, and, above all, the person providing the knowledge should be credible;

- educational activities, aimed at helping individuals/groups to develop psychosocial ("navigation") skills important for building good relationships, functioning in society, and entering into social roles; these include communication skills, coping with stress, self-motivation, goal-setting and decision-making skills, self-awareness and insight, as well as building and regulating adequate self-esteem; these are by far some of the most effective preventive interventions; two types of such strategies are distinguished in the literature:

    1. affective education (aimed at evoking feelings, making it possible to gain self-knowledge from an intra- and interpersonal point of view, confronting one's own unique and exceptional nature); and
    2. social skills.

- alternative activities, otherwise referred to as "strategies of alternatives" to negative behaviours; preventive activities consist in creating space for participation in health-promoting and constructive forms of activity, in organising and engaging in forms of activity that make it possible to experience a sense of belonging, success, satisfaction, regulation of adequate self-esteem, development of interests and potential; they can include "tailor-made" activities in sports clubs, as well as drama or art classes in schools or community centres;
- interventions which generally fit within the area known in the past as secondary prevention (in which they are most important) and tertiary prevention; these intervention activities are dedicated to individuals/groups already experiencing difficulties and specific crises; they are generally carried out taking into account the need for individualisation and within the framework of what is referred to as early intervention programmes, implemented either by professionals or by trained and prepared peers/peer leaders;
- environmental changes aimed at modifying specific social attitudes (especially those of a pathological or discriminatory nature), verifying norms and standards of morality, and orienting a development-promoting and at the same time health-promoting climate in the environment, e.g. at school or at work, to make sure that people functioning in the respective environment can be safe in a broad sense;
- amendments to laws, ordinances, and regulations to strengthen solutions of value;
- harm reduction strategies, formerly included in tertiary prevention, today rather associated with a particular expression of helplessness in the face of serious and severe social problems; it is a choice of the "lesser evil" (or even reinforcing this "evil"), as it is assumed that there is a certain group of people who will not give up risky behaviours, but what can be done for

them is to reduce the scale of an already serious risk, e.g. exchange of needles and syringes for people in extreme stages of drug addiction and substitution treatment; here, social support is also mentioned nowadays (Borzucka-Sitkiewicz & Kowalczewska-Grabowska, 2013; Gaś, 2006; Poleszak, 2017; Szymańska, 2015).

In the contemporary, positive sense, prevention is part of a holistic vision of health, of health-related quality of life as a multidimensional, dynamic construct. Biological, social, psychological, and spiritual factors all co-determine health in acting in synergy. A key factor strengthening and developing health is a health-oriented attitude, i.e. the individual's knowledge-based, informed and active participation, and the involvement of their environment. Working on potentials makes it possible to obtain better resilience, optimal adaptation to changing conditions, and satisfactory coping with difficult situations (Curyło-Sikora & Kaczmarska, 2016).

In contemporary definitions of health, a distinction is made between health and disease, as well as their causes. While the biomedical model taking into account pathogenesis will apply better in the understanding of disease, prevention and health promotion fit more fully within the context of health (Heszen & Sęk, 2007). While in the case of prevention, dedicated activities were generally created with the intention of avoiding a specific "evil" posing a realistic threat, health promotion is a "positive" alternative to the interventions, focusing on resources, pointing to good role models and practices, and emphasising the value of health (Salamucha, 2016). Bearing in mind this juxtaposition, however, the existence of a positive prevention model should also be mentioned. The idea of contemporary practical prevention is to support protective factors, at the same time minimising the impact of risk factors related to specific problem behaviours and diseases. Positive prevention focuses above all on protective factors, especially those inherent to the individual (strengths, resources whose strengthening and development – through psychoeducational measures – builds resilience). In parallel, it also focuses on the individual's closest environment, i.e. the family, peer group, classmates, and school (preventive socioeducational interactions), orienting activities around the creation of a positive environment, abundant in protective factors (Kania, 2016; Ostaszewski, 2006). In this positive approach, positive prevention is already very close to health promotion, which will be described further on in this chapter.

Another aspect linking prevention and health promotion is the activity of health educators. They play an important role, both in the field of prevention and health promotion, that fits within the aims of what is referred to as curative medicine. They educate patients, who consequently become more effectively involved in the treatment process. This profession is already known in many countries. With their professional background, not only do they educate (for example, within the framework of primary care), but also support the development and improvement of health-oriented activities in the field of interventions, policy, or creating systems of solutions dedicated to improving the health of individuals, groups, and communities (Rezner et al., 2013).

Inspired by the point of view featured by the ICF concept, but also by the vision of holistic health, of the importance of resources for the realisation of aspirations, and constructive adaptation to life with a disability, we suggest that prevention dedicated to persons with disabilities or FASD should be considered as preventing the loss or failure to realise real potentials and overlooking resources, as preventing the reduction of health-related quality of life. In our opinion, the current situation of adolescents with disabilities can potentially generate negative potentials threatening their quality of life related to broadly perceived health, e.g. overdependence on others, difficulty in adapting to the disability and to independent life in a dynamically changing reality, negative self-image resulting from comparisons, decreased motivation for development, and reduced participation in the treatment/rehabilitation/therapy process due to difficulties in accessing them. It is important to remember that all of this is happening at the extremely unfavourable time of the pandemic, the threat of war, economic crisis, and unsatisfactory systemic solutions in education, health care, and psychoeducational care.

On the basis of analyses of our research results, referring to the assumptions underlying the individual prevention strategies mentioned earlier and to the idea of positive prevention, we have formulated proposed interventions that we dedicate to adolescents with disabilities and FASD, as well as to representatives of milieus important for them (parents, management of educational institutions, teachers, but also decision-makers in the area of law and applicable regulations). These include:

- information activities,
- educational activities,
- improving the coping skills of adolescents aimed at achieving independence in adulthood, e.g. by organising SST – social skills training dedicated to adolescents with disabilities, and
- participating in experiential activities (e.g. elements of psychodrama) to raise awareness of strengths and resources.

Health promotion is another area corresponding to our research intentions, but also to the prevention described here. Sometimes, health promotion tends to be erroneously equated with health education, the promotion of a healthy lifestyle, or disease prevention (Cianciara et al., 2018). The Ottawa Charter, drafted at the International Conference on Health Promotion held in Ottawa in 1986, became the base document defining the assumptions. According to the charter, health promotion is an important link on the path to gaining and enhancing control over one's health. The document became a response to the then-prevailing needs and growing expectations related to the vision of public health in light of the social, economic, and cultural changes of the contemporary world. Its starting point is a holistic view of health perceived as a resource for realising one's aspirations, satisfying needs, or adapting to changing conditions. Wellbeing depends on various conditions, e.g. environmental, social, and economic ones, and is an indisputable basis for development in various dimensions of life (Barcić & Osińska, 2006; Charzyńska-Gula, 2001). Health promotion activities should therefore focus on ensuring social equality in access to health resources, i.e. health potential. They can essentially be classified into three areas:

- health education,
- disease prevention, and
- health protection (Karski, 2009).

In practice, they are expressed in the following actions:

- building a public health policy – pursuing a health-promoting policy, i.e. making a number of decisions at the political and organisational level, aimed at protecting and enhancing health; however, it should be noted that the policy understood in this manner is above the medical care system, in the area of law, economics, and administration;
- creating supportive, health-promoting environments for people, which means above all creating and enhancing a climate of safety and satisfaction, a balance between work and rest; this area includes promoting health-generating lifestyles; moreover, it promotes involvement of the local community and of the family, but also taking into account the work, education, and leisure environments;
- strengthening community activities – animating local communities in the area of health-promoting activities, enhancing social mobilisation and participation, with health promotion in this approach taking place by the "delegation" of social responsibility for health; such proposals include various self-help movements involving the community in identifying and solving health problems present in them;
- developing health-promoting skills making it possible to control and enhance health (also in situations of disease or disability), promoting the idea of lifelong learning, in line with the principle that at each stage of life, our health is shaped and it is possible to preserve and strengthen health resources; the idea of health education fits most strongly within this area;
- reorienting health care, whose activities should be aimed not only at eliminating diseases, but also at promoting healthy lifestyle; health care in this model should inspire people to look after health and teach behaviours whose aim is to multiply the chances of maintaining good health (Charzyńska-Gula, 2001; Cianciara et al., 2018; Health, 2020).

While the nature of activities in the area of prevention is individual, health promotion takes social and environmental factors into account to a greater extent. Prevention essentially confronts threats and seeks to minimise them, whereas health promotion focuses directly on enhancing resources. "Health promotion makes intensive use of the salutogenetic approach, characteristic of prevention" (disease prevention – ed.) (Cianciara et al., 2018, p. 11). In health promotion, the community is empowered and activated. However, this happens as strategic aspects are pursued related to health management and governance, and improving health literacy. Health promotion is based on the principles of partnership and social justice. It involves actors not only from the health sector (Cianciara et al., 2018; Rootman et al., 2001).

Seeking potential applications of the results of our research on health-related quality of life, we selected prevention and health promotion as areas that are close and intertwined, and which mutually reinforce each other's effectiveness. They represent comprehensive interventions whose intention is to care for health, protect it, and enhance its resources from the individual's point of view. Specifically, we formulate the following recommendations for practice:

1 Strengthening personal resources, with particular emphasis on the development of ego-resiliency understood as optimal regulation of emotions and behaviour, strengthening the ability to adjust the level of control to the situation and building openness to life experience. According to the results of our research, this resource is important both directly for health-related quality of life of adolescents with disabilities and FASD, and indirectly, enhancing and shaping health-promoting lifestyles and high self-rated health.
2 Promoting intergenerational transmission of health-promoting behaviours. Our findings indicated that parents had higher personal resources than children. Parents should learn how to constructively model behaviours resulting from personal resources when raising an adolescent with a disability or FASD.
3 Orienting interventions towards the family, which, as our research indicates, constitutes a strong resource for maintaining adolescents' HRQoL. Work with parents should be oriented towards the normative changes taking place in the family and the aspects faced by parents raising an adolescent entering adulthood, taking into account the disability-related issues. An important aspect resulting from our research is the need to emphasise, through various interventions, the importance of the autonomy and independence of the adolescents and the family, which enables and facilitates this developmental crisis for the individual as well as for all those who make up the family.
4 Our results are very similar to those obtained for the normative population in terms of the issues presented, e.g. autonomy in

relationships with parents and the role of peers. It therefore seems important to consider the problems of adolescents growing up with disabilities as developmentally typical of the period of transition to adulthood, despite their limitations. The differences between parents and adolescents in the assessment of health-related quality of life linked to independence and social support from peers support this direction of proposed actions (e.g. parent-oriented psychoeducational interactions, focusing on proper development during adolescence regardless of the disability, or support for autonomy and relationship building outside the family for adolescents with disabilities).

5 Adolescents with physical disabilities seem to be the group that requires the greatest attention, in light of our findings concerning health-related quality of life, self-rated health, and resources. In the dyads of parents with adolescents with a physical disability, we observed the greatest differences in personal and relational resources between the parents and the adolescents, and the largest discrepancies were seen there, while acceptance of the child's disability was also lower in this group of parents. This may suggest that aid interventions should be addressed to this group to a greater extent.
6 Supporting beneficial online activities of adolescents with disabilities and FASD, while at the same time reducing the risks resulting from being online, taking actions to bring together in social media people struggling with similar difficulties from different regions of Poland and the world by forming self-established support groups of sorts.
7 Educational support for adolescents with disabilities and FASD. As indicated by the results of our research, the school environment requires special monitoring in the context of the functioning of adolescents with FASD within it. Health-related quality of life in the area of assessing one's own cognitive abilities, the school environment, and relationships with teachers seems to be particularly problematic for this group of adolescents.

References

Barić, L., & Osińska, H. (2006). *Oświata zdrowotna i promocja zdrowia. Podręcznik dla studentów i praktyków*. Polskie Towarzystwo Oświaty Zdrowotnej.

Beisert, M. (2006). *Seksualność w cyklu życia człowieka* [*Sexuality in the Human Life Cycle*]. Wydawnictwo Naukowe PWN.

Bielski, J., & Blada, E. (2014). *Zdrowie i kultura fizyczna na przestrzeni dziejów* [*Health and Physical Culture Over the Centuries*]. Impuls.

Borzucka-Sitkiewicz, K., & Kowalczewska-Grabowska, K. (2013). *Profilaktyka społeczna. Aspekty teoretyczno-metodyczne* [*Social Prevention. Theoretical and Methodological Aspects*]. Wydawnictwo Uniwersytetu Śląskiego.

Charzyńska-Gula, M. (2001). *Szkolna edukacja zdrowotna jako element strategii działań na rzecz zdrowia publicznego* [*Health Education at School as an Element of the Strategy of Actions for Public Health*]. Wydawnictwo Akademii Medycznej.

Chlipała, P. (2020). Możliwości i ograniczenia prowadzenia wywiadów pogłębionych w przestrzeni realnej i wirtualnej [Potential and Limitations for Conducting In-Depth Interviews Offline and Online]. In K. Mazurek-Łopacińska & M. Sobocińska (eds.), *Badania marketingowe w gospodarce cyfrowej* [*Marketing Research in the Digital Economy*]. Wydawnictwo Uniwersytetu Ekonomicznego.

Churska-Nowak, K., Gulczyńska, A., & Jankowiak, B. (2018). Modele wychowania seksualnego w rodzinach pochodzenia współczesnych kobiet na tle przemian obyczajowych w sferze seksualności [Sexual Education Models in Families of Origin of Today's Women Against the Background of Morality Transformations in the Sphere of Sexuality]. *Przegląd politologiczny* [*Political Science Review*], *2*, 101–112. 10.14746/pp.2011.16.2.10

Cianciara, D., Urban, E., Piotrowicz, M., Gajewska, M., & Lewtak, K. (2018). Jak ulepszyć programy promocji zdrowia. Część I. Istota promocji zdrowia [How to Improve Health Promotion Programmes. Part. I. The Essence of Health Promotion]. *Hygeia Public Health*, *53*, 9–15.

Cuyło-Sikora, P., & Kaczmarska, A. (2016). Rola profilaktyki pozytywnej w kształtowaniu zdrowia holistycznego [Role of Positive Prevention in Shaping Holistic Health]. *Medycyna Ogólna i Nauki o Zdrowiu* [*General Medicine and Health Sciences*], *22*, 253–259.

Daszkiewicz, M., & Wrona, S. (2014). Zogniskowane wywiady grupowe online jako alternatywa dla tradycyjnych metod gromadzenia danych - szanse rozwoju i wyzwania dla badaczy [Online Focus Groups as an Alternative to Traditional Data Collection Methods – Opportunities for Development and Challenges for Researchers]. *Prace Naukowe Uniwersytetu Ekonomicznego we Wrocławiu* [*Research Papers of the Wrocław University of Economics*], *336*, 321–330. 10.15 611/pn.2014.336.31

Doroszuk, J. (2017). Kryzys rodziców dziecka z niepełnosprawnością w perspektywie nowych narzędzi normalizacyjnych [Crisis in Parents of a Child with Disabilities in the Perspective of New Standardisation Tools]. *Interdyscyplinarne konteksty Pedagogiki Specjalnej* [*Interdisciplinary Contexts of Special Needs Education*] *19*, 51–67.

Dymowska, A. (2019). Seksualność w dorastaniu. O potrzebie edukacji seksualnej w wychowaniu ku zdrowiu [Sexuality in Adolescence. On the Need for Sex Education in Health-Oriented Education]. In A. Dymowska & P. Prósinowski (eds.), *Innowacja – integracja – inspiracja. Kierunki odpowiedzi na zjawisko uzależnień* [*Innovation – Integration – Inspiration. Directions for Responding to the Phenomenon of Addiction*] (119–141). Wydawnictwo Libron.

Firkowska-Mankiewicz, A. (2006). Zmiana paradygmatu w postrzeganiu osoby z niepełnosprawnością intelektualną – z podopiecznego na pełnoprawnego i niezależnego uczestnika życia społecznego [Paradigm Shift in the Perception of People with Intellectual Disabilities – from a Person in One's Charge to a Full and Independent Participant of Social Life]. In B.E. Abramowska (ed.), *Z Warsztatów Terapii Zajęciowej do pracy – rozwiązania systemowe* [*From Occupational Therapy Workshops to Work – Systemic Solutions*] (11–23) PSOUU.

Gaś, Z.B. (2006). *Profilaktyka w szkole [Prevention at School]*. WSiP.

Goetting, A. (1986). The developmental tasks of siblings over the life cycle. *Journal of Marriage and the Family*, *48*, 703–714.

Health, 2020: a European policy framework supporting action across government and society for health and wellbeing. WHO, Copenhagen 2013. https://www.euro.who.int/__data/assets/pdf_file/0011/199532/Health2020-Long.pdf [access: 28.11.2022].

Heszen, I., & Sęk, H. (ed.). (2007). *Psychologia zdrowia [Health Psychology]*. Wydawnictwo Naukowe PWN.

Izdebski, Z., & Wąż, K. (2014). Zdrowie seksualne i reprodukcyjne młodzieży [Sexual and Reproductive Health of Adolescents]. *Zdrowie Publiczne i Zarządzanie [Public Health and Management]*, *12*, 45–55. 10.4467/20842627OZ.14.005.2897

Jewtuch, K. (2020). Współczesna edukacja seksualna dzieci i młodzieży w Polsce – rekonesans, diagnoza, perspektywy [Contemporary Sex Education of Children and Adolescents in Poland – Reconnaissance, Diagnosis, Prospects]. *Filoteknos*, *10*, 470–480.

Jurkiewicz, P. (2017). *Rodzeństwo osób z niepełnosprawnością intelektualną – w drodze od osamotnienia do zaradności, zrozumiałości i sensowności [Siblings of Persons with Intellectual Disabilities – on the Way from Solitude to Resourcefulness, Comprehensibility and Sense]*. Wydawnictwo Akademii Pedagogiki Specjalnej.

Kania, S. (2016). Profilaktyka pozytywna jako tendencja w zapobieganiu zachowań ryzykownych [Positive Prevention as a Trend in Preventing Risky Behaviours]. *Ogrody Nauk i Sztuk [Gardens of Science and Arts]*, *6*, 255–262.

Karski, J.B. (2009). *Promocja zdrowia dziś i perspektywy jej rozwoju w Europie [Health Promotion Today and Prospects for its Development in Europe]*. Wydawnictwa Fachowe CeDeWu.pl

Miller, P. (2012). Wprowadzenie do obserwacji online: warianty i ograniczenia techniki badawczej [Introduction to Online Observation: Variants and Limitations of the Research Technique]. *Przegląd Socjologii Jakościowej [Qualitative Sociology Review]*, *8*, 76–97. 10.18778/1733-8069.8.1.05

NIK – Najwyższa Izba Kontroli [Supreme Audit Office] (2020). *Informacja o wynikach kontroli. Dostępność lecznictwa psychiatrycznego dla dzieci i młodzieży – w latach 2017–2019 [Information on Audit Results. Availability of Psychiatric Treatment for Children and Adolescents in the Years 2017–2019]*. Departament Zdrowia NIK.

Nomejko, A., Dolińska-Zygmunt, G., & Zdrojewicz, Z. (2012). Poczucie jakości życia a satysfakcja z życia seksualnego – badania własne [Perceived Quality of Life vs Satisfaction with Sexual Life – Own Research]. *Seksuologia Polska [Polish Sexology]*, *10*, 54–60.

Ostaszewski, K. (2006). Pozytywna profilaktyka [Positive Prevention]. *Świat Problemów [World of Problems]*, *3*, 6–10.

Pisula, E., & Danielewicz, D. (2007). *Rodzina z dzieckiem z niepełnosprawnością [Family with a Child with Disabilities]*. Wydawnictwo Harmonia.

Poleszak, W. (2017). Standardy i kierunki pracy profilaktycznej z rodziną [Standards and Directions of Prevention Work with the Family]. *Uzależnienia [Addictions]*, *4*, 10–16.

Rezner, A., Rezner, W., & Kosecka, J. (2013). Edukator zdrowia w podstawowej opiece zdrowotnej jako szansa na podniesienie poziomu promocji zdrowia i profilaktyki w Polsce [The Health Educator in Primary Health Care as an Opportunity to Improve the Level of Health Promotion and Prevention in Poland]. *Problemy Higieny i Epidemiologii* [*Problems of Hygiene and Epidemiology*], *94*(3), 407–412.

Rootman, I., Goodstadt, M., Hyndman, B., McQueen, D.V., Potvin, L., Springett, J., & Ziglio,E. (2001). Evaluation in health promotion. *Principles and perspectives*. WHO Regional Publications, European Seiers, 92. https://www.euro.who.int/__data/assets/pdf_file/0007/108934/E73455.pdf [access: 2.12.2022].

Salamucha, A. (2016). Pojęcie profilaktyki (analiza semiotyczna) [The Concept of Prevention (Semiotic Analysis)]. *Roczniki Pedagogiczne* [*Annals of Pedagogy*], *8*, 7–48.

Stopikowska, M. (2016). Spektrum Płodowych Zaburzeń Alkoholowych (FASD): fakty i mity [Fetal Alcohol Spectrum Disorder (FASD): Facts and Myths], Ateneum *Przegląd Familiologiczny* [*Familiology Review*], *4*, 197–216.

Szczupał, B. (2010). Zasada pomocniczości w systemie opieki nad rodziną z dzieckiem z niepełnosprawnością intelektualną – założenia a rzeczywistość [The Principle of Subsidiarity in the System of Care of a Family with a Child with Intellectual Disability – Assumptions vs Reality]. In A. Żyta (ed.), *Rodzina osób z niepełnosprawnością intelektualną wobec wyzwań współczesności* [*Family of Persons with Intellectual Disabilities Faced with Contemporary Challenges*] (85–99). Wydawnictwo Edukacyjne Akapit.

Szymańska, J. (2015). *Programy profilaktyczne. Podstawy profesjonalnej psychoprofilaktyki* [*Prevention Programmes. Foundations of Professional Psychoprevention*]. Ośrodek Rozwoju Edukacji.

Śliwa, S. (2016). Neurodydaktyka a profilaktyka w kształceniu zintegrowanym [Neurodidactics vs Prevention in Integrated Education]. In F.A. Marek, U. Strzelczyk-Raduli & K. Błońska, (eds), *Wspieranie rozwoju dzieci i młodzieży* [*Supporting Development of Children and Adolescents*] (11–18). Wyższa Szkoła Zarządzania i Administracji.

WHO (2014). Basic documents. https://apps.who.int/gb/bd/PDF/bd48/basic-documents-48th-edition-en.pdf [access: 12.10.2022].

Woolf, S.H. (2009). *The economic argument for disease prevention: distinguishing between value and savings*. Washington, Partnership for Prevention.

Żyta, A., & Ćwirynkało, K. (2015). Wspieranie rodzin dzieci z niepełnosprawnością – perspektywa zmiany [Supporting Families of Children with Disabilities – Prospect for Change]. *Wychowanie w Rodzinie* [*Education in the Family*], *1*, 377–396. 10.23734/wwr20151.377.396

Index